Arranging the Meal

A HISTORY OF TABLE SERVICE IN FRANCE

Jean-Louis Flandrin

Translated by Julie E. Johnson
with Sylvie and Antonio Roder

Foreword to the English-Language Edition by Beatrice Fink

UNIVERSITY OF CALIFORNIA PRESS

BERKELEY   LOS ANGELES   LONDON

The publisher gratefully acknowledges the generous contribution to this book provided by the General Endowment Fund of the University of California Press Foundation.

Publié avec le concours du Ministère français chargé de la culture, Centre national du livre. Published with the assistance of the French Ministry of Culture's National Center for the Book.

University of California Press, one of the most distinguished university presses in the United States, enriches lives around the world by advancing scholarship in the humanities, social sciences, and natural sciences. Its activities are supported by the UC Press Foundation and by philanthropic contributions from individuals and institutions. For more information, visit www.ucpress.edu.

Originally published in French as *L'Ordre des mets,*
© ÉDITIONS ODILE JACOB, JANVIER 2002.

University of California Press
Berkeley and Los Angeles, California

University of California Press, Ltd.
London, England

Library of Congress Cataloging-in-Publication Data

Flandrin, Jean-Louis.
   [Ordre des mets. English]
   Arranging the meal : a history of table service in France / Jean-Louis Flandrin ; translated by Julie
E. Johnson with Sylvie and Antonio Roder ; foreword to the English-language edition by Beatrice Fink.
      p.   cm.
   Includes bibliographical references and index.
   ISBN 978-0-520-23885-5 (cloth : alk. paper)
      1. Food habits—France—History.   2. Dinners and dining—France—History.   3. France—Social
life and customs.   4. Food habits—England—History.   5. Food habits—Poland—History.   I. Title.

GT2853.F7F63   2007
394.1'20944—dc22   2007007628

Manufactured in the United States of America

16   15   14   13   12   11   10   09   08   07
10   9   8   7   6   5   4   3   2   1

This book is printed on New Leaf EcoBook 50, a 100% recycled fiber of which 50% is de-inked post-consumer waste, processed chlorine-free. EcoBook 50 is acid-free and meets the minimum requirements of ANSI/ASTM D5634–01 (*Permanence of Paper*).

CONTENTS

FOREWORD

Georges Carantino

Jean-Louis Flandrin had finished writing more than three-quarters of this book, originally published in France as *L'Ordre des mets,* by the time he passed away in August 2001. The knowledge that it would present the conventions of the table in a totally new light must have driven him, in the last months of his life, to see it completed. This act of will surely helped him carry on for nearly a year in spite of the illness that eventually overcame him. It is with gratitude that we acknowledge here the contribution of his closest students, who sustained and assisted him in his final effort.

Having often discussed his book and its outline with him, we were steeped in his approach and reasoning, but would never take it upon ourselves to finish it in his stead. Nevertheless, being familiar with his other writings and comments on the subject, we supplemented the completed portion of his manuscript with selections in which he presents the traditional structure of meals in other European countries and ponders the reasons behind these customs. Many of the points he would have wished to make will no doubt be lost, but to presume to speak for him—not that anyone could—was unthinkable.

While this book establishes a few axioms, it may also inspire new questions and new discoveries. There could be no greater tribute to its author.

Georges Carantino is a historian, a former student of Jean-Louis Flandrin, and now president of De Honesta Voluptate, Société des Amis de Jean-Louis Flandrin (Friends of Jean-Louis Flandrin Society).

Jean-Louis Flandrin's World Order

Beatrice Fink

Bernard Loiseau's dramatic disappearance from the French culinary scene in February 2003—like his illustrious forebear Vatel he committed suicide rather than experience the downfall of his reputation as a chef—generated impressive tremors throughout France. The great culinary artist was declared a martyr by those wishing to undermine the all-powerful restaurant critics' *Diktats*. "Regicides" was the term used by one of Loiseau's followers to characterize this tyrannical cohort. More significantly, this chef extraordinaire was given a hero's farewell by his horde of admirers. His funeral was the occasion for what amounted to a summit meeting of France's culinary crème de la crème. For the thousands unable to enter the small church at Saulieu in which the funeral was held, the ceremony was projected on a huge outdoor screen.

Had Jean-Louis Flandrin been alive, he would have been elated at such a projection of cuisine's grandeur, and would in all likelihood have been among the privileged few invited to attend the funeral service inside the church. Flandrin was a luminary in his own right, not only in his capacity as a member of France's exclusive—at times elusive—image-conscious gastronomic elite, but also as a standard bearer of Academe, more precisely as someone who had devoted a sizable part of his professional career to teaching, researching, writing on, and otherwise fostering all aspects of food in historical perspective. The context he drew on knew no limits: his real and not-so-secret grand design was to carve out a niche for himself as a renowned authority on what he termed historical anthropology, thus tying together the various strands of his work on family structures, sexuality, and, as one of his subtitles suggests, ethnology of the meal.[1] As cook and entertainer par excellence in his own home, as conceiver and overseer of period meals with an emphasis on the Renaissance era, he fitted into the world of practitioners. As scholar and searcher of meanings, he inclined toward the realm of the theoreticians. In one of his food seminars I happened to attend, Flandrin delighted in pointing out the conflation of language and tongue, the linguistic and the gustatory. Historical dictionary in hand, he exclaimed, "Look at all the words in the food lexicon beginning with the letter *g: goût, gourme, gourmet, gourmand, gastronome, glouton . . .*" One might say, consonance for consonance, that Flandrin the scholar was in search of an archetypal order tying together *les mets, les mots, et les mœurs* (dishes, words, and mores).

Unsurprisingly, my first contact with the author was occasioned by a dinner. Not just any dinner. It was in celebration of Easter, invariably a festive occasion in his wife's native Poland. The year was 1980. A mutual friend and colleague had mentioned my culinary interests to the Flandrins, which prompted them to invite me to their holiday feast, sight unseen. There were half a dozen or so of us gathered around the dining table. The setting, in all senses of the term, was one of high drama and anticipation. One of the guests turned out to be a food critic on the staff—I remember my host's insistence on this fact—of a leftist newspaper. This was significant, because at that time an important change was in the air. *La droite* (the political right) was no longer the sole turf of the gastronomic scene. A postwar shift had taken place, and for the left it became fashionable, at first in a radical-chic way, then more systematically, to become an aficionado of things gastronomic. Haute cuisine and its concomitants—celebrated chefs, star-bedecked restaurants, *grands crus,* and the like—while fully maintaining their traditional prestige as status symbols, were no longer being associated with a particular social class or political milieu, but had been embraced by a much wider social spectrum, in the process producing a cultural conflation of conservative and mobility-oriented France. This phenomenon was reminiscent of a shift that had occurred two centuries earlier, when the fine art of preparing dishes and of connoisseur dining became accessible not only to the private sphere (largely upper nobility) but also to the public (mostly well-to-do bourgeoisie). This was almost entirely the outgrowth of the restaurant's coming of age in postrevolutionary France. The food critic guest in question, I should add, was suitably informally garbed, with the obligatory *foulard* draped over his shoulder.

Aside from this venture into the contemporary social climate, the Easter meal, while retaining a suitable historical component (the *gigot* or roast leg of lamb, for instance, was larded not with the usual garlic but with tiny bits of cornichons—French mini-pickles—as was customary, according to Flandrin, in sixteenth-century France), was first and foremost a guessing game. What, the guests were asked, was the principal ingredient of the multitextured soup we were served? It turned out to be a special variety of cabbage. Alongside the main lamb dish, we were served a small bowl of something resembling, in appearance and consistency, pieces of artichoke hearts whose taste, I conjectured, had been modified by various seasonings. The answer, which no one arrived at, turned out to be a beef palate that his wife, Maria, emitting a great sigh, informed us had simmered for more than twenty-four hours so as to render the cartilaginous palate palatable. It was likewise a road sign pointing to the French cookery of yesteryear, when it was not uncommon to use parts of a beef's head (jowls, palate, snout, even ears) in various dishes, whereas today this part of the animal tends to be used exclusively in charcuterie. And so it went from beginning to end with this memorable prandial guessing game, not to mention the sorbet dessert subtly flavored with champagne.

Flandrin's playful side was manifest in other types of challenges. Being acquainted with my anglophone background, he would question me on arcane English terms: What does the word *neats* designate in cookery? This was thrust at me orally, that is to say, without benefit of spelling. Having recently returned from Scotland, I unhesitatingly answered, "Rutabaga." "Oh?" he replied. Shortly thereafter, I realized that I had confused *neeps,* a Scottish term for large yellow turnips, with *neats,* a now-obsolete designation for oxen, bullocks, or cattle and, by British culinary extension, their feet (beef trotters?), once again according to Flandrin. Needless to say, I became as flushed as a piece of raw beef, avoiding the twinkle in my inquisitor's eye.

Whenever I visited the Flandrins, there were exquisite goodies to eat or drink. The last time I saw the author alive, the occasion being an article he was working on for a special food issue I was preparing for publication, a young Moroccan student happened to drop by, bearing mouthwatering pastries from his homeland (he had been working on a dissertation under Flandrin's directorship).[2] These precious tidbits were immediately passed around and shared. Such visits were far from rare, since Flandrin held a quasi-permanent open house for his diverse array of students and was clearly both venerated and beloved by them. Former students Philip and Mary Hyman, an American couple who live and work in France, are currently culinary consultants of note and have been tasked by the French government to record French culinary history region by region. Another former student, Georges Carantino, took it on himself to put together and edit the present work, continue his mentor's unique food history seminar, and head De Honesta Voluptate, Society of the Friends of Jean-Louis Flandrin.[3] I won't ever forget how on the occasion of that last visit the then-ailing historian (several major operations had left the cancer-stricken scholar with reduced mobility and strength) insisted on going by himself to the new, and at that time still unfriendly for the less mobile, Bibliothèque nationale in order to check on and complete several references for the article to be included in my special issue. Nor have I forgotten how, several years earlier, he had given me a lovely little cookery book full of health-maintenance recipes and tips on which kinds of processed edibles should be avoided because they were said to contain health hazards.

Jean-Louis's wife, Maria, while also a historian, did no joint research with him but was his inseparable companion and, when health problems got the better of him, watched over him with a hawk's eye. No more hawkish, however, than the gaze both of them directed toward their two pet dogs, Finek and Grisby. These two vocal mischief makers were ever on the move, and the Flandrins were ever taking them for walks, feeding them dainty (doubtless period gourmet) morsels, and—confided Maria when I went to see her shortly after her husband's death—spoiling them outrageously. Visitors approaching the Flandrins' front door from down the hall would hear the dogs barking. Clearly, they were a therapeutic distraction that kept the Flandrins' minds off their mounting health problems.

The kitchen, however, reigned supreme in their lives. Be it never forgotten that in eighteenth-century France *cuisine* had been elevated to the rank of a fine art, where it remains to this day.

Flandrin's open-house policy was equally an open-door policy. Maria told me that her husband, ever sensitive to those who appeared undernourished, once returned to their apartment with a homeless person he had come across on the street and invited to a meal. Watching another fill an empty stomach was for the food historian a source of great satisfaction.

I had always been in awe, and more than a little envious, of Flandrin's impressive personal library. Bookshelves, often two rows deep, lined the walls of his study as well as other areas of the apartment. There were, of course, the rows and piles of general and of specialized reference books alongside recent and less-recent publications in the field to be expected in any respectable scholar's working library, especially if he or she happens to be a historian. But what attracted me were those precious gems usually found only in the rare-book reserves of a few privileged libraries, and even then not always, not all, and to be handled only under a variety of constraints. Just try to find and, moreover, purchase one of these gems at a rare-book dealer's, at auction, or by some other means! If you are fortunate enough to locate what you are seeking and it is in good condition, your eyes will pop when you find out the price. I'm referring not only to leather-bound period editions of early food-related works but also, and more especially, to those wonderfully useful and infinitely caressable (even though most are bulky folio editions) historical dictionaries, encyclopedias, almanacs, and other assemblages of knowledge and language at a specific point in time. Arguably, nowhere did matters of food and food preparation, nutrition, or the fine art of cookery make greater inroads in such books during the "long" eighteenth century than in France. Flandrin possessed several, in particular one of the eighteenth-century editions of the famed *Dictionnaire de Trévoux,* whose Jesuit editors were involved in more than one polemic as concerned matters of food and recipes with those of Diderot's *Encyclopédie.*[4] The *Dictionnaire de Trévoux* has always been an invaluable research tool for me, as well as a tangible link with a prized culinary epoch.

Generous with his books as in other matters, Flandrin, his wife informed me, had donated the greater portion of his library to the Maison des sciences de l'homme, a prestigious social sciences learning and research center located in the heart of Paris.[5] His manuscripts and other assorted documents have been deposited in France's Archives nationales. Needless to say, an endless number of articles remain encased in learned journals, volumes of Proceedings, and Festschriften. Dog-eared copies of books Flandrin had himself authored naturally remained on his own bookshelves (eleven in all according to the Bibliothèque nationale de France catalog, several in multiple editions and/or translated into other languages, some coauthored or edited). The most recent, and presumably the last, is a charming posthumous booklet on the quintessentially French *blanquette de veau* that amounts to an ode in praise of a classic French dish. *L'Ordre des mets,* as the original French edition of this book is titled, is thus not last on the list of Flandrin's publications, but rather the penultimate. It is, however, the final panel of his unfinished magnum opus, of his not-quite-completed dream of constructing an ethnology of the meal.

I return to the term *unfinished*. The reader may be taken aback by a book whose table of contents, from chapter 9 on, gives the appearance of being fragmented and even somewhat disjointed. There is, however, method in this seeming chaos. Georges Carantino points out in the preceding foreword that in undertaking the task of completing Flandrin's thought without in any way modifying, abridging, or adding to the author's original text, he and a select group of students were not only thoroughly familiar with the author's intentions but were likewise sufficiently cognizant of his writings as a whole to be able to locate fragments in various stages of completion that deal with the ordering of meals in countries other than France, as well as the author's attempts at an explanation. The same holds true for the material in the appendixes.

While the inclusion of an English component in the body of the text is hardly surprising, given the many connections across the centuries between English and French table mores, the interjection of a Polish one may strike the reader as unseemly. Again, this inclusion is not happpenstance. For one, there is more than a single historical tie between France and Poland. More important, the author's wife, as mentioned above, comes from Poland, which might explain the historian's special interest in, and knowledge of, that nation's prandial culture. Reminiscing about the legendary Easter dinner held at the Flandrins' in 1980, I questioned Maria during one of my visits about Polish festive meal traditions. At Eastertide, she replied, there were no specific dishes or rituals (except for the eggs), but the meal was bound to be a fine one, because Easter marked the end of Lent, a period of abstinence taken very seriously by Polish Catholics to this day. The case was different for Christmas. On Christmas Eve, a lean meal is customary, most likely including herring, salted cucumbers, and some form of vegetable soup in copious quantities. A roast-centered meal with trimmings is reserved for Christmas Day, the grand finale consisting of some mouthwatering variety of poppy-seed dessert. In *L'Ordre des mets*, chapter 11 deals with Polish banquets from the sixteenth century to the eighteenth, including how and in which order the dishes were served, according to the observations of French travelers. While the ordering may have changed, soups and poppy-seed preparations were even then much in evidence.

England and Poland, each for its own reasons, clearly ranked high on Flandrin's non-France priority list. Regrettably, Italy, with its all-important contributions to prandial history, is one of the missing pieces, except for some ultrabrief notations on Italian Renaissance meals. The subordination of topography to chronology, at least in the present work, may be explained not only by the fact that its author was a historian but, more significantly, by the fact that "other" meal tables are given extensive coverage in a collection of articles coedited by Flandrin and published shortly before his death.[6] These include, aside from a substantial article by Allen J. Grieco on Italian meals in the late medieval and Renaissance periods, a contribution over eighty pages in length by Flandrin himself titled "Meals in France and the Other Countries of Europe from the Sixteenth to the Nineteenth Centuries."[7] In these pages as elsewhere, Flandrin's gaze invariably focused on the how, when, where, and why of meal order and on attendant questions of civility. Aside from this group of articles, two previous publications brought up the subject: parts of Flandrin's seminal edition of essays on *Histoire de l'alimentation* and a section of the beautifully illustrated book on medieval gourmand feasts he coauthored with C. Lambert that deals with matters of *ordonnance*.[8]

Ordonnance is a French substantive derived from the verb *ordonner* ("to arrange, to order, to put in order") designating not only order, but also disposition, grouping, enactment, and, by medical extension, a prescription.[9] Flandrin's use of the word *ordre* is to be understood in this polysemic sense, far outreaching its mere denotation of "sequence." The subject of a meal's successive dishes is certainly not original and has appeared in many writings, typically travelers' journals, memoirs, or correspondence. But such treatment of meals nearly always stops short of systematic analysis and is reduced to a partial, more or less detailed description, interspersed with sporadic comments, comparisons, or exclamations. Flandrin's search for a logic underlying meal structures in terms of dishes—be it cultural, medicinal, nutritional, culinary, religious, or consisting merely of random factors in no way attributable to discernible logical constructs—was an undertaking as ambitious as it was original. Going beyond compilation and empirical observation, Flandrin attempted to synthesize. While some of the questions he raised remained unanswered (thus pointing to future fields of inquiry), a method in cultural modes was more often detected than not. Why, where, when, and how are the fat/lean controversies resolved or the shifting lines dividing the two set straight? Where are the determinants of hot-to-cold or cold-to-hot mutations in dish order to be found? How does the dialectic of light versus rich foods work itself out? Why do some cultures drink during the meal and others only after? When do sweet and savory merge and when do they not? And why or where does sweet not follow but precede savory?

Among less-inspected areas is that of the nature of serving. *Service à la française* or *service à la russe?* Flandrin has provided a revealing look at this fundamental nineteenth-century shift from a paradigmatic (clustered) to a syntagmatic (sequential) pattern in the serving of dishes at the meal table, punctuated with practical and aesthetic considerations emanating from contemporary observers. In the fragments of what was intended to be the conclusion to his book, Flandrin noted not only the frequent convergence of principles and practices in meal modes across time and space but also the many contradictions or paradoxes that are still to be resolved. So be it, and so it is with all far-reaching endeavors.

There is an old French proverb that says one should have a bit of appetite left when leaving the table. Flandrin's eye-opener does just that. The proof, by the way, is in the pudding. A three-day international conference honoring Flandrin took place at the University of Paris/Vincennes at the end of September 2003. Titled "Le Désir et le goût: Une autre histoire," its published version has recently appeared.[10] It will surely provide much post-prandial nourishment.

NOTES

1. *Tables d'hier, tables d'ailleurs: Histoire et ethnologie du repas,* ed. Jean-Louis Flandrin and Jane Cobbi (Paris: Éd. Odile Jacob, 1999).

2. *The Cultural Topography of Food,* a special issue of *Eighteenth-Century Life* 23, no. 2 (May 1999). The article in question is titled "L'Invention des grands vins français et la mutation des valeurs œnologiques," pp. 24–33.

3. In the original French: De Honesta Voluptate, Société des Amis de Jean-Louis Flandrin. The current president is Patrick Rambourg. The SAJLF, as it is familiarly referred to, holds regular seminars during the academic year involving high-level specialists in the field and holds a yearly period-meal banquet with dishes prepared by SAJLF members.

4. Diderot was (justifiably) accused by the *Dictionnaire de Trévoux*'s editors of having swiped certain recipes from their publication. Diderot in turn pointed out that the Jesuits had plagiarized parts of Father Noël Chomel's early eighteenth-century *Dictionnaire économique.* The finger-pointing was ongoing.

5. This is where Flandrin's seminars were held, and currently those of the SAJLF. The quasi-remainder of his library was subsequently donated to the MSH by his wife.

6. *Tables d'hier, tables d'ailleurs.*

7. My translation.

8. *Histoire de l'alimentation* has been translated into English as *Food: A Cul-*

tural History; J.-L. Flandrin and C. Lambert, *Fêtes gourmandes au moyen âge* (Paris: Imprimerie nationale, 1998).

9. As once did *receipt,* better known under its present name, *recipe.*

10. *Le Désir et le goût: Une autre histoire,* ed. F. Joannes, P. Lantz, and O. Redon (Paris: Presses Universitaires de Vincennes, 2005).

In France, it is generally understood that the elements of a meal are to be served in a particular order. As they wait to be seated, guests are first kept happy with drinks. Accompanying savories stimulate thirst and buffer the effects of the alcohol. At the table, the meal proceeds with soup, cold appetizers, and/or hot dishes, followed by the main course of meat or fish with vegetables, then salad, cheeses, dessert, and, lastly, coffee and after-dinner drinks. No one questions this prescribed order. Exceptionally, the salad is sometimes served as an hors d'oeuvre, with tiny goat cheeses specially warmed for the occasion.

Yet, as the French discover the moment they cross national borders, this order of presentation is neither preordained nor universal: in Italy, pasta is invariably the first course, and cold vegetables such as peppers in oil may be served either as appetizers or as vegetable dishes. In England, cheese is generally served after fruit rather than before. In the United States, coffee with cream, iced tea, and even soft drinks are offered with just about every meal, whereas the French drink *café au lait* only at breakfast or between meals. In Poland, Turkey, and China, people drink no liquids with their main meal but like to end it with a hot broth or cold fruit soup, washed down with a big thirst-quenching cup of tea.

The sequence in which dishes are served is a cultural rather than natural ritual that has evolved over centuries in most countries, including France.

This book presents the history of this evolution. It begins with the seventeenth and eighteenth centuries, when French tradition was at its most elaborate and strict; it then examines the customs preceding and following this golden age, from the last two centuries of the Middle Ages to the present. Next, various periods in several other European countries are considered. Finally, this study explores the reasons behind the order in which meals were served in different periods. The rationales that were given at the time are compared to actual practices, both in France and in neighboring lands. As it turns out, various countries cited the same principles as the basis for quite different meal sequences. This book explains why.

PART ONE

The Structure of Meals in the Classical Age

ONE

Composition of the Classical Meal

Today, dishes are served one after the other, so their order of consumption, whatever it may be, is clear. Such was not the case for the *service à la française* meal etiquette that prevailed until the mid-nineteenth century.

At the time, formal meals consisted of several "courses"—usually three or four but at times five or more—each composed of several dishes brought to the table at the same time. Here is how A.-B.-L. Grimod de La Reynière describes such a meal in his 1805 *Almanach des gourmands:* "An important dinner normally comprises four courses. The first consists of soups, hors d'oeuvres, relevés, and entrées; the second, of roasts and salads; the third of cold pasties and various entremets; and lastly, the fourth, of desserts including fresh and stewed fruit, cookies, macaroons, cheeses, all sorts of sweetmeats, and petits fours typically presented as part of a meal, as well as preserves and ices."[1]

In describing the different courses, Grimod de La Reynière puts different types of dishes in the same category. Some are defined by aspect and mode of preparation, like all the desserts he names. Others are defined by their position and function in the sequence, as in the elements of the first three courses, especially hors d'oeuvres, relevés, entrées, and entremets.[2] Entrées, for instance, could vary greatly depending on their main ingredient, method of preparation, and final appearance, but they were defined by their place in the meal, somewhere between the soup and the roast. Likewise, entremets were very diverse, but all were served between the roast and dessert and characterized by this position in the meal.

A number of dishes, such as soups, roasts, and salads, were categorized in two different ways, both by their content and by their place in the meal. The essential element of any soup or potage—from the Latin *potus,* meaning "brew"—was stock, and this is still the primary connotation of the word. But in the seventeenth and eighteenth centuries, soups were also defined by their place at the very beginning of the meal. In fact, dictionaries of the period define them in terms of both characteristics, as in the 1704 edition of the *Dictionnaire de Trévoux:* "Cooked meat juices in which fine slices of bread are soaked or simmered. *Jus, jusculum.* Soup is served at the beginning of the meal." The second part of this definition is probably the more reliable, because the bread that was simmered in soup could mask its liquid character—in the eighteenth century, barely liquid pasta and rice dishes were sometimes presented as soups. A meal for Louis XVI at his castle in Saint-Cloud on 19 May 1788 included "two main soups," namely, "Vermicelli" and "Spanish Croutons," with two secondary ones, Polish "Clouskis" and "Mixed Croutons." Such examples abound, as discussed in the chapters that follow.

Roasts were also classified by their assigned order as well as by the cooking method. The *Dictionnaire de Trévoux* defines them as "meat roasted on a spit," served "at the midpoint of the meal."

The order and function of salads were more significant than how they were prepared. The same source describes them as "a sort of entremets brought to the table alongside the roast. . . . Usually composed of fresh greens seasoned with salt, oil, and vinegar." But salad greens—not just fruit salads—were often seasoned with sugar, and the term *salad* also applied to vinegar-pickled purslane and sea fennel, cornichons, cured olives, capers, anchovies, and quartered bitter oranges served with the roast to refresh a guest's appetite.

Despite this dual classification of soups, roasts, and salads as both entrées and entremets, these two categories must be clearly distinguished. But there exists no general term for dishes that are defined by their order and function within the meal. Since one must therefore be invented, I propose "functions."

Variations in the Number and Content of Courses

A study of menus reveals that meals often consisted of just three courses—a practice that Grimod de La Reynière condemns but whose existence he acknowledges. It also shows that all courses of the same order—first, second, third, or fourth—did not always consist of the same types of dishes. Not only did customs change between the seventeenth and the nineteenth centuries, but the content of courses varied from meal to meal. Unlike these four courses from the kitchen, dessert was prepared and served by the pantry staff and therefore almost never mentioned in culinary treatises.[3]

In the seventeenth century, each course might consist only of dishes having the same function. Accordingly, such meals comprised a greater number of courses. For instance, one 1662 menu suggested by Pierre de Lune in his *Nouveau et Parfait Maistre d'hostel royal* features a little "Table with one platter and two plates" (figure 1).[4]

But most often—in the eighteenth century and even during the seventeenth—dishes with various functions appeared within a single course, as in the time of Grimod de La Reynière. Moreover, the content of courses varied considerably from one meal to another: not only were entremets often served together with roasts and salads, but the second course could consist of relevés and entrées rather than roasts and salads. Two menus from Menon's *Cuisinière bourgeoise* (1746) illustrate these variations. One, "Supper setting for ten" (figure 2), starts with a classic course of soup with a relevé of spit-roasted butcher's meat, two entrées, and two hors d'oeuvres; the second course features two platters of roasts as well as three entremets; and desserts constitute the third course. In the second example, "Dinner setting for twelve" (figure 3), the first course contains just soups and hors d'oeuvres, plus "a joint of beef for the center," which remained on the table through the second course, when four entrées replaced the soups and hors d'oeuvres; the third course consists of two platters of roasts, three entremets, and two salads; and finally, the fourth course features seven dessert dishes. Even though this meal consists of four courses, their composition differs greatly from that of the meal described by Grimod de La Reynière.[5]

Yet this inconsistent grouping of courses does not appear to have affected the order of presentation of functions: soups came first in all cases; hors d'oeuvres, relevés, and entrées came next, followed by the roasts and salads along with all sorts of entremets; and desserts came last. This order essentially prevailed even with the demise of the French-style meal struc-

TABLE WITH ONE PLATTER AND TWO PLATES

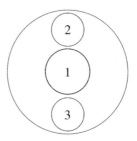

Courses for this table:

SOUPS
Chicken soup with peas at 1
Squab soup at 2
Gosling soup with asparagus at 3

ENTRÉES
Veal breast ragoût at 1
Squab pie at 2
Gosling ragoût at 3

All presented in platter at 1

ASSORTED DISHES
Chicken fricassée at 2
Marinade of squab at 3

ROASTS
Hares and turkeys at 1
Plate of chicken at 2
Plate of squabs at 3
Salads

ENTREMETS
Green peas, asparagus, mushrooms, all presented in platter at 1
Plate of fava beans at 2
Artichokes at 3

———

FIGURE 1. Table with one platter and two plates, based on Pierre de Lune, *Le Nouveau et Parfait Maistre d'hostel royal* (1662). Note that the various entremets vegetables were not combined on one large serving dish, as one might assume, but served on three separate plates, all set within the center platter. The same arrangement was used for the first three entrées of the second course. On the other hand, the threefold design of this meal apparently was discarded for the roast course, where the platter, already laden with hares and turkeys, could hardly have accommodated salads as well.

SUPPER SETTING FOR TEN

FIRST COURSE
1 Soup at the center, if desired
1 Spit-roasted butcher's meat as relevé for the soup

2 entrées, 2 hors d'oeuvres
1 Entrée of vol-au-vent
1 Hen prepared two ways
1 Hors d'oeuvre of rabbit and puréed lentils
1 Hors d'oeuvre of three parchment-wrapped lamb tongues

SECOND COURSE

2 dishes of roast, 3 entremets
1 Pair of small hares
1 Pair of chickens à la reine
1 Entremets of small pastries
1 Small peas
1 Crème brûlée

THIRD COURSE
7 Fruit plates
1 Bowl of waffles for the center
1 Plate of strawberries
1 Stewed cherries
1 Whipped cream
3 Plates of assorted preserves

———

FIGURE 2. Supper setting for ten, from Menon's *Cuisinière bourgeoise suivie de l'Office* (1746).

ture and its replacement by Russian-style service during the nineteenth century.

To preserve the five-dish table layout of the preceding meal, the three dishes of preserves in the fourth course were probably stacked, or arranged on a single tray.

Order of Presentation and Order of Consumption

The exact order of dishes cannot, however, be ascertained from menus. This is because French-style presentation brought a great many dishes simultaneously to the table, and the order in which they appear on the menu does not necessarily reflect the order in which guests partook of them. In the

DINNER SETTING FOR TWELVE

FIRST COURSE

2 Soups, 1 Joint of beef for the center, 2 Hors d'oeuvres
1 Herb soup
1 Rice soup
1 Radish hors d'oeuvre
1 Vambre butter hors d'oeuvre

SECOND COURSE

*Leave the joint of beef in the center and replace the soups
and hors d'oeuvres with 4 entrées*
1 Truffled braised veal tenderloin
1 Mutton chops with basil
1 Claypot of ducks
1 Braised hen

THIRD COURSE

2 roast dishes, 3 entremets, 2 salads
1 Young hare
1 Four small domestic pigeons
1 Entremets at the center, an Amiens pasty
1 Chilled custard
1 Cauliflowers

FOURTH COURSE

Dessert
Pan of fresh fruit at the center
1 Portuguese-style stewed apples
1 Stewed pears
1 Plate of waffles
1 Plate of chestnuts
1 Plate of gooseberry jelly
1 Plate of apricot marmalade

———

FIGURE 3. Dinner setting for twelve, from Menon's *Cuisinière bourgeoise suivie de l'Office* (1746).

Cuisinière bourgeoise supper for ten, for example, was the "spit-roasted joint of butcher's meat as a relevé for the soup" eaten directly after the soup it replaced? Were the entrées then eaten next, before the hors d'oeuvres listed at the end of that menu's first course? Not necessarily. Evidence must be gleaned from other documents.

In the second year of his *Almanach des gourmands,* Grimod de La Reynière explicitly describes the unfolding of an early-nineteenth-century Parisian dinner: "Guests take their seats and their silence bespeaks the power and universality of their sensations. A properly scalding soup does not in the least dampen the general activity; it is as if their palates were lined with mosaic. . . . Now the host . . . skillfully carves a quivering hindquarter of fat beef encircled by a simple vegetable garland studded with lardoons. . . . In the meantime, the hors d'oeuvres disappear and the entrées, eaten after the boiled meats, leave time to apportion the relevés that have replaced the soups."[6]

The structure of meals had not, however, changed significantly since the Revolution: in 1821, a menu for twenty-five people in Archambault's *Cuisinier économe* also mentioned a first-course succession of "two soups" and "two soup relevés" (including a "cut of beef with glazed onion garnish") coming before "eight little hors d'oeuvres" and "twelve entrées." When the first course included relevés, they were mentioned right after the soup they replaced, because what mattered was their placement on the table rather than the order in which dishes were eaten. Still, the order of consumption was not without rules or logic, as the fourth section of this book will show.

A more complicated case is a supper given for Louis XV on Monday 21 June 1751, which lists various categories of dishes without any indication of how they were distributed among the various courses.[7] Included were 2 main entrées, then 2 tureens and 2 soups, 16 entrées, and 4 relevés, all of which probably constituted a first course. Next came 2 main and 2 secondary entremets, 8 roasts, and 16 small entremets, likely adding up to the second course. The question is whether the entremets—or at least the four main and secondary ones mentioned ahead of the roasts—were indeed eaten first. This is doubtful: first of all, the two main entremets echo the two main entrées of the first course, which head the menu listing but were certainly not eaten before the soups. Second, Grimod de La Reynière may have disapproved of serving entremets alongside the roasts, but he never for an instant meant that they should be eaten first.[8] And yet, menus that list main entremets ahead of roasts were even more frequent in the nineteenth century than in the eighteenth.[9]

While it can be assumed that costly cold meat pies and other main entremets, once started, would be eaten before minor entremets, the order of consumption of the latter is still unclear. Of these surprisingly eclectic selections, which were eaten first, hot ones or cold ones, meats (usually cold) or little vegetable dishes (always hot)? Concerning temperature, we have seen that Grimod de La Reynière advocates eating hot food as immediately as possible, but seems to agree that any cold food to be consumed should be eaten first.[10] Were salty dishes consumed before sugary ones?

As for sugared entremets, they were clearly not listed systematically after salty ones. In the supper for ten from *La Cuisinière bourgeoise,* the "Crème gratinée" (a sort of crème brûlée or caramelized custard) does indeed conclude the list of entremets, but the "Entremets de petits gâteaux" (assortment of little pastries) precedes the dish of peas. Similarly, in the dinner for twelve, the "Crème glacée" (frozen custard) precedes a dish of cauliflower. In 1691, François Massialot even starts his entremets selection with sugared preparations.[11] A tendency to list sweet entremets after relevés begins to emerge only in the nineteenth century. But we have seen that the order of listing on menus had little to do with the actual order of consumption. We may thus surmise that in practice, starting in the eighteenth or even the seventeenth century, sweet entremets were eaten after savory ones.

We also lack specific information on the order of consumption of dessert dishes. While fruits were the main dessert items in the seventeenth and eighteenth centuries, other kinds of dishes also appeared, such as ripened or fresh cream cheeses, ice creams, waffles, marzipans, petits fours, candies, and such. But none of these were essential to the dessert course, nor did they structure its sequence. While first-course soups and entrées, hors d'oeuvres, and relevés, as well as second-course roasts and salads, were mandatory and had to be eaten in a precise order, ripened cheeses were optional at the dessert course. Many guests might not even touch the cheeses while others, like the true gourmands mentioned by Grimod de La Reynière, would savor them to the exclusion of all else.[12]

Hence it seems that no protocol of consumption ever developed for dessert, except for ice cream and sherbet. According to the father of gastronomic literature, "Of course, ice creams or curds must appear at the table only at the end of dessert, when they replace a few fruit platters removed in symmetrical fashion."[13]

DISTRIBUTION OF DISHES AMONG "FUNCTIONS"

Acquainted now with the main stages of the classical meal, we begin to grasp what was meant by a soup, an hors d'oeuvre, an entrée, relevés, a roast, a salad, entremets, and a dessert. We can see how dishes were assigned to these various functions according to their basic ingredients and mode of preparation, and depending on whether they were hot or cold, salty or sweet.

Fortunately, many seventeenth- and eighteenth-century cookbooks included guidelines of some sort for the function of their recipes. The 1651 *Cuisinier françois* of François Pierre de La Varenne grouped its recipes by function within the larger categories of meals for meat or meatless days, Lent, and other days: meat-day soups and entrées, "meats suitable for the second course," "entremets for meat days," and so forth. L. S. R. does likewise in his 1674 *L'Art de bien traiter,* and so does François Marin in his 1739 *Dons de Comus.* In 1660, Pierre de Lune organizes *Le Nouveau Cuisinier* by seasons but also groups meat and meatless dishes by function within each season. In his 1691 *Cuisinier royal et bourgeois,* Massialot lists the recipes in alphabetical order, less systematically naming the function of each dish. The function may appear in its name, as in "large pike entrée" or "pike for a meat-day entremets," but is more often indicated at the end of a recipe, as in the one for pike pasties, which "should be cooked slowly and served hot as entrées," and the one for "poached pike," to be served "drained, as an entremets." But all too often the function of a dish—self-evident for Massialot and his seventeenth-century readers—goes unmentioned, thereby reducing his book's usefulness for our present purpose. Finally, Menon's 1746 *Cuisinière bourgeoise* is structured by main ingredient, but each recipe includes a marginal notation of function: hors d'oeuvre, entrée, major entrée, entremets, hors d'oeuvre or entrée, hors d'oeuvre or entremets, roast, and so on. All of these cookbooks thus offer insight into the rules by which a function was assigned to each dish.

In this analysis, we will first consider meals for meat days, when meat was allowed and could be cooked in lard. The rules for meatless days, Lent, and Good Friday were quite different and will be discussed in chapter 4.

TWO

Roasts

WHILE THE PLACE OF MANY dishes in the French meal has changed over the centuries, that of the roast has not. However far back we delve into national history, it has always been the centerpiece of any banquet, from plebeian to aristocratic. Grimod de La Reynière, comparing "the courses of a dinner" to "the various rooms of a building" in his *Almanach des gourmands,* declares that "the roast is the front parlor, the best room, in short the one where the owner's pride resides," adding that "aside from the big exotic cold pasties, it is usually the most noteworthy, the most expensive, and the most eagerly awaited dish. . . . It is important for the roast to meet the guests' expectations of extravagance, preparation, and tenderness, for if it is paltry, burned, or tough, the excellence of everything that preceded it is forgotten." While further verification is in order before asserting that the roast was the most expensive element of any meal, this lordly dish nonetheless offers a good place to begin analyzing the content and functions of various courses.

MID-SEVENTEENTH-CENTURY ROASTS AND ENTRÉES

In the seventeenth and eighteenth centuries, the function of the roast was assigned to roasted meats. A truism perhaps, but it may not always have been so. Meats prepared any other way must therefore have been various kinds of entrées, entremets, or even soups. These would include boiled meats, meats in various sauces, stewed, steamed and simmered, fricasseed, sautéed or fried, or grilled, as well as the pies and pasties of the period, that is, meats wrapped in pastry crust and baked in the oven.[1]

Even more surprising, out of nine recipes in François de La Varenne's *Cuisinier françois* that mention "roast," 6 appear under entrées, 1 under entremets, and only 2 under roasts. Moreover, except for these last 2 roasts, none of the dishes whose name indicates the mode of preparation is itself a roast. Conversely, out of the 80 roasted meat recipes in *Le Cuisinier françois*, only 6 have names indicating the mode of preparation: the 2 roasts just mentioned, 2 "stuffed," 1 "natural," and 1 "à la royale."[2] Moreover, half of them are entrées that were misplaced in the chapter on roasts.

The names of the other 74 recipes in the *Cuisinier françois* chapter on roasts do not specify how these meats were cooked. Thirteen of them involve meats simmered in sauce after roasting, or cooked directly in a sauce, thus referring to dishes that cannot qualify as roasts according to the rules deduced later in this chapter.[3] The 61 remaining recipes call for meats roasted on a spit, with or without lard, but served plain or possibly with a sauce on the side.

At the same time, the meat entrées and entremets whose name did not specify a mode of preparation were never roasted meats. Furthermore, when an entrée or entremets consisted of roasted meat, it was either organ meat or some other cut inappropriate for a roast (a point that will be clarified later), or else the preparation was ultimately a stew.[4]

Criteria defining roasts gradually became more specific and rigid during the period considered here. The second part of this volume will show that during the fourteenth, fifteenth, and sixteenth centuries, the roast course included pasties and sauced meats that would no longer be conceivable in the second half of the eighteenth century. Now that we have examined mid-seventeenth-century reference works, let us turn to the best-seller of the latter half of the eighteenth century, *La Cuisinière bourgeoise* attributed to Menon, for a more exact definition of the roast.[5]

EIGHTEENTH-CENTURY ROASTS AND
SPIT-ROASTED ENTRÉES

Today, a roast means a nice cut of meat cooked in dry heat—on the spit or the grill, in the fireplace or rotisserie, or even oven-roasted. In fact, my butcher would probably consider the oven the best way to roast a good piece of meat. But the concept was formerly much narrower: eighteenth-century dictionaries define the roast as meat "roasted on the spit" in the fireplace, since rotisseries do not seem to have appeared until the early nineteenth century.[6] Even then, meat cooked this way was not always served as a second-course roast dish: it was often brought to the table as a first-course "spit-roasted entrée," "main entrée," or simple entrée, at least according to *La Cuisinière bourgeoise.* How did such entrées differ from the true roast?

Preparation for cooking was the first difference. Grimod de La Reynière states that a small roast must "always be barded, or studded" with lard.[7] Sometimes, in season, domestic pigeons, quail, and woodcock were wrapped in grape leaves as well as barded. These were roasts just the same. On the other hand, if a meat was studded with something other than lard, it became an entrée, like the "Gigot à la Génoise" studded with celery, tarragon, pickles, lard, and a few anchovies; and the "Épaule de Mouton à la Roussie" (i.e., "Russian style"), larded with two handfuls of parsley before being skewered on the spit.[8]

Barded with lard and wrapped in grape leaves, the roast was still ultimately supposed to "brown nicely," even though this is easier to do if the birds are studded.[9] To turn the same meat into a spit-roasted entrée, it was barded with lard and wrapped in buttered paper to keep it from browning, as in this model chicken recipe from *La Cuisinière bourgeoise:* "Cook them on the spit, wrapped in lard and paper. Keep the fire moderate so they won't brown, because a chicken entrée cooked on a spit must be left pale." Paper wrapping defined the spit-roasted entrée in every case: turkey, hen, pigeon, pheasant, teal, partridge, woodcock, quail, thrush, and plover.

Less browned than a roast and therefore less tasty, the spit-roasted entrée usually gained additional flavor from stuffing, sauce, or ragoût: "When your chickens are done, transfer them to the platter . . . & add what sauce or ragoût you wish." The meat was not cooked again in its sauce, as it was in the Middle Ages. It became an entrée when covered with the sauce or, in the seventeenth century, set on top of it.[10] The ragoût was simply arranged on the platter around the meat or, according to *Le Cuisinier royal et bourgeois,* spread underneath it like a sauce.

La Cuisinière bourgeoise never mentions any stuffing in connection with roasts, but its recipe for "pheasant or young pheasant" shows the extent to which stuffing characterized spit-roasted entrées: To serve "as a roast," first clean and stud them, then "cook on the spit and serve when nicely browned." However, "To serve . . . as a spit-roasted entrée, cook on the spit, stuffed with their livers chopped with minced lard, parsley, chives, salt, and coarse pepper; bard them with lard and wrap with paper; serve with Provençale sauce or some other nice little sauce in the modern style."[11]

A bird's cavity could be empty or filled; a roast might retain the liver, heart, and gizzard, or hold an onion studded with three cloves.[12] But as soon as the ingredients were chopped and combined into a stuffing, the dish became a spit-roasted entrée. Plovers are a good example: As roast, they were skewered without emptying the cavity. But "to serve as a spit-roasted entrée, prepare a stuffing from their organs as explained in the article on woodcocks," that is, by discarding the gizzard, chopping the rest of the organs, and mixing with "minced lard or a piece of butter, chopped parsley and chives, a little salt."

There is no proof, however, that stuffing alone turned a roast into an entrée, because the stuffed meats in *La Cuisinière bourgeoise* were always served with a sauce or ragoût.[13] The stuffed, spit-roasted veal breast was served "with any sauce or vegetable ragoût you please"; the stuffed partridges, "with any sauce and ragoût you deem appropriate," and likewise for stuffed woodcock and plover.[14] Stuffings and ragoûts often had one ingredient in common, such as the chestnuts for stuffing spit-roasted goose—a main entrée of former times that has become the Christmas roast.

CHOOSING SUITABLE ROAST MEATS

Various kinds of meats were suitable for the roast. According to the *Almanach des gourmands,* "The roast can be large or small. The first group includes butcher's meat and venison, such as sirloin, lamb shoulder, veal loin, quarters of boar, deer, or roe deer; the second type includes fowl, game, and small birds."[15] Some meats, however, were not appropriate except for entrées or entremets, and even the suitable roast meats were not evenly distributed among the various functions.

La Cuisinière bourgeoise contains no roasts of organ meat, not even calf's liver or beef tongue, which were sometimes served that way at the time of La Varenne.[16] In addition—despite Grimod de La Reynière's comments a few decades later—butcher's meat was not considered suitable for roast: out of 127 such cuts whose function is known, there is only one, the lamb quarter (or possibly two if we count the lamb haunch), that can be called roast. The cookbook's three menus confirm the instructions of the recipes.

The status of fowl and game is entirely different. Most feathered game could be used for roast: lark, woodcock, snipe, quail, mallard, various wild ducks, pheasant, thrush, blackbird, grouse, plover, ortolan, wood pigeon, robin, teal, and lapwing. The exception was the scoter [a sea duck], the one bird that could be eaten on meatless days and that, if served without sauce, would have been a true mortification.

The same applied to domestic fowl: Rouen duckling, turkey, various domesticated pigeons, guinea fowl, hen and capon, Caux hen and nonmated rooster, fattened chicken with eggs, and chicken *à la reine*. There were three exceptions: gosling and especially goose, as well as domesticated duck, whose meat, long said to be indigestible, came to be considered vulgar. The best tables replaced them with turkey toms and hens and with wild ducks.

La Cuisinière bourgeoise did not introduce this distribution of various meats among entrée and roast. The preface to the 1750–1751 edition of Massialot's *Cuisinier royal et bourgeois* states that "with respect to entrées, half of them must consist of large joints that are butcher's cuts and other meats like beef, veal, mutton, veal organs, lamb trotters, tongues and tails, fresh pork, salt pork, sausages, andouilles, and blood pudding; while the other half must consist of lighter selections such as delicate meats—chickens, hens, pigeons, turkeys, ducks, and ducklings—or game, partridges, quail, pheasant, or hares. The roast must feature half white and half dark meat, game and fowl, studded and barded preparations."[17]

It is true that game and especially domesticated fowl provided more recipes for entrées than for roasts. In *La Cuisinière bourgeoise,* feathered game accounts for 25 *[sic]* entrées and 18 roasts, while domestic fowl is used for 114 entrées or hors d'oeuvres and only 8 roasts.[18] But this is mainly because entrées were much more varied than roasts.

An analysis of menus discloses the real proportion of each category of meat in entrées and roasts. The three *Cuisinière bourgeoise* menus, for instance, are unequivocal. In the dinner for twelve, fowl and small game provide 2 of the 4 entrées and both roasts (a hare and four small domestic pigeons); in the supper for ten, they account for 1 of the 2 entrées and both roasts (2 small hares and 2 chickens *à la reine*); in the setting for fourteen, 2 of the 4 entrées and all 4 roasts (a hen, three partridges, eighteen skylarks, and one Rouen duckling). Neither fowl nor game appears in the soups, the centerpieces of the first course, or the entremets of any of those three meals. It is significant that all told, wild hare included, fowl and game account for 1 hors d'oeuvre out of 10, half of the 10 entrées, and all of the roasts.

Furred game, especially small game, was similarly distributed. Out of the six varieties mentioned in *La Cuisinière bourgeoise,* the 3 young rabbits, young hares, and young boars provided the roasts. But the same six species of game furnished a much higher number of entrées (11 of young rabbit, 5 of rabbit, 2 of hare, and 2 of young hare) and hors d'oeuvres (3 of young rabbit, 2 of rabbit, and 2 of hare fillets) for a total of 27 hors d'oeuvres or entrées. Still, the menus reveal that furred game was used for roast less often than feathered game but more often than butcher's meat and even domestic fowl: the same three menus feature furred game as a roast and as an hors d'oeuvre with equal frequency (twice) and never as an entrée or soup.

In conclusion, the various types of meat were distributed very differently among the stages of the meal: Organ meats were used only for hors d'oeuvres and entrées or entremets. Butcher's meat provided hardly any roasts (1 to 3 out of 127 butcher's meat recipes), few entremets (19), but many entrées (103) and hors d'oeuvres (23). Domestic fowl and especially furred or feathered game were essential for roasts. Menus show this better than recipes, since they list these three categories under roasts more often than under entrées and hors d'oeuvres.

FROM *LE CUISINIER FRANÇOIS* TO *LA CUISINIÈRE BOURGEOISE*

La Cuisinière bourgeoise reveals some rules concerning the distribution of meats between roasts and entrées, but do these rules apply to the whole of the seventeenth and eighteenth centuries? It would seem that some of them were still a little hazy at the time of *Le Cuisinier françois* (1651) but then generally and rather rapidly became more precise.

No organ meats figured among roast recipes in *L'Art de bien traiter* in 1674, nor even earlier in 1660 in Pierre de Lune's *Nouveau Cuisinier*. But the 1651 *Cuisinier françois* gave three such recipes in its roast chapter: one for calf's liver, larded, studded, skewered, basted with pepper sauce during roasting, then simmered in the sauce; and two for fresh beef tongue (out of five such cuts in the whole book), boiled before roasting, one of which was then simmered in a mild sauce and the other served with a ragoût. Should we then conclude that organ meats were not yet excluded in 1651 and that this rule emerged only about 1660? Before deciding, I must question the reliability of *Le Cuisinier françois* on the subject. As mentioned earlier, its 80 entries in the roast chapter contained 13 recipes for meats cooked in sauce, which contemporaries were not likely to mistake for roasts! Can the same be said of the organ meats in question?

The example of butcher's meat is certainly more revealing: it is featured as roast much more often in the seventeenth century than at the time of *La Cuisinière bourgeoise* (table 1). This higher frequency prompts a new remark.

TABLE I
Percentage of recipes classed as roast

	Le Cuisinier françois (1651)	Le Nouveau Cuisinier (1660)	L'Art de bien traiter (1674)	La Cuisinière bourgeoise (1774)
Butcher's meat	13 R / 81 B = 16%	6 R / 74 B = 8.1%	13 R / 52 B = 25%	1 to 3 R / 127 B = 0.8% to 2.4%
Game	25 R / 62 G = 40%	24 R / 68 G = 35%	40 R / 47 G = 85%	18 R / 43 G = 42%
Poultry	15 R / 76 P = 20%	12 R / 99 P = 12%	26 R / 78 P = 33%	8 R / 122 P = 7%

B = butcher's meat; G = game; P = poultry; R = roast

Most cookbooks presented the young rather than the adult animal as roast: lamb in *La Cuisinière bourgeoise;* lamb, veal, and suckling pig in *L'Art de bien traiter* as well as *Le Nouveau Cuisinier;* and veal, lamb, and pork in *Le Cuisinier françois,* the only book that also features roasts of adult animals—beef sirloin; loin, ribs, and leg of mutton; and even fresh pork. The exclusion of butcher's meat thus seems to have become increasingly strict, except as noted above regarding organ meats. One further caution may apply here, in this case regarding *La Cuisinière bourgeoise:* Was butcher's meat as clearly excluded in other eighteenth-century works? Based on research to date, all that can be said is that butcher's cuts are just as rare among the roasts (3 out of 200 = 1.5 percent) in *La Science du maître d'hôtel cuisinier,* which is by the same author.

Large furred game animals also appear to have been excluded only gradually (and incompletely) as roasts. In *La Cuisinière bourgeoise,* antlered game are all prepared in marinades or pasties. Only wild boar is roasted on a spit, and even then, only young wild boar is explicitly indicated for roast. In the 1674 *L'Art de bien traiter,* the only large wild game appears in 5 recipes for adult and young wild boar, the latter accounting for 3 roasts or 60 percent of the recipes for this type of food. In 1660, *Le Nouveau Cuisinier* offers 7 roasts out of 26 large wild game recipes, or 27 percent. Adult animals (antlered game and boar) are mentioned as well as young ones (fawns and young wild boar).[19] Lastly, *Le Cuisinier françois* in 1651 contains 9 roasts out of 26 large-game recipes (a ratio of 35 percent), and it likewise accepts the roasting of adult animals. Note that the most tender cuts are selected: fillet, loin, or even shoulder.[20] Still, for large game, full-grown animals became unacceptable for roasts beginning in 1674, while the same was already true in 1660 for butcher's meat.

TABLE 2

Birds not used for roast

	Le Cuisinier françois (1651)	Le Nouveau Cuisinier (1660)	L'Art de bien traiter (1674)	La Cuisinière bourgeoise (1774)
Game	sparrows	—	—	scoter
Poultry	duck	adult males: rooster, tom turkey	duck, gosling	duck, goose

Comparable if less steady changes occurred regarding smaller furred game, namely, hares and wild rabbits. While these furnish as many roasts as hors d'oeuvres, entrées, and entremets combined in the menus of *La Cuisinière bourgeoise,* this is not true of the recipes: 27 hors d'oeuvres or entrées and 8 entremets against only 2 roasts (barely 6 percent). This is a less significant ratio to be sure, but the marked drop since the seventeenth century is worth noting: all 8 of 8 rabbit, young rabbit, and young hare recipes in *L'Art de bien traiter* are roasts; in *Le Nouveau Cuisinier* roasts still account for 2 out of 16 preparations (12.5 percent); and in *Le Cuisinier françois* they number 3 out of 10 (30 percent). Is this because the variety of true culinary preparation required for entrées, hors d'oeuvres, and entremets increased between 1651 and 1774? Or does it illustrate a trend, already established for other types of meats, toward stricter choices for roast meats? This trend is certainly clear in terms of animal age: the three seventeenth-century works include a few adult animals, while only young ones remain in the eighteenth century, at least in *La Cuisinière bourgeoise.*[21]

The four cookbooks cited are in closest agreement concerning feathered game and domestic poultry, which they all consider to be the ideal choices for roasts. And while each book contains a different percentage of such roasts, no steady trend emerges over time (see table 1). Likewise, no clear trend emerges toward an increase or decrease in the number of birds never used for roast (table 2).

Let us conclude with a final examination of the mention of cooking techniques in the titles of recipes. As we have seen, not much precision is to be found on this point in *Le Cuisinier françois:* not a single meat-day recipe title indicates "spit-roasting," but 12 of them mention "roasted." These include 2 roasts and 3 soups and entrées. Conversely, of the 80 recipes in the chapter on meat-day roasts, the titles of only 6 specify mode of preparation: 2

"roasted," 2 "stuffed," 1 "natural," and 1 *"à la royale"*; but as noted, 5 of these 6 dishes were more like entrées than roasts. Things are clearer in later publications. *Le Nouveau Cuisinier* contains 3 recipes called "on the spit" and 4 "roasted," none of which appears to have been a roast. Conversely, none of the 50 actual roast recipes is described as "roasted" or "on the spit." Likewise, no cooking technique is indicated for the roasts mentioned in *L'Art de bien traiter,* and there are no roasts among the 4 recipes labeled "roasted." Lastly, no title among the 31 roasts in *La Cuisinière bourgeoise* indicates a cooking method. In other words, in the matter of naming as well as in the selection of meats for roast, the rules became set between the middle of the seventeenth century and the latter half of the eighteenth century.

THREE

Entrées and Entremets

UNLIKE THE ROAST, WHICH WAS the domain of the rotisserie master, and the salad and dessert, which belonged to the pantry, entrées and entremets were true productions of the kitchen. Both were highly eclectic.

Entrées were subcategorized as small entrées, large entrées, spit-roasted entrées, relevés, and hors d'oeuvres; some were dry, some moist; they could be made of butcher's meat, organ meat, fowl, feathered or furred game, animals large or small, fruits or vegetables, or, on meatless days, eggs, fish, or any manner of aquatic life. These foods—like melon and artichoke, or oysters on meatless days—could be served raw or cooked in any number of ways: roasted, grilled, oven-baked in crust, simmered in sauce, or just boiled. Entremets were even more varied. They, too, could consist of organ meats, large cuts of meat, fowl, or feathered or furred game; many were egg or vegetable dishes, cold meats, aspics, creamed dishes, pasties, pies or tarts, all sorts of other savories, fritters, or fried specialties.

This chapter aims to establish criteria by which to distinguish entrées from entremets, and to ascertain what had to be served during the first course before the roast, and what was to be eaten afterward as part of the final course from the kitchen. This is not as simple as recognizing roast, soup, salad, or dessert dishes. As was the case for the roast, we shall see that relevant factors included the ingredients themselves, their mode of preparation, and their serving temperature.

Vegetables

On meat days, vegetables served various functions. They were a prime component of soups, entrées, and hors d'oeuvres, salads to garnish the roast, and entremets. Cooking and presentation changed with function. Soups are straightforward: along with the requisite bread simmered in the broth, they could contain any of the vegetables also found in entrées, salads, and entremets.

Concerning entrées, Grimod de La Reynière wrote, "All animal products find their way into entrées, which are built around butcher's meat, organs, lamb, game, fowl, and saltwater or freshwater fish, often with vegetables or pasta as a support. But the latter never constitute entrées by themselves; all entrées come from the animal kingdom." Most entrée recipes do in fact include vegetables, but in the seventeenth century, they appeared as components of a sauce, a ragoût, or at most a garnish rather than as an actual dish, and were rarely included in the name of the dish.[1] In the eighteenth century, judging by *La Cuisinière bourgeoise,* vegetables were more often named in recipe titles and became more abundant in the composition of dishes.[2] However, they remained mere accompaniments to meats; never presented alone, vegetables were always of secondary importance.

In contrast, entremets with vegetables were essentially vegetable dishes, with or without meat. The 1660 *Nouveau Cuisinier* offers such vegetable entremets as "Truffles in lamb juices," "Spanish cardoons," "Mushroom casserole," "Ragoût of morels," "Forest mushrooms," "Artichokes in white sauce," "Asparagus in melted butter," "Cauliflower with lamb juices," "Creamed peas," "Young green peas with lard," "Fried cucumber pâté," and so on.[3] The 1739 *Dons de Comus* still lists entremets like "Morels in cream," "Truffles à la provençale," "Asparagus with peas," "Spanish cardoons with parmesan," "Swiss chard in fat," and "German-style artichokes."[4] These vegetable entremets are easy to distinguish from the vegetables served as a garnish for an entrée, even when dishes in both categories contain some meat. The "Young green peas with lard" entremets, for example, can hardly be confused with the entrée "Pigeon with peas"![5]

Vegetables could also be served as salads, distinct from hot entremets in that they were either raw, served at a different temperature, or differently seasoned. Salads were usually a purely vegetable dish, considered as "a sort of entremets brought to the table to accompany the roast." As we saw in the *Dictionnaire de Trévoux,* they were "usually composed of raw greens seasoned with salt, oil, and vinegar." But *Le Cuisinier méthodique* (1685 edition), one of the rare cookbooks to devote any attention to salads, confirms this definition only up to a point. Along with raw greens, it featured salads made of roots, all sorts of fruits, flowers, and even some animal ingredients like anchovies.[6] In addition, the ingredients were not always raw but sometimes cooked.[7] Finally, salads—and not just fruit salads—could sometimes be seasoned with sugar instead of salt, oil, and vinegar.[8]

Eggs

There should not be any confusion over the place of eggs in meat-day meals: no matter how they were prepared, eggs were considered entremets. They could be served as omelets; scrambled; fried; variously seasoned with sauces, cooking juices, meat, fish, vegetables, or fruits; salted or sugared; or could constitute the main ingredient of a whole variety of dishes.[9]

Eggs tended to be eaten mainly on meatless days, and only then were they served as entrées. Consequently, cookbooks contain many more egg recipes for meatless than for meat days.[10] Although there was no church ruling against eating meatless dishes on meat days, egg entrée recipes for meatless days may not be the ideal example of what could be served as entremets at other times.

La Cuisinière bourgeoise, with no mention of meat or meatless days, categorizes "Eggs à la jardinière" as an entrée. As hors d'oeuvres, it lists soft-boiled eggs in various sauces, "Eggs in brown butter," eggs stuffed with lettuce or chicory, "Eggs with tripe and cucumbers," "Eggs with garlic," and "Eggs en sur-tout." Under "hors d'oeuvre or entremets" it includes "Scrambled eggs in the shell," "Eggs in cream," "Fried eggs," "Eggs on bread," "Eggs Parmesan au gratin," "Eggs à la bourgeoise," and "Grilled eggs."[11]

But let there be no confusion: whatever their preparation, eggs served on meat days could be served only as entremets.

Large Meat Cuts

The large butcher's cuts of meat, so rarely found among the roasts, were most often eaten as entrées or main entrées (table 3).[12] But butcher's-meat recipes in these categories steadily increased from 52 percent in *Le Cuisinier françois* to 84 percent in *La Cuisinière bourgeoise.* This is due partly to the decreased proportion of butcher's meats that served as roasts—a drop from 9 percent to 3 percent (although this figure did spike to 12.5 percent in *L'Art de bien traiter*)—and partly to the disappearance of soups calling for such cuts of meat.

TABLE 3

Use of butcher's meats (excluding organ meats)

	Soups	Entrées, etc.	Roasts	Entremets	Pasties	Total
Le Cuisinier françois (1651)	11 = 15%	33 or 39 = 44% or 52%	13 or 7 = 17% or 9%	6 = 8%	12 = 16%	75
Le Nouveau Cuisinier (1660)	12 = 18%	38 = 56%	5 = 7%	3 = 4%	10 = 15%	68
L'Art de bien traiter (1674)	6 = 12.5%	31 = 65%	6 = 12.5%	5 = 10%	—	48
La Cuisinière bourgeoise (1774)	0	125 = 84%	4 = 3%	20 = 13%	—	149

The proportion of large cuts served as entremets remained far lower, but may have been on the rise. What matters is that throughout this period, these large cuts were distinct from others in two ways: by their very nature, and by the manner in which they were cooked and served. In the four books under consideration, most of the large-cut entremets are ham dishes: 6 out of 6 in *Le Cuisinier françois;* 3 out of 3 in Pierre de Lune's *Nouveau Cuisinier;* 3 out of 5 in *L'Art de bien traiter;* 4 out of 20 in *La Cuisinière bourgeoise.*[13] By the same token, all of the ham dishes of known function were entremets, even the fresh hams roasted on the spit and served hot.

Change did occur, however. The proportion of ham among large meat cuts for entremets diminished steadily, and the most recent of these cookbooks includes suckling pig, but not for the same purpose as ham: all of the suckling pig dishes were served cold, which is probably why they were considered entremets, like all other cold meats. Yet even in *La Cuisinière bourgeoise,* suckling pig was not always an entremets: served hot in white sauce, it was an entrée; and spit-roasted, it was a roast.[14]

Organ Meats

With the rather ambiguous exception of *Le Cuisinier françois,* organ meats never served as roasts, but were long used in soups and for entrées, hors d'oeuvres, and entremets (table 4) during the whole period under discussion.[15] Since pasties could be served as either entrées or entremets, we can assume that organs were considered entrée or entremets meats. The two categories combined represent 86 percent to 100 percent of organ-meat preparations.

TABLE 4

Use of organ meats

	Soups	Entrées, etc.	Roasts	Entremets	Pasties	Total
Le Cuisinier françois (1651)	4 = 7%	18 = 30.5%	3 = 5%	31 = 53%	3 = 3%	59
Le Nouveau Cuisinier (1660)	8 = 14%	20 = 34%	0	22 = 37%	9 = 15%	59
L'Art de bien traiter (1674)	4 = 12.5%	13 = 41%	0	15 = 47%	—	32
La Cuisinière bourgeoise (1774)	0	99 = 82%	0	22 = 18%	—	121

Now let us examine whether the organ meats used for entremets can be distinguished from those used for entrées. Those routinely served as entremets include most pork organs (tongue, ears, knuckles, and head but not the liver or chitterlings); foie gras and occasionally deer and rabbit liver; veal and potentially lamb sweetbreads; rooster and veal kidneys, as well as ram white kidneys; salted, dried, smoked, or stuffed beef tongue (fresh tongue was usually an entrée); deer innards; and wild boar trotters. Other organ meats were sometimes prepared as soups but most often as entrées, or as entrée hors d'oeuvres.

We might speculate further about the fact that some organ meats—lamb innards, cock's combs, lamb and fresh beef tongue, veal ears, beef palate, veal knuckle, veal and lamb sweetbreads, veal head, and cow udder—are presented sometimes as entrées and sometimes as entremets. In the first two cookbooks, some of these ambiguities may be due to the fact—already noted—that rules solidified by the mid-eighteenth century were not always so strict a century earlier. Such is the case for the *Nouveau Cuisinier* veal sweetbread entrées and beef palate entremets, and for the lamb organ meats and fresh beef tongue presented as entremets in *Le Cuisinier françois*. Also, as seen in table 4, organ meats tended to be listed more as entremets in the mid-seventeenth century, and more as entrées or hors d'oeuvres beginning in 1674.

Did other factors contribute to eighteenth-century ambiguities (calf's liver, lamb tongue, and veal ears, knuckle, and head being presented as entremets, while veal and lamb sweetbreads were served as hors d'oeuvres)? Sometimes the same meat was an hors d'oeuvre if hot, an entremets if cold;

such is the case with the beef tongues, which were hors d'oeuvres if cooked fresh and served hot, but "cold entremets" if salted, smoked, dried, or stuffed. However, there may have been other differences besides serving temperature. A more conclusive example is the "stuffed veal head *à la bourgeoise*": served hot, it was an entrée; served cold, a "cold entremets."

Kidneys are another example: beef and possibly lamb kidneys were served as an hors d'oeuvre, but veal kidney, according to *La Cuisinière bourgeoise* as well as *Le Nouveau Cuisinier*, was presented as an entremets. Is this just because it was veal, or because it was roasted—all roasted meats being entremets? In *Le Nouveau Cuisinier*, it was served twice as an entremets, once roasted and once in an omelet—the latter preparation, as we have seen, also being an entremets (on meat days).

But *La Cuisinière bourgeoise*, usually so disciplined about the distribution of dishes, is sometimes more lax than seventeenth-century works, as in the case of its "Veal liver à la bourgeoise," "Lamb's tongue en sur-tout," and six veal sweetbread dishes.[16] All were served hot yet could be served as either an hors d'oeuvre or an entremets.

Fowl and Game

We have seen that fowl and small game were prime choices for roast, but were also used for entremets and especially entrées, particularly in the case of domestic poultry. Table 5 provides two sets of entremets figures: the first includes the fowl and game organ meats discussed earlier, and the second does not. But both include pasties, which I have not explicitly listed as entrées or entremets, but which I will show can be categorized. Feathered and furred game, in addition to their much higher ratio of roasted meats, also accounted for a greater proportion of entremets than domesticated animals.[17] In addition, furred game consistently surpassed feathered game as an entremets choice over the course of both centuries.

But these trends do not explain why the same fowl or game was sometimes used for an entrée or hors d'oeuvre and at other times for an entremets. A comparison of the dishes listed in note 17 hints at some answers that will be more systematically examined later in this chapter. The fowl and game entremets, for example, include dishes of aspic and meat in aspic, as well as cold galantines, braised preparations, and pasties that do not appear among the entrées.

Other comparisons leave one wondering: the "Marinated chickens" and fried chicken found among the *Cuisinier françois* entremets are no different from the many marinated and then fried meats and fowl included among

TABLE 5
Fowl and game entrées and entremets

	Le Cuisinier françois (1651)	Le Nouveau Cuisinier (1660)	L'Art de bien traiter (1674)	La Cuisinière bourgeoise (1774)
Domestic fowl	18 E / 7 (3) Em	38 E / 15 (7) Em	27 E / 7 (3) Em	110 E / 11 (6) Em
Feathered game	11 E / 10 (10) Em	13 E / 9 (9) Em	0 E / 1 (1) Em	25 E / 2 (2) Em
Furred game	7 E / 11 (3) Em	10 E / 11 (7) Em	0 E / 2 (0) Em	25 E / 7 (5) Em

E = entrées; Em = entremets

the entrées. Furthermore, *Le Cuisinier françois* and *Le Nouveau Cuisinier* list ragoûts of fowl and game that served as entremets yet are identical to those listed under entrées. But such entremets no longer appear in either *L'Art de bien traiter* or *La Cuisinière bourgeoise*. Here again, distribution rules became more specific and rigorous starting in the mid-seventeenth century.

TYPES OF PREPARATIONS

Pasties and Pies

In the seventeenth and eighteenth centuries, pasties and pies were served only as entrées or entremets, but references do not always specify which. *Le Cuisinier françois,* for instance, has a chapter on "Pastries served throughout the year," and one on "Fish pastries to be eaten hot, including pasties & pies."[18] *Le Nouveau Cuisinier* has chapters on "pasties to be eaten cold," "pasties to be eaten hot," "meat pies," "fish pasties to be eaten hot," and "fish pies."[19] Fortunately, some indication of where each of these dishes belonged in the meal can usually be found either in the chapter heading or in the recipe.

The entrées and entremets were not distinguished by whether they were savory or sweet, as we might think today, but by whether they were served hot or cold.[20] For example, in his 1691 *Cuisinier royal et bourgeois,* Massialot writes, "Pasties are served hot or cold: the former as Entrées, and the latter as Entremets."[21] This distinction is not contradicted by any of the books under consideration. Among the rare pasties it lists, *La Cuisinière bourgeoise* indicates that "Pasty of hare à la bourgeoise" is to be "served cold as an entremets," and its "main centerpiece entremets" include "pasties of any sort of meat you wish to wrap in crust." The recipe provided ends as follows: "After it is cooked, place it where it will cool down."[22] All of the entremets pasties in *Le Cuisinier françois* are cold as well, and the pasties for entrées are all hot.[23] The rule also applied to pies.

Many recipes could, with a few minor variations, make either an entrée or an entremets. For the "Pasté de chapon," *Le Cuisinier françois* explains: "If you want to serve it hot, do not season it as much as when you serve it cold."[24] When served hot, the pasty was usually dressed with a sauce poured through the steam vent or after removing the lid, just before serving. This was the case for the "capon pasty": "Make a white sauce for it or add any juices to it, and serve it hot and uncovered."[25]

Hot and Cold Food

Pasties and pies were not the only dishes served hot as entrées and cold as entremets; this was also true of the *à la daube* (braised) meat and fowl dishes in *L'Art de bien traiter*.[26] *Le Cuisinier françois* mentions such braised dishes only in its chapter on entrées, and ambiguously at that, since four of them are to be served dry on a napkin; but nothing says they were cold.[27] They probably were not because the fifth braised recipe offers two serving suggestions: either "parsleyed" like the others—therefore drained on a napkin—or cold in a jellied sauce reduction.[28] *Le Nouveau Cuisinier* serves its braised dishes as entrées except for the braised pig's knuckles, which are presented as an entremets, not because of their temperature—since they are quickly grilled before serving—but because of the nature of the meat itself, as we have already seen. The book's braised dishes for the entrée course are sometimes served heated in a sauce, but more often at room temperature and plain.[29] Massialot does likewise in his *Cuisinier royal et bourgeois*. Half a century later, *La Cuisinière bourgeoise* serves only cold braised dishes and always labels them as "cold entremets" or "main cold entremets."[30]

La Cuisinière bourgeoise even extends the hot and cold conventions to *à l'étouffade* (smothered) meat and fowl, serving the hot version as an entrée and the cold one as an entremets; similarly, it presents its "Veal's head à la bourgeoise" as a hot entrée and as a "cold entremets"; the same is true of oven-baked beef and "Young hares in galantine"—with the "Suckling pig in galantine" always eaten as a cold entremets.[31] This classification system, like many others, seems to have crystallized during the period in question, for our seventeenth-century books did not apply it to meats that were *à l'étouffade*, stuffed, baked, or in galantine. The "Cold grilled turkey" and the "Cold turkey with cabbage or cucumber" in *Le Nouveau Cuisinier* can be skipped, since they are hot entrées from which some meat is set aside, grilled, and simmered in a sauce. The principle of hot preparation for entrées and cold for entremets did not extend to braised dishes until 1674 in *L'Art de bien traiter.*

Aspics, Custards, Fritters, and Toasts

Aspics were cold by definition and, at least by the mid-seventeenth century, always an entremets. We are not talking about fruit jellies—which belonged in the dessert course like all preserves—but meat-day aspics made from capon and veal knuckles or deer antlers, and the meatless-day versions made with tench and carp scales, as in *Le Cuisinier françois.*[32] To be sure, *Le Nouveau Cuisinier* does suggest aspics in the chapter on "entrées for Good Friday"; but they are combined with all sorts of other dishes with entremets characteristics, for reasons explained in the next chapter.[33]

While the aspics named in recipe titles are all sweet, less-noticeable savory aspics also figure in the body of recipes, such as the puzzling *Cuisinier françois* "Braised pork" served cold (p. 43), and several other cold entremets recipes in *La Cuisinière bourgeoise.*[34]

Custards were also served at the entremets course—at least in meat-day meals, because here again the practice was different for meatless days. For example, in 1660, *Le Nouveau Cuisinier* suggests such meat-day entremets as "Pistachio custards," "Melon custard," "Pea custard," and elsewhere a "Custard pie," two "Almond custard pies," "Apple custard pie," "Sugared artichoke custard," and so on—not counting the various creamed vegetables that were served at the entremets course as vegetables, not for their creamed sauces. Similarly, in 1739 *Les Dons de Comus* suggests 45 entremets of assorted custards and *La Cuisinière bourgeoise* lists 21, excluding the dessert custards—whipped custards, creamed cheeses, and fruit custards—that proliferated at the time.[35]

The entremets course also brought a wide selection of fritters. *Le Cuisinier françois* offers 9, all of them as entremets; there are 18 in *Les Dons de Comus,* including "Early dawn fritters," "Royal fritters," "Fallen fritters," "Fritters à l'Italienne," "Cup-and-ball fritters," "Extruded fritters," "Elder blossom fritters," "Fritter poppies," fruit fritters of all sorts, and a few vegetable ones. *La Cuisinière bourgeoise* has 12 such entremets selections, plus one hors d'oeuvre of "Calf tripe fritters" and one meat-day entrée, "Pigeon fritters"—not to mention the "Cod fritters" as a meatless hors d'oeuvre or entrée.[36]

Pierre de Lune, in his *Nouveau Cuisinier,* presents 11 fritters as entrées for

Good Friday, but as we have seen, these are not relevant to our search for the rules by which meat-day dishes were organized. The hors d'oeuvres and meat-day entrées in *La Cuisinière bourgeoise* are a different matter. Why were these not served as entremets? Comparison with those that were suggests that fritters served as entremets were all composed of fruits, vegetables, dough, custard, or cheese, while those brought as entrées and hors d'oeuvres consisted of organ or other meats, poultry, or fish. The same holds true in *L'Art de bien traiter,* where "Fritters of veal fricassee" are an entrée, while entremets include "Little fritters," "Fritters of sliced artichoke bottoms," and "Mushroom fritters." Another of the book's entremets consists of "Marinated veal sweetbreads fried or as fritters," suggesting that the crucial difference was not between meats and vegetables but between foods typical of entremets and foods that characterized entrées. In other words, where fritters and all fried foods were concerned, classification as an entrée or an entremets depended on the food ingredients and not on their preparation.

The final two dish types typical of entremets were toasts and ramekins. The two terms seem nearly synonymous as used in the recipe for "Kidney ramekin" in *Le Cuisinier françois:* "Remove the kidney from a cooked veal loin, chop with parsley or garlic and an egg yolk; season the mixture and spread on bread toasted in the skillet, and serve plain or with sugar. Veal kidney toast can be made the same way but without parsley or onion: spread the well-seasoned kidney on bread slices toasted to a nice color in the skillet. You may sprinkle it with sugar and serve or even mix sugar into the preparation if you wish."[37] In recipe names, this book mentions only ramekins, whereas *Le Nouveau Cuisinier* uses only the term *rôties.*[38] *L'Art de bien traiter* ignores them both, while *Le Cuisinier royal et bourgeois* lists "toasts" of veal kidneys, woodcock, and foie gras, as well as cheese "ramekins"; *La Cuisinière bourgeoise* contains ten toasts, all as entremets; *Les Dons de Comus* has twelve, including "Toasts à l'Italienne," "Toasts à la prieure," "Toasts with marrow," "Toasts glazed with eggs," and a single recipe for "Ramekins," all of which are also intended as entremets.[39]

Raw Food: Shellfish, Vegetables, and Fruit

Raw food today may mean oysters or other shellfish at the start of the meal, first-course fruits such as melon or possibly grapefruit, hors d'oeuvres of raw vegetables, possibly a salad eaten after the main dish and before the cheese (if not with it), or else some fruit for dessert. In the seventeenth and eighteenth centuries, raw oysters sometimes began the meal. But this was unusual except at the seashore, and they usually made a complete meal, as in the *Déjeuner d'huîtres* painted around the mid-eighteenth century by Jean-François de Troy. Raw fruits were sometimes also presented as entrées, but became increasingly typical of dessert. "Salads"—which could mean olives in brine, vinegar preserves, or bitter orange quarters—were closely linked to roasts, but the *Dictionnaire de Trévoux* defines them as entremets. As for fruits, they already typified dessert in the seventeenth century— much more so than today, since "dessert" now also means pastries, custards, and all sorts of other sweet entremets. Raw foods were thus eaten more or less as they are today, but with some interesting nuances, notably the absence of raw vegetable hors d'oeuvres—except perhaps for artichokes in a pepper sauce, which in *La Cuisinière bourgeoise* constituted an hors d'oeuvre as they do today, but were considered an entremets in the time of *Le Cuisinier françois*.[40]

FOUR

Composition of Meatless Meals

MEATLESS AND LENTEN MEALS, FASTING, AND ABSTINENCE

Christian food regulations having become extremely lax since the mid-twentieth century, we will first review what they were during the fourteenth, fifteenth, and sixteenth centuries and how they loosened in the seventeenth and eighteenth. We will also touch on the very strict conventions that prevailed in the late Middle Ages.

Early medieval and Renaissance rules focused only on fasting and abstinence. Fasting initially meant no food at all for periods of various lengths, emulating Jesus' forty-day fast in the desert. During the late Middle Ages there were three forty-day fasts: one before Easter (our present-day Lent), one from St. Martin's Day to Christmas, and a more elusive one after Pentecost. Short fasts were also observed, including ember days and the eves of certain major celebrations. During fasting periods, no food was eaten before nightfall, a custom Muslims still observe during Ramadan—except that these Christian nights of abstinence from meat or even any nourishment save bread and water were much less enjoyable than the nights of Ramadan.

The Pentecost fast disappeared even before the eleventh century, while the one before Christmas dwindled to the twenty-odd days of Advent. The rules then gradually eased over the next centuries. The single meal of fasting days was now allowed at the "none" or ninth hour of the day, which is about three in the afternoon. This was soon supplemented by a morsel at bedtime and liquid food in the morning, which were not viewed as breaking the fast.

Lent contrasted with the remainder of the year, called *charnage,* itself divided into meat and meatless days. The Lenten abstinence from meat did not prohibit Western Christians from eating fish, unlike the Greeks and other Eastern believers for whom this was forbidden during part of their extensive fast. In the Western world, Lent ruled out cooking with lard and other animal fats but also with butter, thus distinguishing Lenten abstinence from the ordinary meatless Fridays and Saturdays of the *charnage* period. Another difference from ordinary meatless days was that the Lenten diet also excluded eggs, cream, and cheese. Moreover, seventeenth-century cookbooks disclose an even stricter Good Friday diet that also excluded fish, leaving only vegetables.[1]

For northern Europeans who consumed butter and generally did not care for olive oil or even food cooked in oil, the Lenten abstinence was a real deprivation. Luther denounced it emphatically, accusing the papacy of using this interdiction to promote the sale of inferior Italian oils. In a more serious vein, it appears that aversion to oil cookery may have contributed to northern Europe's Reformation movement.

In subsequent decades, the papacy did in fact grant more dispensations in countries that did not produce olive oil and therefore did not have a taste for it. In the seventeenth and eighteenth centuries, nearly all French provinces were among these exempt regions; French cookbooks thus use butter in Lenten recipes—still distinct however from simple meatless dishes. Here is La Varenne's method for making fish soup during Lent: "Make broth with half water, half purée; add carp or other fish bones, an onion studded with cloves, bouquet garni, & salt; cook everything together with crustless bread & butter; sieve and use the broth as desired." And, in general: "All Lenten soups are prepared and seasoned like meatless-day preparations, except without eggs; but some can be mixed with purée, and others may contain almond broth for serving white or swirled."[2]

SEQUENCE OF MEATLESS MEALS

Like meat-day meals, meatless ones were organized in several courses fulfilling the same functions: soups, entrées, hors d'oeuvres, relevés, roast, salads, entremets, and desserts. The meatless ingredients, preparations, and types of dishes typical of these functions are reminiscent of what we have seen for meat-day meals, but with some major and surprising differences, as illustrated below by meatless-day roasts.

Meatless soups could contain fish and other aquatic life, or vegetables. *L'Art de bien traiter,* for example, suggests crayfish soup, puréed bean soup with green peas, garnished with heads of lettuce & stuffed cucumbers, asparagus soup, meatless soup *à la reine,* turtle soup, smelt soup, Milan cabbage soup, turnip soup, scoter and turnip soup, and so forth. The meat stock that enriched all meat-day soups was replaced by either purée or almond milk (crushed almonds moistened not with meat stock but with water or meatless broth or, increasingly, with milk), or a meatless broth of freshwater fish bones and mixed herbs. In the seventeenth century, these broths were flavored with various "juices" (e.g., crayfish or mushroom) and garnished with meatless tidbits like mushrooms, asparagus tips, carp roe, artichoke bottoms, morels, wild mushrooms, little fish sausages, and so on. For Lent, lard and other animal fats were replaced by butter and sometimes, though less and less, by oil.

After the soup but generally during the same first course came meatless entrées and hors d'oeuvres of fish in sauce or ragoût, various shellfish, "eggs for entrée," or hot fish pasties and various pies. The second course usually brought fish roasts such as those found once again in *L'Art de bien traiter:* flounder in court bouillon, brill, fresh salmon, sturgeon, large pike, red mullet, trout, perch, and so on. The names of these meatless roast dishes, like those of meat-day roast recipes, rarely indicate their mode of preparation. Alongside the roast or following as a separate course came meatless entremets, still nearly as diverse as their meat-day counterparts. The meal ended with desserts that were not strikingly different from those of meat days.

Having reviewed the basic structure of meatless meal sequences, we can now more closely examine these successive functions. We will analyze what sorts of foods and modes of preparation were involved, especially when it comes to the three functions whose dishes are problematic, namely, entrées (and hors d'oeuvres), entremets, and roasts.

FOOD CATEGORIES

Vegetables

On meatless as well as meat days, vegetables were served at two points in the meal—in soups and in entremets—the only difference being that vegetable soups appeared more often in meatless meals. Lenten meals also included vegetables as entrées. For example, the "Table of Entrées for Lent Containing no Eggs" [in *Le Cuisinier françois*] lists 74 fish dishes, 12 of vegetables, and 3 of fruits. Vegetables were served on Good Friday throughout the whole meal, which apparently consisted of just soups and entrées in *Le Cuisinier françois,* but which according to *Le Cuisinier royal et bourgeois* included a roast made entirely of root vegetables as well as some entremets.[3]

Certain vegetables—artichokes, cardoons [related to artichokes], asparagus, peas, mushrooms, and truffles—were fashionable and served at meatday meals. Others always or nearly always appeared on meatless days. This was true of spinach, cabbage, pumpkin, celery, leeks, greens, lentils, carrots, turnips, white and black salsify, and so on.[4] One might surmise that these vegetables, served only at meatless meals, were less attractive to gourmands and therefore ignored in meat-day meals; they were useful for Lenten and meatless meals, when there were few other options. However, they included delicacies like morels, wild mushrooms, and even skirret [a root vegetable related to caraway], reputed to be the most delectable of roots.[5] Conversely, some of the often-served meat-day vegetables could be fairly pedestrian, like fava beans and dried peas.[6] These may have been compatible with large cuts of salted meat, while cooking in butter was more suited to the delicate flavor of wild mushrooms or skirret.[7] But this is pure speculation.

Some vegetables—cabbage, broccoli, lettuce, onions, leeks—were more readily chosen for soup.[8] Others were used also, or only, for entremets or Lenten entrées. Such was the case for cauliflower, spinach, artichoke, celery, chard and cardoons, Paris mushrooms, and especially morels, wild mushrooms, and truffles, which were only rarely made into soup.[9] A great number of entrées called for skirret, at least in the mid-seventeenth century, when it was prized.[10]

Eggs

On meatless days, as in meat-day meals, eggs were served as entremets and sometimes in soups. But on meatless days they were also served in the entrée course, in fact much more often than at other points in the meal. The 29 meatless egg recipes in *Le Cuisinier françois,* for instance, include 3 soups, 4 entremets, 2 pastries, and 20 entrées. Similarly, 9 of the 10 egg recipes in *L'Art de bien traiter* are for entrées.[11]

Fish and Other Aquatic Life

Fish appeared in every segment of meatless-day meals: in soups, entrées, and hors d'oeuvres, roasts, entremets, and even salads. Dessert was the sole exception. But let us see whether any type of fish would do for these various functions.

The books considered here show that many of the fish listed were used for meatless roasts, some of them surprising on account of their small size or minimal gastronomic interest. But when we see small fish like smelt, gudgeon, red mullet, or weever, we should keep in mind that meat-day roasts did not come from the largest animals either, but from all sorts of succulent selections including lark, quail, ortolan, woodcock, and partridge. The real surprise is the many fish of very low gastronomic status that were considered acceptable for meatless roasts, including barbel, bream, herring, dab, mackerel, whiting, chub, skate, sardine, and tench—especially since their mediocrity was acknowledged even at the time. Concerning barbel, chub, gudgeon, and bream, Menon wrote, "Although these fish are not highly valued, some of them are nevertheless quite good"; and on the dab, L. S. R. comments, "At times when sole is unavailable, one is only too happy to resort to these ocean rejects."[12]

Fish suitable for roasts were not all used as such with equal frequency. Some—like shad, brill, pike, carp, smelt, sturgeon, plaice, salmon, sole, turbot, and weever—are selected for roasts in all or nearly all the books. While they served other functions as well, that of meatless roast was among the most common, ranging from 17 percent for sole up to 43.5 percent for shad, 44 percent for trout, and 45 percent for brill. In addition to these very roast-worthy fishes, marine mammals were also made into roasts, and roasts only, until 1660, after which they were no longer mentioned. Examples from *Le Cuisinier françois* include sea otters and porpoises.

Other fish appear only rarely as roasts. Barbel, catfish, burbot, plaice, sea bream, snapper, herring, lobster, oysters, lamprey, spiny lobster, scoter [actually, a sea duck], whiting, fresh cod, sardine, and chub are mentioned as roasts in only one book, and very seldom at that. Lobster is mentioned nine times, but only once for roast. Likewise suggested only once for a roast are spiny lobster (1 out of 10 mentions), herring (1/14), lamprey (1/17), and oysters (1/27). Note that these uncommon roasts appear only in *Le Cuisinier françois*, whose laxity has already been pointed out, and in *La Cuisinière bourgeoise*, which is thus just as undiscriminating when it comes to selecting fish. I would tend to categorize fish that were only sporadically served as roasts with ones never used that way, at least in the books consulted. These include anchovies, conger, hake, salt cod, and tuna, as well as crustaceans, shellfish, and other marine life no longer classified as fish—shrimp, crabs, crayfish, rock lobster, snails, frogs, mussels, urchins, clams, octopus, and turtles.

All saltwater life was usable for soup: shellfish (mussels, oysters), crustaceans (crayfish), reptiles (turtles), amphibians (frogs), and birds (scoters), as well as many fish including those most readily used for roast such as brill, pike, carp, smelt, sturgeon, perch, red mullet, salmon, sole, tench, turbot, and weever. Entrées were also made from most fish (shad, eel, barbel, catfish, brill, bream, pike, etc.), shellfish (oysters, mussels, clams), crustaceans (shrimp, crab, crayfish, lobster, spiny lobster), and reptiles and amphibians (turtles and frogs). No other function used such a range of aquatic animals.

Entremets were more selective: they included most crustaceans (crayfish, rock lobster, crab, lobster), frogs, turtles, and certain fishes such as anchovies, eels, carp, monkfish, salmon, sole, trout, and turbot.[13] Some of these actual fishes, such as anchovies, may have been entremets on their own merit, but most were used for their organs or because they were particularly well suited for use in cold-cut substitutes and other entremets specialties for meatless days.[14] Monkfish, for instance, was used in entremets mostly for its liver, carp for its roe or because its flesh could be worked into all sorts of delicacies, eel to make cervelat [a type of sausage], anchovies because they worked well as toast spread, and salmon along with "salmon trout, turbot, carp & other firm-fleshed fish" for cold pasties.[15] The entremets course also often featured fish-based preparations of unspecified species: fish aspic, fish ham, fish cervelat.[16]

Entrée and Entremets Preparations

As in the case of meat-day dishes, most of the dishes with sauce or ragoût were entrées; only *Le Cuisinier françois,* at the start of the period under examination, presents an important number of fish dishes in ragoût for the second course. Fish with sauce was presented as roast until 1674.

Other entrée preparations were fish in casserole, poached in demi–court bouillon, steamed, fricasseed, chopped, marinated, stewed, and in pies. Here again, only *Le Cuisinier françois* occasionally presents fish in demi–court bouillon as a second-course dish, and even in this work it is essentially a first-course offering. Fish as entremets were much fewer: fried in nearly every book, and much more rarely marinated, stewed, roasted, or in a sauce. Note that very few of these preparations were typical of soups, entrées, meatless roasts, or entremets: the exceptions were steaming, chopping, cooking in a red-wine stew and perhaps in pies, all typical of first courses—at least judging from just the cookbooks under consideration. Granted, *Le Cuisinier françois* also includes preparations in casserole, poached in demi–court bouillon, stuffed, and fricasseed.

Meatless Roasts in La Cuisinière bourgeoise

It seems paradoxical at first that the meatless-day roasts in *La Cuisinière bourgeoise* are not roasted. The occasional fish roasted on the spit, like sturgeon or large eel, was served as an entrée, covered with a sauce.[17] The same was true for all grilled fish: salmon steak, shad, bass, red mullet, mackerel, weever, sardines, mullet, herring, trout.[18] The few that were oven-baked with a sauce were also entrées.[19]

In this book, only two modes of preparation were deemed suitable for serving fish as the roast course: poaching and frying. It explicitly states, "All manner of fish fried & cooked in court bouillon are served as a dish of meatless roast."[20] Out of the book's 12 roast recipes, 6 are poached—5 in court bouillon and one *au bleu* [in which fish is cooked quickly, immediately after it has been killed]—and 6 are fried.[21] But these two cooking methods were not used only for meatless roasts: out of 13 fried fish recipes in this book, there are only 6 roasts, the others consisting of 5 entrées, 1 hors d'oeuvre, and 1 entremets. The marinated fried skate, cod, and pike, for example, were entrées because they were first marinated; the fried dab, sole, and plaice also constituted entrées, because of the sauce or ragoût served on the same plate. The same held for fried whiting when served in a "white sauce with capers and anchovies." Desalted anchovies fried in batter made an entremets, more because of the anchovies than because of the batter; marinated, floured, and fried frogs were an entrée hors d'oeuvre.[22] Similarly, out of 11 fish in court bouillon, there are 4 roasts and 7 entrées.[23] Only fish *au bleu* was served exclusively as roast, but this preparation occurs only once in *La Cuisinière bourgeoise*.

Other aspects of preparation and service were more typical of roasts than these cooking methods. Choice fish for poaching had to be dropped in court bouillon without being scaled, then served plain on a white napkin garnished only with some parsley. Salmon, for instance: "If served as a roast dish, do not scale it; once cooked, place it dry on a napkin, surrounded by green parsley."[24] The same applied to shad, pike, and especially carp, with its beautiful scales. What distinguished a turbot, brill, or salmon-trout roast, however, was not the scales but the fact of being served on a napkin and garnished with parsley. If presented with a sauce or ragoût on the same dish, they were entrées.

Frying fishes were always scaled first, but still considered roasts. The true characteristic of all meatless roasts, whatever their cooking method, was thus the serving style, on a napkin and without sauce.

The Nature of the Roast

What was this concept of the roast, that in the meatless context it could apply to a poached fish? What defining characteristic could embrace the existence of both fish roasts and meat roasts?

Roast meat and fried fish share the property of being cooked to "a nice color." As explained earlier, chickens prepared as spit-roasted entrées were larded and wrapped in paper "to prevent coloring, because chickens meant for spit-roasted entrées must be served white."[25] If meant for roast, their color had to be "neither too pale nor too browned."[26] The roast even called sometimes for deep browning. Pheasant roasts, for example, were served "when nicely colored." The same instruction applied to fried fish roasts. For dab, sole, flounder, and plaice, *La Cuisinière bourgeoise* recommends cooking "in hot frying oil on a lively fire" so that the fish does not get "mushy and oily," and adds, "When cooked to a nice color, take it out, place it on a cloth, then serve on a napkin as a roast dish."[27] The same instructions are given for river monkfish: "Simply dip in flour and fry; when nicely colored, serve on a napkin as a roast dish."[28] Since fish is more fragile than fowl, less convenient to cook on the spit, and less apt to take on a golden color by that method, it is reasonable to conclude that frying is the best way to give it "a nice color," as for a meat roast.

Fish in court bouillon or *au bleu* is another matter, since poaching is the antithesis of roasting in all respects. Note, however, that poached fish is prepared in a watery medium (court bouillon), while roast fowl is prepared in hot air. It can thus be said that fish roasts and meat roasts are both cooked in their natural element.

We have seen that both kinds of roast were prepared as simply as possible, without stuffing, sauce, marinade, or ragoût. ("Stuffed cod tail" is an entrée because it is stuffed; the twenty-nine sauced and eight marinated fish dishes are entrées by virtue of their sauce or marinade.)[29] Of course, these extremely simple preparations are not the easiest to get right: there is no marinade to compensate for any lack of flavor, no stuffing, sauce, or ragoût to correct a dish that has been overcooked, undercooked, cooked too fast, or cooked too slowly. The utter simplicity of meatless and meat-day roasts requires perfection.

Seventeenth-Century Meatless Roasts

Do the meatless roast rules drawn from an examination of *La Cuisinière bourgeoise* extend to other cookbooks, particularly those of the seventeenth century? Cooking procedures suitable for meatless roasts had clearly proliferated: fish could now be cooked not only *au bleu,* in court bouillon, or fried, but also roasted, grilled, in ragoût, in casserole, in demi–court bouillon, in beurre blanc, and with various sauces.[30] The definition of what could be served in the second course had once again become more strict, while the number of acceptable cooking procedures steadily diminished: eight and seven in the two books from the mid-seventeenth century, five in 1674 and 1691, and only three in 1734 and 1774.

In all our seventeenth-century books, a high proportion of grilled fishes (about one quarter to half of them) are served during the second course, as compared to the 0/64 ratio in *Nouveau Cuisinier royal et bourgeois* and the 0/21 in *La Cuisinière bourgeoise.* It is not quite the same for "roasted" or "spit-roasted" fish, which are clearly more numerous in *Le Cuisinier françois* than in later works. It is worth pointing out that at the time, roasted or grilled fish presented in the second course always included a sauce, like the fish served as entrées.

As already mentioned in connection with meat-day roasts, it is tempting to wonder whether *Le Cuisinier françois* allowed entrée recipes in its chapter on meatless roasts simply by association, especially since this is the only book to propose fish "en ragoust," "en castrolle," or "au demy court bouillon" as second-course dishes. But a note preceding its recipe for "Grenost en castrolle" rules out this conclusion: "Although it is normally served in court bouillon, it must nevertheless be served in casserole for the second course." Here, at least where gurnard is concerned, the author finds the casserole method more characteristic of fish roast than cooking in court bouillon! Note also that fish in casserole are served for the second course seven times out of ten, one of the highest ratios found not only in that particular cookbook but more generally in all the books under discussion. It therefore seems clear that the notion of fish roast in *Le Cuisinier françois* differs greatly from the one that prevailed in the eighteenth century.

Like these cookbooks, this discussion has variously used the terms *meatless roast, fish roast,* and sometimes *second-course fish.* Were all of these notions equivalent? La Varenne, in *Le Cuisinier françois,* has no chapter called

"Roast" but one called "Second Course" for meatless as well as meat-day meals. But we know that the second course also included salads and often entremets, even if the roast was its main feature. Could the fish in sauce or ragoût mentioned as second-course dishes be entremets rather than meatless roasts? *Le Cuisinier françois* and *Le Nouveau Cuisinier* are ambiguous on this point, and *L'Art de bien traiter* even more so when it places a chapter on "Fried Dishes" (type of dish), then another on "Entremets" (function), after the chapter called "For the Second Course" (service), which itself follows a chapter on soups and one on meatless entrées (functions).

Le Cuisinier royal et bourgeois is more consistent and clear: on meatless meals, it devotes a chapter each to the first and second courses. The first is neatly divided into seasonal soups and entrées for the whole year; though less obviously, the second is also organized in its own way (pp. 68–71). It first states that for the second course, "the same fishes are served as above [for the first course] in court bouillon & fried, or on the grill or the spit." After a series of examples, it goes on to say that "you may also serve fish pasties & pies . . . & add several meat-day entremets like mushrooms, artichokes, asparagus, morels, and cucumbers." It concludes with "fish salads, which are also part of this course." In this list of all second-course selections, do the fish "on the grill & the spit" represent meatless roasts like the fish "in court bouillon and fried," or are they entremets like the pasties, pies, and vegetable dishes? There is no clear answer, and the recipes are not much help because they never state whether the dish is a roast. Worse yet, the ones that most seem like roasts are sometimes described as entremets. Take, for example, the "Carp in court bouillon," which is the ideal example of roast in most of the books: "Serve on a napkin with green parsley and lemon slices as an entremets," and the "Pike in court bouillon, or *au bleu*," which is to be "served plain as an entremets."

In the eighteenth century, when *Le Nouveau Cuisinier royal et bourgeois* (1730–1734) and *La Cuisinière bourgeoise* indicate the function of a dish, whether meatless or meat-day, they use the term *roast,* not *second course. La Cuisinière bourgeoise,* for example, gives recipes for turbot and brill in white court bouillon to be "served dry on a towel, garnished with green parsley, as a dish of roast," and for fried whiting "dipped in flour, fried very hot, & served on a plate as a dish of roast."

The last clues for solving this problem come from second-course meatless menus from these various periods. The 1662 *Nouveau et Parfait Maistre d'hostel royal,* by Pierre de Lune, contains several meatless menus. One of the simplest is the "Table with two salvers & three platters" (pp. 89–90), where 1 and 2 stand for the salvers and 3, 4, and 5 represent smaller serving pieces. This meal consists of a first course of five soups, a second course with five entrées, a third course presented as "Fish," and a fourth called "Entremets"—followed of course by a fifth course, dessert, which goes unmentioned. The course of interest here is the third: it features a "dry turbot" in platter 1, probably cooked in court bouillon; "pike & perch in sauce" in 2; "weevers" in 3; and "salmon" in 4—the last two possibly cooked in court bouillon, though no mention is made—and "fried sole" in 5, plus the "salads and olives" expected in this meatless-day fish course as well as for meat-day roast courses.

The 1691 *Cuisinier royal et bourgeois* gives "Meatless Menu Suggestions for ordinary occasions" that refer to the whole second course as roast but that are too vague to satisfy our curiosity about cooking methods for the fish mentioned and about the nature of the entremets.[31] The menus published in *Les Soupers de la Cour* (1755) are more detailed, as for instance the "Table for twenty-five to thirty meatless place settings served to twenty-seven persons" from the "Menus de Printemps."[32] The "Third course" includes 2 principal entremets and 2 secondary ones, plus 12 roast dishes including 3 of sole, 3 of smelt, 2 of whiting, 1 of salmon in aspic, 1 of shad, and 2 of flounder. In no instance is the cooking method specified, but all appear to have been poached. Another "Menus de Printemps" example is a "Table for twenty to twenty-five meatless place settings served to twenty-three persons": the third course features "2 Principal Entremets" and "2 Secondary Entremets," along with "8 Dishes of Roast," namely, "2 of monkfish, 1 of sturgeon, 1 of fried carp, 1 of shad, 1 of salmon in aspic, 1 of pike fillets, 1 of perch." In this meal, as in the preceding one, the "Fourth Course" consists of "18 Hot Entremets as Relevés for the Roasts, Sauces, & Salads," with no fish save a "ragoût of carp tongues," the fifth and last course being dessert.

The Sequence of Dishes in the Classical Period

To conclude part one, it is clear that during the classical period, from 1650 to 1789, the sequence of dishes did not remain static but varied constantly for meat days as well as meatless ones. There were changes in the various stages of a meal during that period: hors d'oeuvres appeared in the seventeenth century, and relevés in the first half of the eighteenth century. At first they were part of different courses; later they were served only during the first course. Courses also became more elaborate. Each contained only one type of dish in Pierre de Lune's *Nouveau et Parfait Maistre d'hostel royal*, several in Massialot's *Cuisinier royal et bourgeois* (soups, entrées, and hors d'oeuvres for the first course, roasts, salads, and entremets for the second), and even more in the second half of the century. This progression is evident in the menu of the supper for Louis XV on Monday 21 June 1751—a menu that seems to have been composed of three courses, though its presentation is ambiguous.[33]

The definition of dishes suitable as meat and meatless roasts also evolved. By the second half of the eighteenth century, the only acceptable meat-day dishes were roasted meats nicely browned—on the spit, of course—and served without sauce or ragoût; and meatless options were limited to fish cooked in court bouillon, with their scales if attractive, and served dry on a white napkin; or fish fried without having been marinated, and served the same way. By contrast, as we have seen repeatedly, the mid-seventeenth century was far less selective, for both meat and meatless days.

But while the meal sequence in the classical period was not immutable, the variations were greater before 1650 and again during the nineteenth and twentieth centuries. Part two will address these developments.

Fourteenth to Twentieth Centuries

Variations in the Sequence of Courses in France

FIVE

French Meals in the Fourteenth and Fifteenth Centuries

DID FOURTEENTH- AND FIFTEENTH-CENTURY French meals follow a pre-scribed order? The question is raised not by me but by the few historians who have even broached the subject, and who describe medieval meals as disorganized collations of dishes. Alfred Franklin, probably misled by the ambiguity of the term *mets* ("dish" or "course"), finds not only that there was no orderly sequence of cooked foods, but that the most disparate dishes were served pell-mell on a single large platter.[1] Preconceived notions about the barbarity of the medieval table have in fact remained so ingrained that many historians have perpetuated them, unchallenged, for a whole century.[2]

While in his sixth volume Franklin devotes a few equivocal words to the absence of any order in the service sequence of meals,[3] Bridget Ann Henisch develops this premise in a much more reliable study:

> The arrangement of a medieval menu differs sharply from a modern one. In the latter, ideally, a certain attempt is made to balance the flavors and textures of the different items, and each course of the meal is planned as part of a whole. In the former, there is simply a profusion of dishes, each regarded as an isolated, self-contained unit, served with its own sauce or accompaniments and judged on its own merits. . . . The great advantage of this approach was its flexibility: Anything could be added or subtracted at a moment's notice without wrecking the delicate balance of the dinner.[4]

Admittedly, the sequence of dishes in fourteenth- and fifteenth-century meals is not easy to grasp: it clearly differs from both our own custom and that of the "French-style service" practiced in France between the seventeenth and nineteenth centuries. But this alone does not prove that there were no rules, expressed or implied. Starting from the opposite hypothesis, we will attempt to uncover some signs of such order by analyzing the twenty-nine French menus (694 dishes) figuring in *Le Ménagier de Paris* of circa 1393 and the six others published in the printed edition of *Le Viandier de Taillevent* about 1486.[5]

DEFINING THE NOTION OF COURSES

The Concept of Course: "Dish" and "Platter"

In fourteenth- and fifteenth-century France, courses were sometimes called "dishes" *(mets)* and sometimes "platters" *(assiettes)*. The two terms were equivalent and interchangeable in most cases, but could occasionally have different meanings.

Dish is the only word used in eighteen of the twenty-nine menus.[6] Menu 1 uses only the word *platter,* with exactly the same meaning, and menu 2, alternately using *platter* and *dish,* confirms this interchangeability: the first and second platters are followed by the third, fourth, and fifth dishes, with a sixth and final platter. Similarly, menu 5 lists the "third platter" and "fourth platter" after the "second dish," which itself came after a "first dish and platter." This seeming redundancy occurs again in menu 19, while menus 16 and 17 refer to a "first platter," then to "dishes" for the next courses.

Yet the terms *dish* and *platter,* used in the same menu, could also mean something quite different: menu 1 is a "Dinner . . . of thirty-one dishes with six platters"; menu 2, a "Dinner . . . of twenty-four dishes with six platters"; and menu 15, a "dinner of twenty-four dishes with three platters." In all three cases, it is the term *platter* that designates the sequences of the meal, while the word *dish* seems to indicate the contents of a preparation, just as it does at present. The absence of reliable criteria for distinguishing foods combined in a single dish from those constituting distinct dishes makes it difficult to count some 30 dishes in the first menu and only 24 in the second.[7]

In some cases the unnumbered term *platter* refers to the first course. This occurs in menu 26, which attaches no number to any sequence of the meal but assigns a particular name to each: "Platter," "Soups," "Roast," "Entremets," "Dessert," "Finish," and "Sendoff."

In retrospect we may wonder if the expression "First dish and platter" in menus 5 and 9 is truly redundant, or if *platter* is used there, as in menu 26, to name the first dish—something like "entrée," or "hors d'oeuvre," or "appetizer." In the same vein, the term *finish* expresses the nature of the closing course in menus 2 and 5.[8]

Variable Number of Courses

Great variability in the number of courses in fourteenth-century French menus makes them especially difficult to study: the second course of a menu containing only two or three courses might well serve a very different function than the same course would in a menu of six or more courses.[9] The researcher's task is further complicated by probable copyist errors. For example, menu 19 may well consist of only two courses because the copy clerk forgot the third and fourth, as suggested by a glance at menu 20.[10] But what of the other two- or three-course menus?

Systems for Identifying Courses

In the fourteenth century, courses were most frequently identified by number. But some menus identify each course by a particular name. We have seen that menu 26 designates a "Platter," "Soup," "Roast," "Entremets," "Dessert," "Finish," and "Sendoff," as do menus 25 and 27. Several other menus mix numbered and named sequences. Menu 24, for instance, presents three numbered sequences ("First dish . . . ," "Second dish . . . ," "Third dish . . ."), followed by four named sequences: "entremets, then Dessert, Finish, and Sendoff." Since this menu does not indicate the contents of the last four sequences, we may wonder whether these truly represent courses in the same sense as the numbered sequences. I tend to think so, by analogy with menus 25, 26, and 27, where the same words obviously indicate groups of dishes forming courses likely to be distinct. In fact, menus 2, 5, 7, 14, 16, and 20 show that the "finish" is a course. And there is no evidence to the contrary for the "dessert" in menus 24, 25, and 26.

The status of entremets is more uncertain: menu 24 mentions it last in a list of dishes forming the "Tiers mets" [i.e., third course] as if it were merely one of them. The same is true for menus 10 and 13.[11] In menu 18, it clearly does not count as a full-fledged course even though it consists of two dishes ("pheasant and swan") because it is mentioned within the second *mets* and is followed by the *tiers mets*. Furthermore, when the entremets is composed of several dishes it sometimes appears in two parts, as in menu 14, with no way to know if those two entremets amounted to two successive courses or just one, or did not count as courses at all.[12]

Before and after the Meal

We may wonder if the "Garnache" that opens menu 25 in *Le Ménagier de Paris* and the "Platter" mentioned in menu 26 are part of the meal proper. In any case, the waffles and *hypocras* [a spiced red wine] served during the "finish" *(issue)* do constitute part of the meal, as indicated by menu 2 ("the sixth and last platter for the finish"), menu 5 ("Fourth platter: *hypocras* and sweet wafers for the finish"), and menu 14, whose finish includes all sorts of meats and fish before the waffles and the claret.

The "sendoff" *(boute-hors)*, always composed of wine and spices, was another matter. This association of wine and spices is always mentioned after the finish and after the guests have washed their hands and risen from the table. Take, for example, the finish of the meal described in menu 25: "Wine and spices constitute the Sendoff. Wash, express thanks, and move to the dressing room; dinner for the servants, followed soon by wine and spices; then, leave-taking." The meal of 27 similarly concludes, "Entremets . . . Finish . . . Dancing, singing, wine, and spices . . . ."

These extraneous stages of the meal, apparently less frequent than today, correspond to our before-meal aperitifs, appetizers, and other finger foods, and our after-meal coffees and liqueurs. Furthermore, they seemed to serve the same appetizing and digestive functions, and probably other less explicit purposes yet to be identified.

Number of Dishes per Course

Seventeenth- and eighteenth-century *maître d'hôtel* manuals proclaim that each course of a meal must contain the same number of dishes in the same places on the table. In other words, once a "table setting" was adopted, it had to be retained from the first course to the last. This rule was generally followed in the menus that have come down to us. Was this the case in the fourteenth and fifteenth centuries?

It would appear so from the titles of menus 2 and 15 in *Le Ménagier de Paris* ("dinner of twenty-four dishes with six platters" and "dinner of twenty-four dishes with three platters"), since twenty-four is divisible by both six and three. But an examination of these two and other menus is inconclusive. In most of them, the number of dishes per course is similar if not equal—at least for the numbered courses.[13] But problems in identifying the dishes, and even the courses themselves, preclude any definitive conclusion.

French meal sequences give an initial impression of great disorder, but merit a closer look.

While courses identified by the same number may not necessarily have served the same function, courses with the same name did. They can thus serve as benchmarks, especially the "meat roasts" featured in seventeen out of eighteen "meat meals." Courses can then be sequenced from this fixed point at the center of the meal.

Among the six numbered courses in menus 1 and 2, two occur before the roast and two between the roast and the finish. In menu 5, with just four courses, a numbered one occurs before the roast and another between the roast and the finish. Menu 7, which appears to have six courses like menus 1 and 2, actually has only five if the sendoff is not part of the meal. Two out of the five come between the roast and the finish, and only one precedes the roast.

If we renumber the courses, using the roast as the zero point, we would assign numbers –2, –1, 0, 1, 2, 3 (finish) to the courses of menus 1 and 2; numbers –1, 0, 1, 2, 3 (finish), and sendoff to the courses of menu 7; and so on.

Thus structured, the menus of *Le Ménagier de Paris* become comparable. We can now ascertain which dishes were presented before the roast, during the finish and the sendoff, at the same time as the roast, and between the roast and the finish.

Opening Dishes

Sorting the 694 dishes alphabetically reveals that some of them are systematically presented at the beginning of a meal, in the sequences –2 and –1.

Sequence –2, which perhaps precedes the actual meal, features Grenache wine (2 out of 2 mentions), fresh cherries (1/1), butter (1/1), "hot scalded pastries" (1/1), blood pudding and sausages (2/2), and little "eel" savories (2/2), veal pasties (2/2), and "northern pies" (1/6)—with two more of the latter in sequence –1.

Beef pasties were always served in sequence –1, at the start of the actual meal (6/6), like all boiled beef (13/13) and "coarse meat cuts" (11/11), as well as "goose with salted fatback" (5/5). Note also that in all meat dinners from menus 1 to 15, the course preceding the roast always included beef or other boiled red meat.[14]

Salt-cured food was also normally served at the start of the actual meal— "Salted meats" (2/2), "goose with fatback" (5/5), "Salted mullet and young lampreys" (1/1), "Salted eels" (8/8), salt herring (10/10)—as were some salads such as watercress (5/6), as well as vinegar dishes like "Vinaigrette" (1/1) and "salt herring in vinegar" (3/3), which often accompanied the watercress.

The first course (–1) was typically devoted to soups, as menus 25, 26, and 28 clearly show. This is where one finds nearly all the "brewets" (22/24), "stews" (12/12), "fish gravés" (4/4), "seymé" (1/1), "comminée" (1/1), "espimbèche" (1/1), "geneste" (1/1), "salmagundis" (3/3), "white fish sauces" (3/3), and "soup prepared three ways" (1/1); as well as other soups, like plain "cretonnée" (2/2), and "eel soringue" (4/5). Besides these meat, poultry, or fish soups, there were also capons or hens, boiled or "herbed" (8/8), "loach in water" or "au jaunet" (6/6). The list must also include all cooked vegetable dishes—"broad-leaf cabbage" (1/1), "Fava beans" (3/3), "Turnips" (4/4), "Leeks" (3/3), "Purées" (7/7), and "Peas" (10/10). In the "Viandier" section of *Le Ménagier de Paris,* all of the above are listed in the chapter on "Light plain soups without spices."

Out of 128 dishes that can be called soups, 97 (76 percent) were served at this first course of the meal. This proportion would be higher were it not for the fact that certain very specific soups discussed below were systematically served in other courses (e.g., "Blancmange," "frumenty," "Rosée," "gravé d'oiselets," "meat cretonnée," "cretonnée d'Espagne"). Excluding these, 97 out of 100 of the soups mentioned above were served in sequence –1, which must reflect an inflexible rule. The same sequence also included all boiled coarse meats (29/29) and all salted foods—27/27 if we include "crapois" or whale blubber.

The inclusion of other dishes in this first course is more random: ocean fish (4/11), possibly salted though this is not mentioned; "tanches aux soupes" (2/7) and "venaison aux soupes" (3/3), which may have been soups; and various dishes listed in the entremets chapter of the *Ménagier de Paris* "Viandier": "Fried cheese sticks" (1/5), "Arbalètes" [brochettes] (2/7), "Flans" (1/4), "Cold sage soup" (4/8), "rissoles" (2/5). Remember also that in the same chapter, the *Ménagier* listed "northern pies," which sometimes appeared in sequence –2.

As we have seen, the notion of entremets was ambiguous. It is therefore not surprising that dishes listed in that chapter could be served at various stages of the meal. What eventually became hors d'oeuvres, for example, were long offered at each course before eventually becoming a fixed part of the first course only. These little entremets also took a long time to find their proper place in the unfolding of a French meal.

But overall, out of 236 dishes mentioned thus far, 193 (82 percent) were served before the roast. This cannot be merely by chance.

Closing Dishes

Let's turn now to the "sendoff" explicitly mentioned in four of the menus and to the "finish" mentioned in eleven of them.[15]

The sendoff is not a problem: it always consists of wine and spices. Conversely, we have seen that wine and spices always come after the finish, regardless of whether they are explicitly called a sendoff. We may thus count menus 27 and 28 as implicitly including a sendoff.

The content of the finish is more variable—as is the apparent meaning of the term *finish* itself. It appears to have both a narrow and a wide sense. Narrowly, it is the course that occurs between dessert and sendoff and consists of just *hypocras* and sweet wafers or eventual equivalents such as the "oublies, estrées et claret" cited in menu 14.[16] In fourteenth- and fifteenth-century France, such dishes must have normally signaled the end of major aristocratic dinners. But apparently they were not part of supper, menu 27 calling them "unseasonal" at this always more modest meal.[17]

More broadly, the finish could mean the last part of the meal, including dessert—which was not mentioned in those days—together with the finish itself. In this case, we find dishes more typical of dessert and preceding courses: flans (1/6), *darioles* [pastries with almond cream] (1/8), cheese (1/1), figs (1/6), grapes (1/2), loquats (1/3), shelled nuts (1/4), stewed pears (1/3), and Jordan almonds (1/5), along with the occasional "Venison" (1/30), "savory rice" (1/7), "capon pies" (1/11), and "eels *renversées*" (1/15).

The modern reader's impression of disorder comes from finding these meat and grain dishes served for dessert or for the finish. But this should not count for much because such selections at the finish occur only in menu 14, which is a strange one in many respects. Remember also that the concept of sweet versus salty took root in France only in the seventeenth century and that salty food at meal's end was not yet considered out of place.[18] Besides, the list of dishes in this extended finish usually ends with *hypocras* and sweet wafers or "estrées et claret," at least in the case of dinners (cf. menus 14, 20, 28) as opposed to the plain suppers of menus 16 and 27.

Roasts and Garnishes

The menus in *Le Ménagier de Paris* are often vague about the cuts of meat used for meat roasts: "Roast" is mentioned twice (menus 9, 15), "meat Roast" three times (menus 3, 7, 11), and "Best Roast" seven times (menus 4, 5, 8, 12, 13, 16, 17), with no further details. But 6 menus mention various animals for this stage of the meal (without indicating any cooking procedure, which leaves roasting as the most likely): 8 small quadrupeds and 17 birds, but no large quadrupeds save 1 mention of venison, which normally would belong elsewhere.[19] Out of 26 references to these animals with no indicated cooking procedure, 25 refer to the roast course.

As in the seventeenth and eighteenth centuries, salads and sauces garnished the roasts surprisingly less than one might expect: 2 dishes of lettuce (out of 3), and only 2 sauces (out of the 2 mentioned in these menus).

Even more unexpected are the 31 thickened soups (out of 46 mentioned for all courses combined), including blancmanges, gravés, shredded meat soups, and so on. Most notable among them are the "blancmange," featured in the roast course 12 times out of 15, the lark gravés (2/2), and the meat (2/2) and Spanish (3/3) cretonnées.

Meat roasts and fish roasts rarely appeared in the same course, but menu 16 mentions "Best meat and fish roast" with no further detail. The other menus, be they meat or fish, present the fish roast after the second course: generally during the third (menus 4, 6, 8, 10, 12, 15, 20–24), but sometimes the fourth (menus 3, 11, 13), fifth (menu 2), or even sixth course (menu 25).

Yet the 14 freshwater fish identified as such are all presented during the second course (together with the meat roast on nonfasting menus), as are 8 of the 11 saltwater fish. Explicit designations aside, the same holds true overall for 37 of the 68 freshwater fish and 21 of the 39 saltwater fish. The meat roast course thus features a high proportion of fishes whose cooking procedure is not indicated, but which were most likely poached to correspond to their element, water. It remains unclear how these fish were any different from "fish roasts"—the latter being recognized as such during the classical period by the fact of being poached without scaling and served plain on a white cloth.

In addition to two dishes of organ meats without special significance, the meat roast course also includes 14 mentions of pasties (out of 28 overall), and 29 mentions of other dishes that Le Ménagier de Paris lists in its chapter on "Entremets, fried dishes, and breadings."[20] Some of these entremets were mainly served during the roast course: arbalètes (5/7), fried dishes (1/1), taillis [dense puddings suitable for slicing] (2/3), and pies (5/7). But most were more typically served after the roast: crêpes (5 with the roast and 7 after it), breadings (2 with the roast and 11 after), flan (1 with the roast and 4 after), froide sauge [cold sage soup] (1 with the roast and 4 after), aspic (3 with the roast and 12 after), and sugared milk (2 with the roast and 4 after). In all, 14 diverse entremets are served 29 times with the roasts and 44 times after it.

It is tempting to conclude that, as in the seventeenth and eighteenth centuries, entremets that normally constituted a separate course could be served together with the roast. But during the classical period, this grouping meant no course between roast and dessert, whereas here only menu 9 fits that case. Entremets thus do not yet appear to have acquired an established position in fourteenth-century French meals.

Dishes Served between the Roast and the Finish

Since "dessert" is mentioned in only three menus, let us examine what dishes were presented between the roast course and the finish per se, namely, "*hypocras* and sweet wafers."

This part of the meal, whose number of courses varies greatly, includes a great many different freshwater and saltwater fish dishes: 90 out of 127 references to these fishes in all courses combined—not surprising in that we have already seen that the fish roast was always presented after the meat roast. But certain fishes and certain methods of preparation stand out: "eels *renversées*" (10/15), bream (12/16), lamprey (7/8), crayfish (6/7), "plaice in water" (5/8), turbot (4/6), conger eel (4/4), and "Tanche aux soupes" (4/7).

Nor is it surprising to find some birds without any specific mention of cooking method, but likely to have been roasted. All are large birds with showy feathers—bitterns, swans, pheasants, peacocks, herons, and others. Birds of the kind were presented with their plumage and constituted a quintessential entremets spectacle. A total of 6 out of 8 of these birds are served after the roast. What I do not understand is why this part of the meal also included birds "in a white sauce": capons, goose, mallards, and other "river birds," 8 out of 8 in all. What was so special about this preparation?

Another rule seldom broken: venison was served 14 times out of 17 after the roast, only venison soup being served at the beginning of a meal. The frumenty usually accompanying the venison likewise appears 13 out of 13 times after the roast.

Since this part of the meal included dessert—explicitly mentioned or not—it is normal to find here all the fresh and cooked fruit not served to open the meal. These include dates, fresh figs, loquats, pears, fresh apples, grapes, hazelnuts, and shelled walnuts, for a total of 11 references including the 4 that preceded or replaced *hypocras* and sweet wafers under the "finish" classification.[21]

Finally, all sorts of dishes listed in the "entremets" chapter of *Le Ménagier de Paris* also appear between the roast and the finish: crêpes, breadings, fried dishes, flans, cold sage soup, aspic, sugared milk, fried cheese sticks, rissoles, savory rice, *taillis, talmouses* [savory cheese tartlets], tarts and pies, *blanc-manger parti,* parsnips, and *leschefrites* [shallow custardlike tarts], most of which have already appeared in the roast course. However, out of 131 mentions for all courses combined, these entremets appear a total of 96 times between the roast and the finish. Entremets had not yet been assigned an established place in the meal, but were on the way to finding one.

To conclude this study of dish distribution among courses, I would say that the long-standing impression of disorder derived from medieval French menus arose mainly from variability in the number of courses, and the resulting difficulty of comparing them. But once this problem has been removed, it becomes apparent that most dishes were distributed among the various parts of the meal in a systematic way. While the reasons for this distribution still largely elude us, medieval meals appear to have adhered to most of the implicit rules I have identified.[22]

SIX

Sixteenth-Century Overview

THE SEQUENCE OF DISHES IN the sixteenth century has come down to us essentially through the twelve menus in *Le Livre fort excellent de cuysine* (originally published about 1540 as *Le Livre de cuysine très utile et profitable*)—all but the last of which indicate the stages of the meal.[1]

GENERAL COMMENTS

Courses

The names of these stages had changed: called *assiettes* ("platters" or "dishes") in the fourteenth and fifteenth centuries, they became *services* ("courses") in the sixteenth century and retained this designation in the seventeenth, eighteenth, and nineteenth centuries.

But the number of courses in the meal remained as variable as in the Middle Ages: one menu has 3 courses, three of them have 4, four have 5, one has 8, and one has 9 (for an average of 5.2)—barely more consistent than the menus in *Le Ménagier de Paris,* which have two with 2 courses, ten with 3, six with 4, three with 5, three with 6, two with 7, and one with 9 (average: 4.2).

Courses in these sixteenth-century menus are more often named than numbered: "entrée" or "table platter" to start; then "soups," the "roast," "second roast," "third roast," and so on until the "finish," which systematically comes at the end of each meal. In contrast, the menus of the fifteenth-century *Viandier de Taillevent* show a nameless course for this final stage, except the menu for the banquet of Monseigneur de Foyes, which called it *fruicterie* or "assorted fruit."[2]

When sixteenth-century courses are numbered, the number refers—sometimes implicitly but often expressly—to the number of roasts rather than the number of courses. The third course in menu 4 is a roast followed by a "Second course," a "Third roast course" and a "Fourth roast course," which are the fourth, fifth, and sixth courses of the meal. The numbering of menus 1, 2, 3, 5, and 11 is analogous. This confirms the special importance of the roast: more clearly than in the seventeenth and eighteenth centuries, sixteenth-century meals were organized around it.[3]

As in the Middle Ages, each course offered a similar if not absolutely equal number of dishes (generally from 2 to 8), which varied from one meal to another. The first menu is the most consistent: 4–4–4–4–4–4. The second, with the greatest number of courses, also has an even distribution of dishes: 4–3–3–5–3–3–3–3–3. The third contains more copious courses, including two unnamed ones: [6]–6–[5]–8–9. The fourth is notable for its "Trussed entremets," served alone between the second and third roasts: 4–3–3–3–1–4–4–7. The fifth shows five courses followed by meat and spice tallies (5–2–4–3–4). The sixth is very uneven (18–5–3–6–3). It proposes an enormous entrée course for summer (18 dishes) and a much smaller one for winter (5 dishes). The seventh, for supper on the same summer day, has an endless first roast course of 12 dishes and a finish of *hypocras,* handwashing, Jordan almonds, and digestive spices: 4–4–12–4–7. Only the roast is copious in the eighth: 2–2–5–3. The ninth is a supper with only three courses (3–8–4), presumably for the same day, but in which the roast comprises 8 dishes. The tenth is a menu for a winter banquet. It has two entrée courses of 6 and 8 dishes, the first consisting of pastries and the second of cooked dishes, with no roast after the soups but with a composite "Finish" *(Issue)* followed by an unusual sweet "Tenth dish": 6–8–5–8–7. Finally, the eleventh menu is an abundant supper of 5 dishes plus "digestive spices" that would have been called the "sendoff" *(boute-hors)* in the fourteenth century: 6–6–6–7–9 + 3.

Comparison of First Courses over Time

We have seen that fourteenth-century feasts consisted of one or two courses before the roast, then one or two roast courses, followed by one, two, or three courses between roast and finish, possibly ending with a "sendoff." In the sixteenth century, courses preceding the roast were more obvious and predictable: they always included a course of entrées—more reliably even than the soup course, which is missing in the ninth menu. In the Middle Ages, the soup course was always present but the platter of entrées often missing.

The sixteenth century marked the end of the customary sequence of entrée followed by soup course. By the mid-1800s, if not earlier in the century, soup opened the meal. We saw in chapter 1 that in the early nineteenth century, soups were the first dishes to be eaten, and that throughout the seventeenth and eighteenth centuries (or at least by 1651) they were served before entrées even if not always mentioned at the head of the first course.[4] In the seventeenth century they often appeared in a special course preceding the entrées, as they do in the 1662 *Nouveau et Parfait Maistre d'hostel royal* by Pierre de Lune.[5] We find another convincing clue from that same year in *L'Escole parfaite des officiers de bouche.* It reprints the menus from *Le Livre fort excellent de cuysine,* updating them by switching the position of the entrée course from first to second place, placing the soup course in first position.

The Roasts

Even though the rather frequent mention of "Best roast" in the fourteenth-century menus of *Le Ménagier de Paris* suggested the existence of several roast courses, it always referred only to a "Meat roast"—most often in the second course—followed in 16 out of 29 menus by a "fish roast" (or "bream roast" or "roasted bream"). This fish roast was only one of the many components of the next course, just as the meat roast or best roast constituted only one component of its respective course.

The sixteenth-century *Livre fort excellent de cuysine* is a different matter altogether. The term *roast* now applies to an entire course, even though that course does not consist exclusively of roasted meats. Disregarding the absence of any roast course in menu 10, which is strange in all respects, I would also point out that seven out of ten menus include more than one meat roast; menu 2 even has six.[6]

Another difference is that fish roasts have been dropped from these meat-day meals even though this series of menus predates Charles IX's edict against serving meat and fish in the same meal. The origin and initial date of this interdiction of fish in meat-day meals, as well as the reasons for it, should thus be investigated.

It is also strange that none of the eleven menus is meatless, whereas *Le Ménagier de Paris* offered nearly as many meatless as meat-day menus.

Could this be due to the influence of the Reformation during this first half of the sixteenth century? Granted, meatless menus are also absent from the three offered by *La Cuisinière bourgeoise* in the eighteenth century. But the lack of meatless menus is not as striking in three instances as in eleven. (In fact, Menon's *Science du maître d'hôtel cuisinier,* published around the same period as *La Cuisinière bourgeoise,* still includes two meatless ones among the nine it proposes.) Also, Catholic regulations regarding meatless meals were again being challenged in the eighteenth century, though less fundamentally than in the sixteenth century.

Finally, owing to the regular presence of an entrée course before the soup course, the first roast course is generally the third one in the meal. It appears only once in second position (in menu 9, a supper without soups) and once in fourth position—in menu 6, which mentions two entrée courses and one soup course. But on closer examination, it seems that only one of these two entrée courses should be counted, the first in summer and the second in winter, since the latter is called "alternate table entrée for winter," which contradicts the stated nature of the menu as being for a "summer banquet." The "Roast" in menu 6 thus also comes in third position as usual.

After the Roast

We have seen that in the fourteenth century several courses were often served between the one containing the meat roast and the "finish" that concluded the meal. These intervening dishes were often listed in cookbooks under the entremets chapter.[7] I would hesitate to call them entremets, however, since at that time the term also referred to spectacular dishes, even actual performances that enlivened aristocratic banquets. Yet this "entremets" designation cannot simply be dismissed, especially since it also appeared in certain menus of the fourteenth century, continued to be used, and became more clearly defined in the seventeenth, eighteenth, and nineteenth centuries.[8]

In the sixteenth century, one could thus expect to find one or more courses increasingly coming to resemble the entremets of the classical era. But paradoxically, almost all the menus of *Le Livre fort excellent de cuysine* advance directly from the last roast to the "finish." The exceptional "trussed entremets" in menu 4 appears between the second and third roasts. Similarly, the "peacock entremets" of menu 7 is part of the first "Roast" course, which is followed by a second called "Other course." Finally, the word *entremets* appears a third time for an "entremets salad." But judging by the list of dishes in menu 12, this was probably served as an entrée.

Similarly, the menus of *Le Ménagier de Paris* sometimes mention a course called "Desserte," which seems to herald the dessert of our own time—or of the bourgeois meals of the seventeenth and eighteenth centuries. But *Le Livre fort excellent de cuysine* does not advance this trend either, since its menus mention neither "desserte" nor "dessert."

There is a third disappointment. A menu in *Le Viandier de Taillevent,* printed about 1486, shows a final course called "fruiterie," which seems to herald the "fruict" of aristocratic meals in the seventeenth and eighteenth centuries. But our sixteenth-century menus mention neither "fruit" nor "fruiterie" any more than they do dessert. *Issue de table,* the expression used for the final course, could not be more medieval. It appears in each of the sixteenth-century menus, in other words much more often than in those of the fourteenth century itself.

Though not what might be expected, these Renaissance menus should not be viewed as more archaic than those of the fourteenth-century *Ménagier de Paris.* They are actually modern in their use of the term *service* instead of *mets* or *assiette,* as well as in the clarity of the names of courses and the regularity with which they occur—even though not all of the menus contain the same number of them.

COMPOSITION OF THE ROAST IN THE SIXTEENTH CENTURY

The Cooking of Roasts

We have seen that during the classical period, meat-day roasts consisted of poultry, meat, and game, all spit-roasted to a golden brown and served without sauce, at least not on the same platter. (Sauces and salads could be brought to the table at the same time, as garnishes.) We learned this by analyzing recipes because, you will recall, there is usually no indication of cooking method either in the menus or in the names of these roasts; only the animal species and the cut of meat are specified. Can the 11 menus of *Le Livre fort excellent de cuysine* help us determine if roasts were prepared in the same manner in the sixteenth century, when the "roast" course included everything that was not an entrée, soup, or finish?

The book's 11 actual menus propose 24 roast courses. Let us examine the sorts of dishes that compose them.

1. Among the 117 dishes of these 24 roast courses, only 5 are described as "roasted" *(rôtis),* all of them venison. Outside the roast courses, there is one other dish described as roasted, namely, calf's liver. Being

TABLE 6

Composition of roast courses in *Le Livre fort excellent de cuysine* (1555)

Meal (M=Menu No.)	Course Name (Actual)	Order	Dishes
M2. Banquet or wedding	Fifth course (7)	2.7.2a	Roasted venison
M3. Other banquet	Second course (3)	3.3.0a	Roasted venison
M4. Other course	Fourth roast course (7)	4.7.1a	Roasted venison
M9. For supper	Roast (2)	9.2.1a	Roasted venison
M11. For a supper	First roast (3)	11.3.2b	Roasted venison
M6. Summer banquet	Table entrée (1)	6.1.9a	Roasted calf's liver
M1. Banquet or wedding	Second roast (4)	1.4.4a	*Pigeons en rost*
M1. Banquet or wedding	Third roast course (5)	1.5.1a	*Venayson de rost saulce realle*

organ meat, it was probably presented as an entrée. Even more rare are the dishes described as "en rost" or "de rost"; they occur only twice, both times in the roast courses of the first menu: "Pigeons en rost" and "Venayson de rost saulce realle," which was probably a venison roast (table 6).

2. Just as in the fourteenth, fifteenth, seventeenth, and eighteenth centuries, these sixteenth-century roasts include many types of meats whose cooking method is not specified: 54 out of 117 dishes, or nearly half, counting a few fowls seasoned "with fine grain salt." It is obviously difficult to prove that these meats were roasted, since I am here relying on menus rather than recipes. But their being so is strongly suggested by the fact that this practice endured from the fourteenth to the eighteenth century and has been verified through analysis of seventeenth- and eighteenth-century recipes.

3. Just as in the fourteenth, fifteenth, seventeenth, and eighteenth centuries, the roast courses include sauces eaten with the roast meats but served separately in sauceboats rather than on the platter. Here again we find—also to be eaten with the roast—salads and other salty or acidic dishes similar to salads, such as "olives," "pickled cucumbers" (which we might call cornichons), "Lemon salad," and "Cordial sauce vinaigrette." What strikes me as strange is not the presence of these sauces and salads but their infrequency, which echoes the fourteenth-century menus (table 7).

TABLE 7

Dishes served with the roast course

Meal (M=Menu No.)	Course Name (Actual)	Order	Dishes
M2. Other banquet	Second roast (4)	2.4.2a	Batarde sauce
M2. Other banquet	Second roast (4)	2.4.4a	Batarde sauce
M2. Other banquet	Third course (5)	2.5.1a	Cordial sauce vinaigrette
M4. Other course	Second course (4)	4.4.3a	Olives
M4. Other course	Third roast course (6)	4.6.4a	Lemon salad
M4. Other course	Fourth roast course (7)	4.7.3a	Pickled cucumbers
M7. For supper	Roast (3)	7.3.3b	*Hypocras* sauce
M9. (Supper)	Roast (2)	9.2.4b	Olives

TABLE 8

Pies served with the roast course

Meal (M=Menu No.)	Course Name (Actual)	Order	Dishes
M1. Banquet or wedding	Roast (3)	1.3.4a	Pigeon pies
M1. Banquet or wedding	Third roast course (5)	1.5.4a	Cool venison pies
M2. Other banquet	Roast (3)	2.3.2a	Hot venison pies
M2. Other banquet	Second roast (4)	2.4.5a	Young quail pies
M2. Other banquet	Third course (5)	2.5.3a	Young wild duck pies
M2. Other banquet	Fifth course (7)	2.7.3a	Cool venison pies
M3. Other banquet	Soups (2) [=Roast (3)]	3.2.6a	Hot venison pies
M3. Other banquet	Soups (2) [=Roast (3)]	3.2.11a	Quail pies
M3. Other banquet	Second course (3) [=4]	3.3.6a	Sparrow pies
M3. Other banquet	Second course (3) [=4]	3.3.8a	Cold venison pies
M4. Other course	Fourth roast course (7)	4.7.4a	Cool venison pie
M5. One other banquet	Second roast (4)	5.4.3a	A pigeon pie
M6. Summer banquet	Roast (4)	6.4.3b	Duck pies
M7. For supper	Roast (3)	7.3.3a	Lark pie
M7. For supper	Roast (3)	7.3.5b	Pie of doves
M7. For supper	Roast (3)	7.3.7a	Teal pies
M7. For supper	Other course (4)	7.4.2a	Cool pork pies
M8. Other feast	Roast (3)	8.3.4a	A duck pie
M9. (Supper)	Roast (2)	9.2.3a	Lark pie
M11. For a supper	First roast (3)	11.3.3a	Sparrow pies
M11. For a supper	Second roast (4)	11.4.5a	Cool venison pie

4. Again, just as in the fourteenth century, these roast courses include
    pies: not at every roast course, but 21 pies in 10 menus nevertheless,
    which results in at least one for each menu that includes a roast course
    (table 8). There are also instances of several pies within a single course.

Two of these pies are hot, 6 are cold (or "cool"), and 12 have no specified
temperature. The hot ones are served in the first roast course of menus 2
and 3; the cold ones appear five times in the last roast course and once in
the next-to-last (fifth roast of menu 2). This distribution seems to fore-
shadow practices observed in the seventeenth and eighteenth centuries
when, as we have seen, hot pies are entrées and cold ones are entremets.

But finding hot pies before cold ones in the menus of *Le Livre fort excellent de cuysine* is interesting for another reason: it is an early hint that the
final roast courses do not serve exactly the same function as the first ones;
they occupy the same place as entremets will in the seventeenth and eighteenth centuries.

Stuffing and Sauces for Roast Meats

It is more difficult to interpret the inclusion of stuffed and sauced meats in
these roast courses—or at least meats complemented with a sauce mentioned in the name of the dish.[9] Since most of these dishes are not found
in the recipes of *Le Livre fort excellent de cuysine*, it is difficult to know
whether they were roasted meats served with a sauce—on the same platter
or separately—or if they were cooked in the sauce after roasting, as was
often the case in the Middle Ages, or even not roasted at all.

In fourteenth- and fifteenth-century menus, the roast course often featured numerous sauced preparations most often labeled "thickened soups."
Examples include *blancs-mangers, gravés, cretonnées* [creamy soups with
crisp bits of chicken or veal], and *écartelés* [shredded-meat soups]. The presence of such dishes, which have nothing to do with roasts, supports the notion that in the Middle Ages the roast was not yet a course but part of a
course, or simply a dish.[10] This appears to be an established fact for the
fourteenth century, but very doubtful for the sixteenth century, when the
page layout of *Le Livre fort excellent de cuysine* shows the term *Rost* as designating an entire course.

Sixteenth-century roast courses nonetheless appear to contain plenty of
such roasted meats seasoned with a sauce or even recooked in it, whereas
those of the seventeenth and eighteenth centuries contain none. It is diffi-

cult, however, to know for sure, since our source contains no recipe for most of them. Sometimes the recipe can be found, or guessed from ones given for comparable dishes. The recipe for "Woodcock à l'esquesal" may be impossible to find, but we can imagine what a "Duck à la dodine" is: white *dodine* (made with milk) was a sauce for roasted waterfowl, and the duck recipe involves a *dodine* of verjuice poured into a pie when nearly cooked. The kid recipe is also a pie, in this case served with *sauce Robert* and green gooseberries (which yield a type of verjuice familiar to northern regions). But the "Roast chapter" tells us that roasted kid is eaten *au verjus* as well as *à l'orange* or sprinkled with salt. It also tells us that "Partridges"—like partridge chicks, pigeons, and plovers—were eaten with salt or *à l'orange*. The recipe for pigeon confit—perhaps similar to our *pigeon au sucre*—starts with roasted pigeons that are then cooked again with vermilion wine, sugar, and spices. *Sauce realle* was made with the same vermilion wine enhanced with vinegar, sugar, and spices, then reduced by half and poured over the venison, which was probably roasted. I assume the same was done when this sauce was used with heron chicks.

Thus, the dishes whose titles include the name of a meat and a sauce do appear to be roasts covered with a sauce or, more rarely, cooked in that sauce in the medieval style. In the seventeenth and eighteenth centuries these roasts would constitute spit-roasted entrées. But in the less-exacting sixteenth century, such dishes were part of the roast course just like hot and cold pies and, more lastingly, salads and sauces. Where pies are concerned, the sixteenth century foreshadowed the seventeenth and eighteenth centuries by placing hot pies in the early roast courses and cold ones in the succeeding ones. Yet these roasted meats served or cooked in sauce did not portend spit-roasted entrées, because the first and last roast courses include equal numbers of them.

Meats Suitable for Roasts in the Sixteenth Century

We have seen that in the classical era, the meat of choice for the roast was fowl (domestic, but especially wild), along with small, preferably young fur-covered game (young rabbits and hares). The roast was rarely of large game (always young after 1674), rarely of butcher's meat (only young animals like veal, lamb, kid, or suckling pig) and never of organ meats (at least after 1660). These preferences already existed in the fourteenth and fifteenth centuries, as the roast meats in *Ménagier de Paris* menus include seventeen birds, eight small (or young) quadrupeds, and a single large adult (a boar). What about the sixteenth century?

Examination of *Le Livre fort excellent de cuysine* reveals that butcher's meat, organ meats, and large joints of venison were as rare for the roast course in the sixteenth century as in the seventeenth and eighteenth: no organ meats appear in this course, even though they make up 41 dishes in the book's recipes and menus. Butcher's meat is just as rare: except for lamb (roasted in its only mention) and suckling pig (roasted 8 times out of 10 inclusions), there are just 7 roasts among the 43 other butcher's meat dishes.[11] Large game (deer, doe, boar, and "venison") yields only 10 roasts out of 52 mentions.[12] Just as in the preceding and the following centuries, meats for the roast were domestic fowl (46 roasts out of 95 recipes), most feathered game (20 roasts out of 34), small furred game (14 times out of 17), and suckling pig (10 out of 12).[13]

OTHER DISHES AND COURSES

Without analyzing the other courses as closely, we should nonetheless identify their component parts on the threshold of the classical period.

Entrées

Entrées in *Le Livre fort excellent de cuysine* still bear a medieval stamp. Take, for example, the "White *hypocras*" that opens the tenth menu. Especially medieval are the often, if not always, included juicy fruits: orange salads in the first and seventh menus; apricots and Damascus plums in the second; Damascus plums again in the third, fifth, and eleventh; peaches and grapes in the fourth and fifth; *pompons* (i.e., elongated melons) in the tenth; not to mention various meats prepared with fruit, like the beef palate with gooseberries, wood pigeons with pomegranate, and kid with oranges.

Menu 10, with its two entrée courses—a "Winter table entrée" followed by a "Kitchen entrée"—offers in the first course a series of sugared pastries reminiscent of Italian meals of that period. The "White *hypocras*" is followed by "Marchepains," which are probably marzipan; some "Florets"; "Marzipan skewers"; a mysterious "Chemine"; and something called "Dry cake." Curiously, the "Pompons" and the "Gouges blanches," which might also have been cakes with picturesque names, appear as kitchen entrées. But this could be by mistake, since there are only five table entrées (six counting the white *hypocras*) and eight kitchen entrées.

We mentioned earlier that the hot pies of the first roast course prefigured the seventeenth-century entrée pies (while the cold ones of the final courses prepared the way for entremets presentations). But hot pies and a few other savory pastries also figured among the entrées—these already occasionally being present in the fourteenth century, in the first course of the *Ménagier de Paris* menus. For example, the entrées in the second and seventh menus of *Le Livre fort excellent de cuysine* feature "Capon breast in pastry shell." Similarly, there are "Hot small venison pies" in the second, fourth, and seventh menus, and "Pies with heated sauce" in the sixth and eighth. Also probably served hot—if the explicit rules of the seventeenth century were already in force—are the "Veal pies" in the third and fifth menus, a "Potted veal pie with crust" in the sixth, and "Young wild duck pies" in the tenth.

Typical of entrées in seventeenth- and eighteenth-century banquets are the most varied sorts of organ-meat preparations. Similarly, in *Le Livre fort excellent de cuysine* we find "Browned kid heads" in the first and sixth menus, "Cow udders" and "Stuffed chitterlings" in the third and sixth, and "Beef tongue" in the third. The sixth includes "Salted lamb tongues," "Lamb trotters," "Confiture de fraize de poussin," "Confit of kid stomach," "Roasted calf's liver," "Fricassée de menus droitz à la barbe robert," "Beef palate with gooseberries and chives," "Steamed lamb's tongues," and "Peppered pork tripe." By contrast, these organ meats are nonexistent in the fourteenth- and fifteenth-century menus of *Le Ménagier de Paris* and in the printed version of *Le Viandier de Taillevent*.

While far fewer cold meats were served in the sixteenth century than in the fourteenth, they were also served as entrées: "Stuffed chitterlings" (menus 3 and 6), "Milanese cervelat" and "Sausages" (menu 6), "Chitterlings and sausages" (menu 8), and "Milanese sausages" (menu 10). Cold meats of this type, already served as entrées in the Middle Ages, were still entrées in the eighteenth century—although a new sensibility had to some extent eliminated them from aristocratic meals.

Finally, sixteenth-century entrées included all sorts of presumably sauced meat dishes: "Small venison sirloins" (menu 1), "Venison sirloins" (menu 11), and "Venison sirloins in sauce royale" (menu 7); fricassees (menus 4 and 5); "Pullet breast purée" (menu 5); "Chicken fricassee in grain verjuice," "Confiture de fraize de poussin," "Confit of kid stomach," "Carbonnade à la coulloule," "Pullet fricassee in sauce madame," "Beef palate with gooseberries and chives," "Quail confit in *cameline* sauce," "Stuffed *caillette*" (stomach of lamb or of another animal unrelated to quail), and "Leg of lamb hash" (all menu 6); "Wild pigeons with cabbage" (menu 9); "Wood pigeons with pomegranate," "Kid with oranges," and "Stuffed sparrows" (menu 10); and lastly, "Venison sirloins" and "Sunburst of capon breast" (menu 11). Some of these dishes might have been treated as soups in the fourteenth century, but all are considered entrées in the seventeenth and eighteenth centuries.

The only vegetable dish among these meats in sauce, the "*Burelot* of new fava beans," might have made a soup in medieval times but would have been served as an entremets in the seventeenth and eighteenth centuries.

There were also various salads of greens, roots, and fruits, as well as other acidulous dishes, served raw as fruits, or sometimes cooked: "Vinaigrettes" (menu 1), the already mentioned "Orange salads" (menus 1 and 7), "Beef palate with gooseberries and chives" (menu 6), chicory salad (menu 9), parsnip salads (menus 7 and 11), and "Green salads" (menu 11). We shall see that the placement of these salads reflects the medical theory and practice of most European regions, but not the customs of Paris in the seventeenth and eighteenth centuries, nor those of the Middle Ages for that matter.[14] It is as if French table customs were fleetingly influenced in the sixteenth century in this regard by the practices of Italy and other neighboring countries.

Soups

As we have seen, medieval soups often consisted of sauced meat, which could be confused with seventeenth- and eighteenth-century entrées. This was equally true in the Renaissance: here we find meats in sauce such as "Leg of veal in golden broth" (menus 1 and 6), "Wood pigeon in pepper sauce," and "*Gravé* of small birds" (menu 4), "Rabbit stew" (menu 8), "Nestling with capers" (menu 10), and "Pigeons with cinnamon" (menu 11).

There are a great many boiled meats, with or without a vegetable garnish: "Larded boiled meat" (menus 1, 2, 3, and 11); "Pullets with herbs or steamed" (menu 1) and "Steamed pullets" (menu 2); "Wild pigeons with cabbage" (menus 2, 3, and 6), which were probably boiled, as were "Partridge with cabbage" and "Boar with turnips" (menu 7), and "Partridge chicks," "Young hares," "Chickens," and "Stuffed nestlings" (menu 3); certainly boiled were the "Boiled capons" (menu 4), "Widgeons with leeks" (menu 6), "Claypot pigeons" (menu 7), "Capons coated in court bouillon," "Pullets with peas," and perhaps the "Venison roll with fine herbs" (menu 10).

Many of these soups contained only vegetables—or at least their name makes no mention of meat. These include "Porree braee" (menu 1) and "Poree broyee" (menu 5), composed mainly of white leeks; "Squash soup" and "Stuffed cucumbers" (menu 3); "Frumenty" (menus 7 and 11), which in the Middle Ages came after the roast; "Golden broth" (menu 8), for which it is not clear whether this was more vegetable- than animal-based;

and "Lettuce in apple confit" (menu 10). Somewhat surprising in this array of vegetable soups is that none of the cited menus is for meatless days, whereas in the seventeenth and eighteenth centuries, meatless soups for meat days were rare among the upper classes.

As a final comment, the third menu seems to suggest that a few meat pies figured among the soups, since it mentions "Hot venison pies" and "Quail pies." But a closer look reveals that these belong in the first roast course, whose heading and space separation from the preceding course were omitted by the menu writer.

The Finish

We have seen that all the menus in *Le Livre fort excellent de cuysine* contain a course called the *issue* ("finish"), as opposed to only ten of the twenty-nine *Ménagier de Paris* menus, plus another three with no finish but a "desserts" course. The six menus from the printed edition of *Le Viandier de Taillevent* have courses whose contents are similar to the "finishes" of the nine menus from *Le Livre fort excellent de cuysine*. But while this course is called "fruicterie" in the "Banquet de Monseigneur de Foyes," the others are merely numbered.[15] Although the terms *Dessert* and *Fruit* eventually prevailed over *finish* in the seventeenth and eighteenth centuries, this incipient standardization indicates a future trend.

The contents of this final course were also evolving, with many fresh and stewed fruits as well as fruit pies, just as in today's desserts. There are also various other sweet pastries, as well as custards and all sorts of entremets in the modern sense of the term. Fresh fruits include "Peaches" (menu 3), "Pears" (menus 3, 5, and 6), "Two-headed pears" (menu 11), and "Cherries" and "Capendu apples" (menu 10). Dry fruit included "Almonds and green walnuts" (menu 3) and "Almonds and peeled walnuts" (menus 5 and 11).

Stewed fruit and fruit pies include "Apple papillons" (menus 1 and 4), "Pears in *hypocras*" (menus 3, 4, 9, and 11), "Apple tarts" and "Cooked pears" (menu 4), "Quince pies" and "Fried medlars" (menu 7), "Cooked pear" (menu 8), "Minced apple tarts" (menu 9), "Candied squash" (menu 10), and "Apple turnover" and "Verjuice tarts" (menu 11).

Other pastries have peculiar names like "Platter of three oven pieces" (menus 1 and 2) and "Three oven pieces on a platter" (menus 3 and 7). There are also a "Cream pie" (menu 4); unspecified "Tarts" (menu 5); a "Flaky pastry cake" (menu 6); "English pie" (menu 8); "A tender cake" and a *talmouse* (menu 9); some "Laiches clavées" (menu 10), which appear to be slices of cake; and "Rozée dangleterre" (menu 11), which could also be a pastry.

Only two kinds of entremets in the contemporary sense of the word are mingled with these cakes. First, there are jellies: "Amber jelly" (menu 1), "Jelly" (menu 2), "Three kinds of jellies" (menu 3), "Clear jelly mold" and "White jelly angels" (menu 4), "Jelly lozenges" (menu 6), "Clear and amber jelly" (menu 7), and "White jelly studded with almonds" (menu 11). There are no pastry custards, but we find crème fraîche and cream cheeses. We have mentioned the "Cream tart" in the fourth menu, but there are also "Cream cheeses" (menu 1), "Cream cheese and curds" (menu 3), and "Cream cheese" (menu 10). While sugar is nowhere specified for any of these cheeses, they are all fresh products of the type most of us eat with sugar today, and none is a ripened cheese.

Nevertheless, these finish courses did contain some dishes likely to be savories: probably not the "Chestnuts" (menu 8), but very likely the "Artichokes" (menu 10)—although sugared artichoke pies did exist in the seventeenth century and possibly earlier. Even more surprising is the "Porpoise" (menu 10), which seems quite medieval both as a dish and because of its place in the meal. But on the whole, these unsweetened dishes were very rare in the finish courses of the time. This was already so at the end of the fifteenth century in the six menus of the printed *Viandier de Taillevent*. The same cannot be said of the twenty-seven menus in *Le Ménagier de Paris*. Not only does the finish course of its menu 14 list venison, "Savory rice," capon pies, and eels *renversées* in among "Cream flans," filled pastries, fruits, wafers, "Biscuits," and the honeyed wine known as "Claré," but most of the meals without a finish course (i.e., most meals at the time) ended with savory dishes.

CONCLUSION

If *Le Livre fort excellent de cuysine* and its menus are any indication, sixteenth-century customs heralded those of the classical age in many respects. The various stages of the meal were no longer called "platters" or "dishes" but "courses"; and several of these courses were already labeled "entrées," "soups," or "roast," as they would be known—or begin to be known—in the seventeenth century, for example in Pierre de Lune's *Nouveau et Parfait Maistre d'hostel royal*. Furthermore, hot pies were systematically served before cold ones, as in the classical period: the hot ones among the entrées or first roast courses, and the cold ones among the last (or last two) roast courses. It seems that, in the cited work, *roast* refers to a course, whereas in the fourteenth century it may have meant merely a dish. Nevertheless, the sixteenth-century roast course retained many meat dishes that were not roasts in the seventeenth- and eighteenth-century sense of the word, or that were roasts with a sauce. Remember that these will still appear in *Le Cuisinier françois,* though fewer in number, and then gradually disappear.

The first thing one notices about sixteenth-century entrées and soups is their medieval quality: the white *hypocras* and especially the juicy fruit in many entrées; the sauced and boiled meats considered "soups" as in the Middle Ages, which came to be seen as entrées as in later centuries. Next one notes the salads—of greens or fruit—suggesting a fleeting Italian influence, since they would more likely have been served with the roast in the fourteenth and fifteenth centuries, and again in the seventeenth and eighteenth centuries.

Finally, we see elements that announce future trends, like the presence of many organ meats among the entrées. While the last course, the finish, retains a content as medieval as its name (in the classical period the custard and pastry entremets will be separated from the dessert fruits), the consistent presence of this finish course is a new feature prefiguring that well-known characteristic of modern French gastronomy: the separation of sweet and savory foods.

SEVEN

Classical Order in the Seventeenth and Eighteenth Centuries

DESPITE ALL OF THE SIXTEENTH-CENTURY elements prefiguring the classical order of courses, the true revolution probably happened in the seventeenth century. I say "probably" because of the dearth of accessible references from the mid-sixteenth century to the mid-seventeenth. As we have just seen, the classical order was barely emerging in the mid-sixteenth century and nearly established by the mid-seventeenth century, with hardly a trace of the stages by which it solidified in between. Fortunately, the last detectable phases of this development occurred at the end of the seventeenth century and during the first decades of the eighteenth century, periods for which there is no lack of documentation.

Immediately apparent are changes at the start of the meal. We find a curious transposition of the entrées and the soups. As the name indicates, entrées traditionally started the meal, but soups now preceded them. Then, as if a single first course combining soups and entrées were not substantial enough, we see the emergence of relevés and hors d'oeuvres, new concepts aimed at palliating the diner's initial hunger.

As to the rest of the meal, we find a trend, at times striking, toward less, not more: fewer roasts and entremets, especially when brought to the table together in the second course. Yet complicating this evolution toward fewer entremets was a second major trend that ultimately prevailed in the seventeenth century: all sweet dishes came to be concentrated in the two major concluding courses, the entremets and dessert. This development will be examined in the last part of this chapter.

Soups and Entrées

Between the mid-sixteenth century and the mid-seventeenth, soups and entrées exchanged places; soups were now served—or rather, eaten—first, and entrées second, in spite of their name.

The first signs of this permutation, to my knowledge, date from the mid-seventeenth century. In *Le Cuisinier françois* (1651), for instance, the list of chapters begins with soups, followed by entrées. And in 1660, Pierre de Lune's *Nouveau Cuisinier* places soups at the head of the chapters for each season. The implication of this ranking is confirmed in the 1662 menu book *Le Nouveau et Parfait Maître d'hostel royal,* also by Pierre de Lune, where soups are listed before entrées in each menu.

Another particularly interesting confirmation comes in 1662 from *L'Escole parfaite des officiers de bouche.*[1] As already noted, this work duplicates the menus of the 1542 *Livre fort excellent de cuysine,* simply reversing the entrées and soups. As we shall see, other changes did occur between the mid-sixteenth century and the mid-seventeenth, but the publishers of *L'Escole parfaite* apparently considered them of lesser importance. This particularly significant and corroborating example shows that seventeenth- and eighteenth-century meals uniformly began with soups. Whatever their placement on the menu, they were eaten first.

Indeed, soups might not appear at the top of the menu. The supper of Thursday 29 April 1751 at the château de Choisy, for example, first mentions the "Dormant" [a large gold or silver centerpiece], which was to remain at the center of the table throughout the meal (figure 4). Similarly, the supper of Monday 21 June 1751 mentions the "Dormant," followed by the "Two major entrées"; and only then the "Two *oilles* [stews]" and "Two soups."[2] But this tells us nothing about the order in which all these dishes were eaten. It seems even certain that at this meal, as at all other seventeenth- and eighteenth-century meals, such stews and soups were eaten first, before major or secondary entrées. In this regard, I would again cite Grimod de La Reynière's comments in his 1804 *Almanach des gourmands* about the order in which dishes were eaten: "Guests take their seats and their silence bespeaks the power and universality of their sensations. A properly scald-

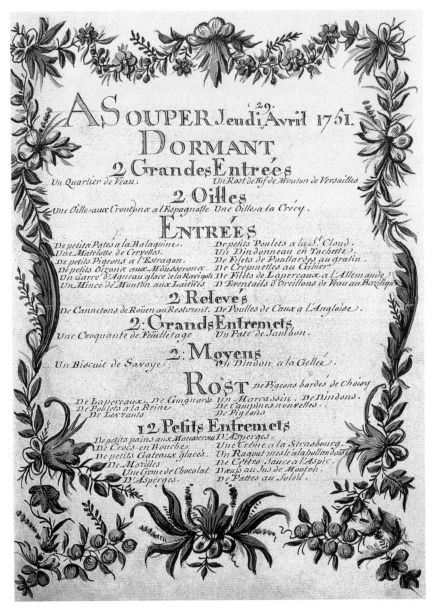

FIGURE 4. Menu for a 29 April 1751 meal at Choisy for Louis XV, in the collection *Voyages du Roy au château de Choisy, avec les logements de la cour et les menus de la table de Sa Majesté,* by F.-P. Brain de Sainte-Marie. 1751. India ink on paper. Châteaux de Versailles et de Trianon, Versailles, France. (Réunion des musées nationaux/Art Resource, NY)

ing soup does not in the least dampen the general activity. . . . Now the host . . . skillfully carves a quivering hindquarter of fat beef encircled by a simple vegetable garland studded with lardoons. . . . In the meantime, the hors d'oeuvres disappear and the entrées, eaten after the boiled meats, leave time to apportion the relevés that have replaced the soups."[3] This rare account provides much more direct evidence on this point than do menus.

Hors d'Oeuvres

Hors d'oeuvres seem to have materialized at the end of the seventeenth century. None are to be found in La Varenne, Pierre de Lune, or L. S. R. *[L'Art de bien traiter]*, but only in the 1691 first edition of Massialot's *Cuisinier royal et bourgeois.*

Dictionaries of the period—such as the *Dictionnaire de Trévoux* in 1704—derive this word from the vocabulary of architecture but recognize several figurative meanings, including, with respect to meals: "Something is said to be *hors d'œuvre,* figuratively, when it is a digression, a thing that does not pertain to the subject at hand. The term *hors d'œuvre* also refers, at grand feasts, to certain dishes served in addition to those one might expect in the normal composition of a feast."

Seventeenth- and eighteenth-century hors d'oeuvres were mostly hot dishes (as opposed to today's cold ones) but smaller than entrées. Thus the five hors d'oeuvres that Massialot names for the first course of a June menu—comparable to the meals served to the king on ordinary occasions—are "Stuffed sheep trotters and croquettes, Chicken breast with oysters, Grilled sheep tongues in sauce remoulade, Chicken fricassee with pike, and Young turkey stuffed with herbs."[4] All these dishes, served in definitely smaller vessels than the entrées of the same meal, do seem to have been less copious: a "Fawn leg with its rear quarter, half studded, half breaded, garnished with little savories, in sauce poivrade," a "Cut of half-salted beef, cooked on hot coals," and, as the main entrée, a "Roast beef garnished with marinade, and fried veal chops."

At first, as *Le Cuisinier royal et bourgeois* testifies, hors d'oeuvres found their place not only in the first, but also in the second course, composed of roasts and entremets. The June meal, whose five first-course hors d'oeuvres we have just enumerated, had four more in the second course, after the entremets: "One of fritters, one of rissoles, one of mushrooms in cream, one of eggs with orange." Hors d'oeuvres sometimes even figured among the entremets without appearing in the first course. One April dinner menu, for example, contains none in the first course but two in the second: "One of artichoke bottoms in cream, and one of sliced salt pork."[5]

First-course hors d'oeuvres were served after the soups and entrées and, in Massialot, second-course hors d'oeuvres came after the entremets. In *La Cuisinière bourgeoise* (1746), they no longer appear except in the first course, but still at the end of the course, after the entrées. In *Les Soupers de la Cour* (1755), hors d'oeuvres combine with the entrées at the end of the first course, but before the relevés constituting the second.[6] Several of the dinners in Menon's *Science du maître d'hôtel cuisinier* (1789 edition) place "Four hors d'oeuvres" after the soups, at the end of the first course but before the second course, composed of "Two entrées as relevés for the soups."[7] But in the "Supper" menus, where the entrées were part of the first course, the hors d'oeuvres followed them.[8] There is also a "Fall and Winter dinner" in which "Four hors d'oeuvres" precede "Two Entrées" even though these entrées are part of the first course.[9]

Hors d'oeuvres did not skip ahead until later. In 1821, for example, in Archambault's *Cuisinier économe,* "Eight small hors d'oeuvres" are mentioned (if not eaten) after "Two soups" and "Two relevés," but before the "Twelve entrées."[10] These were all cold hors d'oeuvres, much more common in the nineteenth century than in the seventeenth and eighteenth. In 1804, as we have seen, Grimod de La Reynière was already writing in his *Almanach des gourmands* that hors d'oeuvres were to be eaten immediately after the soups, while the host was carving the boiled meat.

Soupless Suppers

In the 1691 first edition of Massialot's *Cuisinier royal et bourgeois,* most meals are simply called "meals" or "ordinaries," while some are called "dinner" and others "supper."[11] But whatever their name, they all have a first course containing soups, entrées, and hors d'oeuvres. Later, this was not always so. The menus of *Les Soupers de la Cour* in 1755 almost always include soups and stews; but the supper menu of *La Cuisinière bourgeoise* suggests a "Soup for the center" only "if you judge it appropriate." The 1789 edition of *La Science du maître d'hôtel cuisinier* includes soups only in its dinner menus and never for suppers, which generally contain one less course.[12] This rule—linguistically odd since one would expect soup at a *souper*—persisted into the nineteenth century.

Relevés and Spit-Roasted Entrées

The verb *relever* was already used in the seventeenth century to mean "to clear away one dish and replace it immediately with another." But the noun *relevé* ["remove" in English culinary terminology] does not appear to have entered the vocabulary of the table until the eighteenth century. It is often used to designate the large spit-roasted *entrées de broche* that replaced the soups—usually during the first course, although they sometimes introduced the second, as we just saw in *La Science du maître d'hôtel cuisinier*. We have also seen, in part one, that these spit-roasted entrées were neither browned to the same degree as roasts nor studded with diced bacon or lard, but usually wrapped in fat and oiled paper, and that their bland taste was corrected with a sauce.[13]

These relevés could also be all kinds of dishes other than roasted meats, as widely illustrated in *Les Soupers de la Cour*: for meat days, a rice casserole, hot quail pie with lettuce, lamb quarter with cucumbers, leg of veal in cream, and spit-roasted ham in champagne sauce; for meatless meals, shad (probably poached), fish stew, perch *à l'anglaise*, and fish pie.[14]

Prior to the nineteenth century, there were always as many relevés as soups, but this later changed.[15] We have already seen that relevés appeared in menus at various points that did not always match their order of consumption. In the royal menu of 21 June 1751, the four relevés were noted after the sixteen entrées and may have introduced the second course; similarly, in *Les Soupers de la Cour*, the "Soup relevés" constituted a "second course" each time they were mentioned. But they could also appear elsewhere in the menu: about the same period, in the supper for ten place settings from *La Cuisinière bourgeoise*, the spit-roasted joint of butcher's meat listed as a relevé for the soup occurs immediately after the soup it replaces; likewise, in the 1821 menu for a "Table with twenty-five place settings" by Archambault, the two soup relevés—namely, a joint of beef garnished with glazed onions, and a turbot or other fish—immediately follow the two soups, just before the eight small hors d'oeuvres and twelve entrées. But they were no more eaten at that point in the meal in 1821 than they would have been in 1746. They were probably eaten at the very end of the first course, as suggested by the first menus cited and as recounted by Grimod de La Reynière.

FEWER ROASTS AND FAR MORE ENTREMETS

The first part of the meal is striking for its neologisms describing new culinary functions; the second, for its trend toward reduction, certainly at least in the number of roast courses. Whatever the final tally of roast dishes, so variable from one meal to another, there remained only one roast course in seventeenth- and eighteenth-century meals, in dramatic contrast to previous centuries.

Fewer Roast Courses

Most meat-day meals in the fourteenth-century menus of *Le Ménagier de Paris* featured a meat roast and a fish roast in one of the courses. By the sixteenth century, fish had almost disappeared from the menus in *Le Livre fort excellent de cuysine,* but far from decreasing, the number of roasts had expanded, with some menus listing three, four, or even six of them—an average of more than two per meal.

But this multiplication of roasts was no more than a passing trend: in the seventeenth and eighteenth centuries, only one roast course remained in both meat-day and meatless meals, the several roasted meats being served either on the same serving platter or on different ones. For example, the "Table with three platters" in *Le Nouveau et Parfait Maistre d'hostel* by Pierre de Lune presents a first platter with a combination of roasted lamb, capons, and partridges; a second platter with roasted chickens and plovers; and a third one filled with quails and young pigeons.[16] The whole series is accompanied by salads and by olives, which were also called salads.

The eighteenth century brought no significant changes. For example, Massialot's *Nouveau Cuisinier royal et bourgeois* of 1742 has a "Table with 6 to 8 place settings, served with one large, two medium, and four small dishes"; its second course consists of "Three dishes of roast: one of Campine chickens, one of two young hares, and another of eight pigeons, accompanied by two salads and two sauces." The number of roasts could sometimes be higher (e.g., eight appear in the royal supper of 21 June 1751 in Choisy) without destroying the unity of the roast course.[17]

Fish for Meat-Day Meals

As just recalled above, the late-fourteenth-century meat-day menus of *Le Ménagier de Paris* often included a fish roast in the course that followed the meat roast course. In contrast, *Le Livre fort excellent de cuysine* not only contains no meatless menus, but features practically no fish in its meat-day menus—even though they nearly always include several roast courses.[18]

One might ascribe the absence of fish in meat-day menus to Charles IX's edict against eating meat and fish at the same meal. But if we are to believe the menus consulted, the practice seems to have preceded this royal law and continued throughout the seventeenth and eighteenth centuries, up to the Revolution. Even so, cookbooks, especially those of the eighteenth century, contain many fish recipes suitable only for meat-day meals containing meat. *Le Cuisinier gascon* (1740), for example, mentions "conger eels for meat and meatless days."[19] *Festin joyeux* (1738) has "meat-day sole soup," "meat-day stuffed carp soup," and "meat-day carp stuffed on the bone."[20] The 1774 edition of *La Cuisinière bourgeoise* suggests "Meat-day turbot and brill cooked with nice slices of veal"; "Meat-day sturgeon on a spit"; eel, "which can also be served on meat days in various ways, including as a fricandeau or a garnish for meat-day entrées"; carp, which "is also served in many other ways for meat and meatless days"; trout, which "can also be prepared like salmon for meat days"; "monkfish or catfish," which "also make very good meat-day entrées as a fricandeau, studded with lard, or natural, with good ragoûts of cockscomb or such"; and so on.[21] The inclusion of all these good meat-day fish recipes in so many eighteenth-century works suggests that there must exist menus in which they appear, though I have not yet encountered any.

A Plethora of Entremets

There were no major changes, yet seventeenth- and eighteenth-century menus differ widely according to whether the entremets and roasts are combined in the same course or separated into two consecutive courses. A proliferation of entremets could especially be achieved through various tricks of presentation.

Pierre de Lune was the master of such seventeenth-century techniques. His "Table with two platters and two dishes," for instance, has only four soups in the first course and four entrées in the second, but four roasts and "Three different salads at the saltcellar" by the time the third course appears and, most remarkably, "Ten entremets with four dishes per platter" in the fourth course. To take another example, his "Table with three platters and four dishes" includes an "Entremets with five dishes per platter," for a total of nineteen entremets selections.[22] The entremets in *La Science du maître d'hôtel cuisinier* (1789) are simpler but still plentiful. "Summer supper serving nine," for example, features a "Flaky pastry for the center," four dishes of roast, four salads, and two sauces, resulting in a second course of eleven dishes, and a third course of "Nine entremets," both savory and sweet.[23]

In contrast, there are far fewer entremets when combined with the roasts in a single course. Examples include the second and third menus of *La Cuisinière bourgeoise*: only three entremets in the second menu ("Amiens pie," "iced custard," and "cauliflower") for a dinner with twelve place settings; three also in the third menu, namely, "Small cakes," "peas," and "cream au gratin," for a supper table with ten place settings. Some menus and cookbooks emphasize savory entremets, while others, like this one, favor sweet entremets. Considering how vast the array of entremets could be, there are really very few of them here, especially compared with the seven dishes of desserts included in both menus.[24]

It is time to note that starting in the seventeenth century one of the four major flavors—sweet—branched out into its own category. Up to then, sugar was not excluded as seasoning for any type of food—meat, fish, or vegetables—and could be found at any stage of the meal. Any dish could contain sugar, and sweet dishes could appear in any course, although, even as of the sixteenth century, they were more plentiful at dessert.

Starting in the seventeenth century, however, some foods could be seasoned only with salt, and others only with sugar. Furthermore, sweetened dishes increasingly gravitated toward the last two courses of the meal, the entremets and dessert. From the seventeenth century to at least the end of the nineteenth century and even the early twentieth, the sequence of dishes was rearranged so that the sweet ones were always eaten after the savory. This change did not happen overnight, but rather as a slow but persistent and continuous process of reorganization over several centuries. While this movement took place in several countries—as we shall see in part three—it seems to have occurred first and foremost in France.

Separation of Savory and Sweet

This reorganization began with the cuisine itself. Even today, French people exposed to foreign table customs are most struck by differences in cuisine—whether to their taste or not. They are surprised not by the presence of sugar but by how it is used: the sweet flavoring of Moroccan tagines; the corn (or maple) syrups served over an American breakfast of bacon and eggs, and pancakes with salted butter; the "Cremona mustard" offered for Italian pot-au-feu. But in fact the French did not always shy away from such combinations. A marked reticence is evident by the early nineteenth century, when Horace Raisson, for instance, grumbled about what he called romantic cuisine: "Soon all the aberrations of an art that knows neither limits nor rules will be transplanted here: our tables will exhibit rabbits stretched out on a bed of gooseberry jelly, hares surrounded by applesauce. And soon, we will be eating dessert after the soup and entremets before entrées, just as our neighbors do."[25]

Although the proportion of recipes containing sugar was on the increase until the sixteenth century (figure 5), the percentage of sugared meat and fish reached its peak in the fifteenth century (figure 6). Such combinations

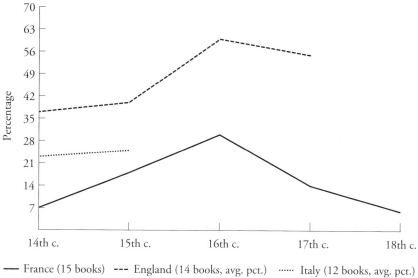

── France (15 books)　--- England (14 books, avg. pct.)　····· Italy (12 books, avg. pct.)

FIGURE 5. Percentage of recipes containing sugar

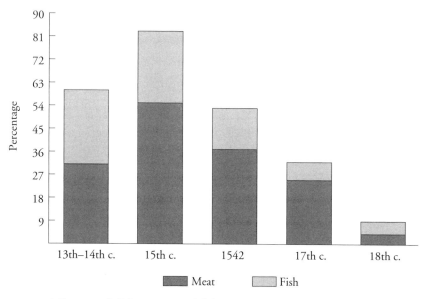

▨ Meat　▧ Fish

FIGURE 6. Sweetened dishes: meat and fish

became increasingly exceptional through the seventeenth and eighteenth centuries. *La Cuisinière bourgeoise,* in 1746, mentions a little sugar in "Breast of veal with peas" and in "Caux pigeons with peas." But just like today, it was the peas, not the meat, that called for the sugar. The book's only recipe likely to shock modern taste is for a "Marrow custard," which mixes sugar and marrow.

In 1651, *Le Cuisinier françois* was still presenting a sweet sauce with young hares, fawn, and beef tongue; the "veal pie," "English pie," rissoles, and "kidney ramekins" were all sugared, as were the capon and veal-shank aspics for entremets. Likewise, in 1660 the *Cuisinier méthodique* recipes for "Stewed meat," "Cold minced meat," "Meat in aspic," "Gallimaufry," "Restaurative," "Whimsical soup," "Jacobine soup," and "Chicory soup" all included sugar—and were all meat preparations.

Sugared poultry was by then much less frequent than in the Middle Ages and the Renaissance, but *Le Cuisinier françois* still suggested "Teal soup with *hypocras*" and "Young wild duck in sweet sauce"; *Le Cuisinier méthodique* still had "Sweet [pigeon] compote" and "[Capon] stew with sweet sauce"; lastly, *L'Art de bien traiter* listed a poultry "blancmange." Likewise for fish: *Le Cuisinier françois* sugared its "Salmon soup," "Salmon ragout," "Roasted stuffed sole," "Lamprey in sweet sauce," "Fish aspic," and "Meatless blancmange"; and *Le Cuisinier méthodique* sugared "Preserved oysters" and "Fish fritters."

While the practice of combining sugar with meat or fish steadily waned, it increased steadily with eggs and dairy products (figure 7).

The growth of this practice as applied to dried and fresh fruits is harder to track, despite what figure 8 might suggest. Fresh fruit was becoming increasingly linked with dessert, which was the province of the steward rather than the cook. That is why, as we have seen, cookbooks usually skip the essentials of fresh fruit handling and sweet preparations. When a pantry manual is included at the back of a cookbook, as in *La Cuisinière bourgeoise suivie de l'Office,* we glimpse the tangible uses of sugar in more recent centuries. But including these recipes distorts the statistics.

The association of sugar with other produce is similarly skewed because salads were normally under the care of the steward. The chapter devoted to them in *Le Cuisinier méthodique* thus introduces a heterogeneous factor into our statistics. The 1685 edition of the work still uses sugar on some green salads, like "Firm lettuce & others," "Violet salad," "Wild white chicory," "Sugared capers," "Pomegranate," or even a "Health salad" as well as on plain and mixed fruit salads such as "Crowned salad" (a mixture of

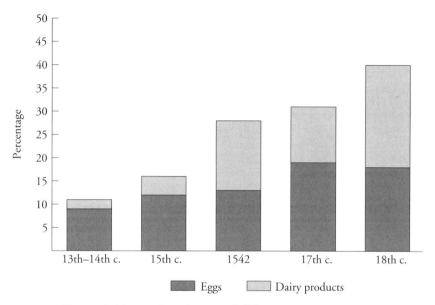

FIGURE 7. Eggs and dairy products in sugared dishes

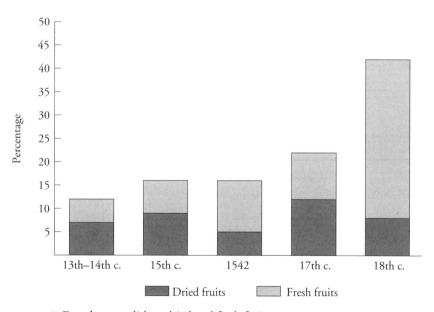

FIGURE 8. French sweet dishes: dried and fresh fruits

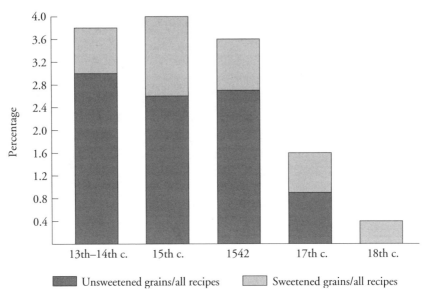

FIGURE 9. Grains as a percentage of all recipes

lemon, pomegranate, pistachios, and lettuce and other greens), "Salad of preserved lemon peel," "Almond salad," a lemon salad, salads of "Sweet lemons, oranges, and Seville oranges," "Wild green chicory," "Capers with sugar," "Pomegranate," and "Pistachio."[26] Yet references such as those found in Jouvin de Rochefort's *Voyageur d'Europe* (1675) suggest that sugared salads were out of fashion in France even before the end of the seventeenth century.[27]

A graph illustrating the use of sugar with other plant-based foods would be chaotic and barely readable for two reasons: the ratio of grain dishes in cookbooks lessened steadily after the fourteenth century, and these grain dishes were increasingly served sweet. Figure 9 shows the relative proportion of grain dishes containing sugar.

The picture is even more complex with respect to vegetables. While the upper classes ate them much more often in the seventeenth and eighteenth centuries than in the fourteenth and fifteenth, vegetables seasoned with sugar seem to have become much rarer in the eighteenth century as compared to the seventeenth. However, *La Cuisinière bourgeoise* continued to use sugar with peas, broad beans, pumpkin, and squash, as well as—more oddly to the contemporary palate—on several mushroom dishes.

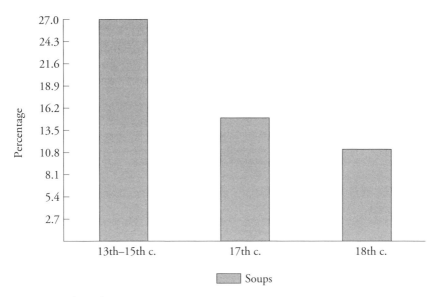

FIGURE 10. Sugar in soups

Sweet after Savory

Not only does our traditional gastronomy find it strange and questionable to use sugar on meat, poultry, or fish and most vegetables, but it also assigns sweet dishes to the end of the meal. Served as entremets for centuries, these sweet dishes are now, with few exceptions, eaten only at dessert. The point is that these positions took even longer to become established than savory versus sweet seasoning.

Many cookbooks are organized around chapters devoted to specific types of dishes: soups, entrées, roasts, entremets; others indicate the function of the dish in the margin of each recipe. We thus see that since the Middle Ages, sweet seasonings have disappeared from certain types of dishes, such as soups (figure 10) and roasts (figure 11), while multiplying in others such as entremets (figure 11).

But over the course of the period in question, the meaning of some of these designations changed. In the fourteenth and fifteenth centuries, soups were often meat preparations with minimal sauce, very different from the almost entirely liquid soups of the eighteenth century. The fact that some of these medieval soups would have been considered entrées in more modern times skews the statistical data.

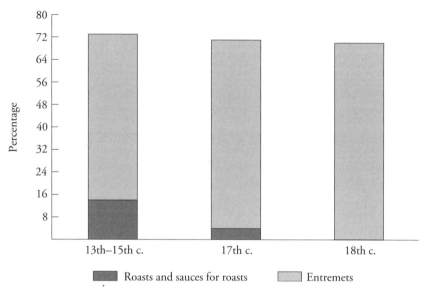

FIGURE 11. Sugar in roasts and entremets

Legend: ■ Roasts and sauces for roasts   ▧ Entremets

While fourteenth- and fifteenth-century recipe collections contain no entrées as such, they did exist. This is clear from menus, particularly those dating from the sixteenth century. Their entrées include some prepared dishes but also many others that required no cooking, such as the fresh fruit already mentioned in preceding chapters. Dishes that could be defined as sweet included both fresh raw fruit—which is inherently sweet rather than flavored with sugar—and sweet pastries to which sugar was added, such as "Florets," "Dry pastries," and "Marzipan brochelets." This collection of recipes thus also fails to convey a clear picture of the use of sugar in entrées.

As mentioned earlier, salads and desserts appear only rarely in cookbooks because they were the responsibility of the steward rather than the cook. But certain salads were long seasoned with sugar, as demonstrated by *L'École des ragoûts*.[28] Desserts have always included sweet dishes, though in highly varied proportions depending on the period. This final course was not ordinarily listed in the menus but a few examples do exist, and their study rounds out information on the developing uses of sugar. The small corpus of menus I have collected shows, above all, that desserts constituted an increasingly high proportion of the dishes brought to the table (figure 12).[29]

The occurrence of sweet or sugared dishes outside of dessert can be

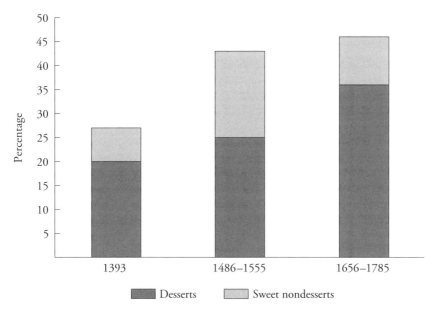

FIGURE 12. Desserts and sweet nondessert dishes

analyzed once identified by their name, if self-explanatory, or through knowledge about how these dishes were commonly prepared. At first, their proportion grew along with the increasingly frequent use of sugar: from 7.20 percent in the fourteenth century to 17.91 percent in the fifteenth and sixteenth centuries. It then dropped to 9.15 percent in the seventeenth and eighteenth centuries (figure 12), when sweet dishes progressively migrated to the end of the meal. The eighteenth-century menus no longer show any sweet or sugared dishes except as entremets or desserts.

Medieval meals not only began with all sorts of fruit and other sweet dishes that today we do not eat until dessert, but included in dessert various meat and savory dishes that we would now find out of place at that point in the meal: venison in frumenty, turtledove and lark pie, crayfish, fresh herring, artichokes, porpoise, chestnuts, olives, cheeses. These incongruities also gradually disappeared, declining from 24.1 percent in the fourteenth century to 5.6 percent in the fifteenth and sixteenth centuries and 2.5 percent in the seventeenth and eighteenth centuries (figure 13). The most persistent custom was the inclusion of ripened cheeses among desserts, which lasted into the early twentieth century and even tended to increase.

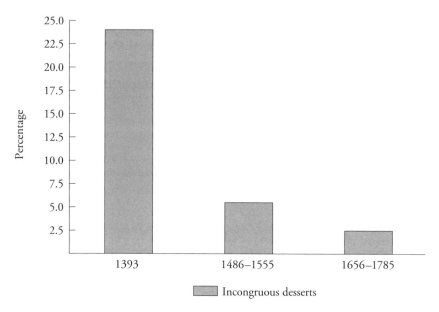

FIGURE 13. Meat or savory desserts

Conclusion

French attitudes regarding sweet selections clearly do not date from time immemorial but have gradually evolved over the centuries. Sweet flavors, disregarded in the fourteenth century, gradually came to be accepted by the upper classes in the fifteenth and sixteenth centuries, doubtless to emulate our neighbors for whom the use of sugar was a sign of distinction.

At first used as a seasoning for all sorts of food, sugar in modern times increasingly came to be considered incongruous with meats and vegetables. Since the eighteenth century it has been used with hardly anything but eggs, dairy products, flour, and fruit.

Furthermore, fruit and sweetened foods, which in the late Middle Ages were served with any course, gradually came to be reassigned to the end of the meal. But this evolution took longer than the preceding one. Until the early twentieth century, sweet entremets appeared alongside savory ones in the penultimate course. And when ripened and sometimes quite pungent cheeses were offered to guests, they figured among the fruits, compotes, and preserves of dessert.

In the twentieth century, cheese was finally uncoupled from this association with sweets and relocated between salad and dessert. This disassociation occurred as part of a much wider movement that deserves greater notice than it has received. Before delving into it, however (see chapter 9), let us review how courses changed in the nineteenth century.

EIGHT

Innovations from the Revolution to World War I

TO WHAT EXTENT AND OVER what time frame did the Revolution trans-
form French eating habits as it ended the absolute authority of the church
in France? I raise the question here although it cannot be answered as precisely as I would like within the scope of this book. Remember that no meat
was eaten on Friday or Saturday before 1789, and that even Wednesday was
a semi-meatless day on which egg dishes were featured. After the Revolution, meatless menus grew scarce, even for Fridays and Saturdays. Does this
mean that the French who continued to fast and restrict their diet were now
a definite minority?

The impact of religious rules should not overshadow that of individual
economic means: it is not clear what proportion of the French population
could afford fresh or salted meat before or after 1789, on days allowed by
the church. Ill-equipped to answer this historical question, I will continue
to focus on the social classes for whom the decision to eat meat, fish, or even
eggs was a matter of conviction rather than material resources. I will also
focus on their various reasons for eating fish: as a substitute for the forbidden meat of fasting days, or to combine the pleasures of both.

I will also discuss the Russian-style service that replaced the French style
in the nineteenth century and that many authors consider the most notable
development in this domain. Russian service reduced the number of
courses and dishes served at meals for the wealthy. The present chapter is

mainly devoted to showing how this shift affected every stage of the meal. I will conclude with a curious transition in the phrasing of menus from the singular, which almost certainly described courses, to the plural, which probably designated dishes.

Fish in Meat-Day Meals

In the previous chapter, I stated that from the sixteenth century until the Revolution, I found no fish on any menu except meatless ones, because Charles IX had issued an edict against eating meat and fish in the same meal. But the number of fish recipes for meat days in cookbooks—especially in the eighteenth century—raises doubts that this prohibition was strictly observed up to 1789.

After the Revolution, fish reappeared in meat-day menus just as in the Middle Ages, and even became systematically served as a relevé. See, for example, the "Service for 25" in Archambault's 1821 *Le Cuisinier économe,* where the two relevés are a dish of "Beef garnished with glazed onions" and a "Turbot or other fish," as well as Dugléré's spring menu for fifteen, reported by Alexandre Dumas, where the two major dishes are "Stuffed carp à la Chambord" and "Sirloin à la Sunderland."[1]

While this association of fish and meat is less systematic for the roast course, it nevertheless occurs throughout the nineteenth century, as confirmed by many menus. In Archambault, the "Four roast dishes" consist of a "Hen with watercress," "Red woodcocks or partridges," "Salmon trout," and "Smelt." The "Dinner menu for 24" by Verdier at the Maison dorée offers "Two roasts" consisting of "Turkey and ortolans" and a "Mound of crayfish."[2] The dinner menu served to the royal family of Belgium includes two roasts, one of "Saddle of boar in venison sauce" and the other of "Fried smelt."[3]

These combinations seem to revert to the Middle Ages. But remember that in the *Ménagier de Paris* menus, the meat roast and the fish roast were served in two different courses, which was no longer the case in the nineteenth century. Note, however, that just as in the seventeenth and eighteenth centuries, these fish and shellfish "roasts" were still poached or fried—never spit-roasted, grilled, or oven-baked as one might expect them to be today.

The nineteenth century was most notably marked by efforts to diversify the various types of dishes as much as possible. As Archambault writes in his *Cuisinier économe,* "Because variety contributes to a dinner's merit, the four or six entrées of a meal must include one of butcher's meat, one of poultry, one of fish, and one of pastries. The roast must consist of game if the entrées contain none, and of poultry if they do. If vegetables are in season, they can make up two out of four entremets."[4] As we have seen, other authors relied on fish more than did Archambault in this quest for diversification.

Fish as a Stage of the Meal

For some restaurateurs, fish constituted a first-course stage of the meal in the same manner as soups, hors d'oeuvres, entrées, and relevés. It was included in every menu of the restaurateur Magny. When the stages of the meals are not specified, the menu lists a fish dish described no more specifically than the dishes that precede and follow it. The "Lunch menu for two," for example, offers "Sole in white wine" between "Two salt-meadow lamb chops with chestnut purée" (which seems to be an entrée) and "Two roast quail" (which certainly constitutes the roast). The opening dishes of his "Dinner menu for four" definitely stress seafood, starting with "Marennes oysters" and proceeding to an hors d'oeuvre of "Butter and shrimp," a "Crayfish bisque," and "Trout in hollandaise sauce." Then come "Filets à la Rossini"— evidence, among other indications, that this was not a totally meatless meal.[5]

Where the types of dishes are specified, fish is one of them. One long menu begins with "Soup" ("Faubonne with quenelles") followed by "Fish" (namely, "Fillets of sole Dieppoise"). Another follows this same format, the soup consisting of "Turtle soup à l'anglaise" and "Royal spring soup," and the fish being "Salmon fillets à la Daumont" and "Turbot in lobster and hollandaise sauce." Similarly, in a "Russian-service dinner for 25," Urbain Dubois and Émile Bernard present two fish dishes between the hors d'oeuvres and relevés.[6] Other examples include English-service dinners for 12 and for 20, where the fish course arrives between the soups and the relevés; a "French-service dinner for 48," where the fish course fits between the hors d'oeuvres (which did not exist in English service) and the relevés; and a "French-service dinner for 100," which presents its "Four fishes" between "Eight hot hors d'oeuvres" and "Four relevés."[7]

Were Meatless Rules Still Observed after the Revolution?

After perusing hundreds of nineteenth-century menus, one wonders if the meatless rule still existed during that period. Did the church still impose it, and did the faithful still observe it? Fish and meat dishes are closely associated in the twenty-one menus published by Grimod de La Reynière in his 1808 *Manuel des amphitryons,* but none of them is a meatless menu. The same holds true for the very few menus of Archambault's *Cuisinier économe,* and for the thirty-eight composed by six great chefs of the second half of the century that were reprinted at the back of Alexandre Dumas's *Grand Dictionnaire de cuisine.* Nearly all include fish, but none is a meatless menu. Can this be simply by chance?

Even more surprising, I could not find a single meatless menu among the 131 gathered by Philippe Mordacq in his book *Le Menu.* Likewise, none are to be found in the 1893 to 1899 issues of *La Cuisine française et étrangère,* nor in the twenty-eight menus in the 1897 issues of *L'Art culinaire.* Two of the latter are Friday menus, but both contain meat. Since these are Escoffier menus for London's Savoy Hotel, they shed no light on French customs or on the Catholic tradition of the period. The twenty-one menus of *La Cuisine française et étrangère,* which do pertain, include three Friday meals. But here again, each contains several meat dishes.[8] Are we to surmise that, during this period in France, only freethinkers held banquets on Fridays? As it turns out, the phenomenon extended beyond banquets. Meatless menus are equally absent in *Les 366 Menus du baron Brisse,* which presents a meal menu for every day of the year, each containing the same number of dishes. Not a single one is meatless.

Could it be that the pope dispensed the French from meatless obligations, just as he had done for the Spaniards at war against the Moors in the Middle Ages? Or might this be a historiographic gourmet tradition attempting to erase the memory of ancient prohibitions? The latter possibility seems the more plausible line of research since a careful look at documents collected contemporaneously rather than compiled in later times reveals that meatless menus did indeed exist.

La Cuisine classique by Urbain Dubois and Émile Bernard, for instance, contains menus for a "Meatless dinner for 12," a "Meatless dinner for 10," a "Meatless dinner for 26," and a "Meatless dinner for 14," all four presented in the Russian style.[9] But given that these authors were cooks for the king of Prussia, a Calvinist ruler, what exactly should one make of these artifacts? Let us instead rely on a document by Baron Brisse, author of the 366 meat-day menus already mentioned. He also wrote *La Cuisine en carême avec obédience aux Commandements de l'Église. . . . Menus et recettes pour le déjeuner et le dîner de chaque jour du carême* ("Lenten cuisine in compliance with Church rules. . . . Lunch and dinner Menus for each day of Lent"), published in 1873.

The nineteenth-century displacement of "French service" by "Russian service" is reputed to be a major event in the history of table service. Yet the period when this transition occurred is difficult to pinpoint, as is the actual difference between the two styles. It is not even certain that this table-service innovation changed anything regarding the order in which dishes were presented.

The order of presentation, however, did not remain static throughout the nineteenth century. All sorts of minor changes were taking place, some perhaps resulting from the new serving customs. In their 1856 *Cuisine classique,* Dubois and Bernard wrote, "Table service today is generally based on two methods, French service and Russian service, which share a common goal but start from conflicting if not opposite principles. Each method has its proponents and opponents, converts and critics, but both are practiced equally."[10]

Cooks to the Prussian king and advocates of the Russian style, these two authors defined it by comparison with the French method, which at the time still predominated at prestigious French and English tables. While more pleasing to the eye, the French tradition had a drawback: dishes to be eaten last remained too long on the table and got cold, despite the use of dish-warmers and covers.[11] To avoid this problem, Russian service placed on the table only cold dishes that could wait, while hot ones were passed around to all the guests immediately after being carved in the kitchen. According to our authors, "This serving style makes for a less elegant table than French service, but has the priceless advantage of allowing the food to be enjoyed under the best possible conditions, it being arranged for presentation the moment it is cooked to perfection, and served immediately. It also means that the guests must serve themselves. . . . Although the table is not adorned with hot dishes, the cook always has the option of dressing it with cold selections, pastries and entremets, which can wait without losing quality or flavor." This applied especially to dessert: "It is therefore elegantly, lavishly presented and remains on display throughout the dinner. The visual appeal of such a meal can thus be striking and in fact leave very little to envy about dinners served in the French style."[12]

This Russian service, which apparently came to prevail in France only during the second half of the nineteenth century, was already being discussed fifty years earlier. In the 1804 *Almanach des gourmands,* Grimod de La Reynière wrote,

In Germany, Switzerland, and most of the north, this carving is carried out by an ad hoc steward who performs it with rare skill. This is a valuable custom thanks to which host and guests can put time to better use; it also enhances large pieces of meat by presenting them in all their splendor, properly carved. It dispenses with useless ceremony and rescues the timid, since the serving platters are passed around for all guests to serve themselves according to their appetite and preference. We hope to see this fine method adopted in France, especially for important meals. Our Nation will then, in every regard, deserve complete preeminence in the fine art of cuisine and dining.[13]

The new manner of serving, often described as a sort of revolution, thus did not necessarily change the order in which dishes were presented and eaten. But over the course of the nineteenth century, many other innovations indeed occurred that probably did relate to the Russian style of service.

Reduced Number of Courses

Many nineteenth-century authors suggested or justified a reduction in the number of courses and dishes. We have seen that between the sixteenth century and the seventeenth, fewer courses came to be served at aristocratic tables. But their number was far from fixed in the seventeenth and eighteenth centuries. Important dinners, like those of Pierre de Lune in 1662, usually had five courses—soups, entrées, roasts, entremets, and dessert—while by 1692, those of Massialot included only three. The first consisted of soups and entrées, the second included the roasts together with the salads and entremets, and dessert constituted the third. But *Le Cuisinier royal et bourgeois* was not the definitive word on the matter. In his eighteenth-century *Nouveau Cuisinier royal et bourgeois,* Massialot himself lists menus with an additional course. One example is a "Table for 6 to 8, served in one principal, two medium, and four small platters." It contains four courses: soups and entrées, then roasts and salads, then entremets of all sorts, and lastly desserts. Menon's *Cuisinière bourgeoise,* published in 1746, offers one three-course menu and two four-course menus, which also differ in how the courses are distributed. In the first menu, the second course consists of entrées, whereas in the third it is composed of the two relevés for the soups.

The 1755 *Soupers de la Cour* even proposes menus with five courses per meal, if we count the second course as the two relevés that take the place of the two soups. There are also many five-course menus in *La Science du maître d'hôtel cuisinier* (counting desserts, which the book does not mention). Here again, the second course consists of the two relevés for the soup; the third, roasts and salads; and the fourth, assorted entremets. These are all dinner menus, such as "Spring dinner" and "Fall and winter meatless dinner for eleven." The supper menus have four courses, with no soup or relevé. There are also four-course menus in which the third combines roasts and entremets.

More surprising for its time is a "Table for 25 to 30 for the month of February, served to 27 at supper," which has six courses including dessert. The first consists of four *oilles*, "four terrines for the corners," and "16 entrées or hors d'oeuvres"; the second has four relevés for the *oilles;* the third brings four large and eight small platters of roast, eight salads, and four pastries "as relevés for the terrines"; the fourth offers assorted entremets; the fifth contains "Little pastries as relevés for the 16 entremets"; and since all meals concluded with dessert, there must have been a sixth course consisting essentially of fresh and cooked fruit.[14]

The Midway Pause

In the seventeenth and eighteenth centuries, meals were sometimes served in three courses, dessert included, but this was not yet the rule. In the nineteenth century it quickly became customary. Early in the century, Grimod de La Reynière railed against hosts who served their entremets together with the roasts—apparently the prevailing practice, though some menus still offered four courses.

Adoption of the three-course meal was reinforced by the custom of serving a small glass of chilled or unchilled alcohol between the first course and the second. This *coup du milieu* became a standard feature of every feast menu in the latter half of the century, but was already mentioned between the second course and the third in the 1804 *Almanach des gourmands:*

> It is to the city of Bordeaux, so dear to gourmands and wine lovers in so many regards, that we owe this admirable innovation, this stroke of genius that makes a second dinner possible and has a way of redoubling the vigor of the weakest stomachs.
>
> Between the roast and the entremets, about midway through the meal, dining hall doors in Bordeaux open to reveal a young girl of 18 to 22 years, tall, blonde, shapely, engaging in all respects. Her sleeves are rolled up to her shoulders; in one hand, she carries a mahogany tray bearing as many glasses as there are guests, and in the other she holds a Montcenis crystal decanter of Jamaican rum, absinthe, or vermouth (although the latter is

more a preprandial than a mid-meal drink). Thus equipped, our Hebe walks around the table, starting with the best gourmand or most eminent guest. She pours a glass of the bitter nectar for each and silently retires. For the coup du milieu must always be simple. . . .

The coup du milieu has a quasi-magical effect. Speaking only to its effects and not its causes, which we leave to the doctors to explain, we simply note that each gourmand then feels as he did when he first sat down, and is ready to do honor to a second dinner. Above all, the host must therefore be careful not to unduly delay the midway pause, lest everyone leave with an unsatiated appetite.

This custom has become so popular in Paris in recent years that no respectably decent table has failed to adopt it. Ladies especially, here as well as in Bordeaux, are particularly fond of the *coup du milieu.*

Evidence for the existence of this *coup du milieu* during the first half of the nineteenth century remains elusive. I find none in the menus of Viard's 1806 *Cuisinier impérial* nor in those of Archambault's 1821 *Cuisinier économe,* although it is mentioned in the latter work, a few pages before the menus: "While the second [course] is being readied, one consumes the *coup du milieu,* which is rum, kirsch, or dry madeira." Then, just twenty years later, Joubert, Bouchard, and Louis Leclerc suddenly refer to it as an antiquated custom: "Some people still observe the custom of the *coup du milieu.* In this case, madeira, aged cognac, or rum should be served at the end of the first course."[15] The fact remains, however, that this practice was well established from the middle to the end of the century. It appears, for instance, in most of Dubois and Bernard's menus in 1856, and in those published in gastronomy periodicals like *La Cuisine française et étrangère* and *L'Art culinaire* shortly before 1900. Dubois and Bernard had a favorite, "Roman punch," which they sometimes replaced with "Imperial punch," "Pineapple punch," "Iced punch," "Neapolitan punch," "Alkermès punch," or "Kirsch punch." An incredible diversity of such drinks appears in the menus of *L'Art culinaire* and *La Cuisine française et étrangère.*[16]

At what precise moment of the meal was this midway pause served? In 1804, Grimod de La Reynière put it between the second and third courses, in other words between the roast and the entremets. It occupies the same place—between "Roast Bohemian pheasant" and "French green peas"—in the lunch menu for the coronation of Emperor William I on 18 October 1861.[17] But by then, this was no longer its usual place: after Grimod, most authors generally combined the entremets and the roast into one course and marked the midway pause between the entrées and the roast. Examples include Archambault in *Le Cuisinier économe;* Joubert, Bouchard, and Leclerc in *Le Conservateur;* and all authors in the latter half of the century.

Reduced Number of Dishes

From the very beginning of the nineteenth century, there was a call to reduce the number of dishes, but it took a long time to be heeded. In 1805 Grimod de La Reynière commented,

> In old compendiums we find some first courses that contain up to 128 dishes for only sixty place settings; if we were to enumerate them here, we would see that these 128 dishes are copious enough to feed a small army. We have moved away from such profusion, and with good reason. A glance at this multitude of dishes satiates rather than tempts; and although most of these dishes are duplicates, the overabundance of choice is so confusing that the appetite wanes and the dinner gets cold before one can make up one's mind. . . . The second course consisted entirely of 52 relevés; the third course, granted that it combined roasts and entremets, presented an array of 160 dishes including salads and sauces. Anyone giving such a dinner nowadays would be a laughingstock.[18]

In his *Manuel des amphitryons,* the same author proposes, for fifteen guests, a dinner of 36 dishes described as "rather simple" and "easily prepared in a bourgeois kitchen"; he concludes with a menu for sixty that consists of three courses of 36 dishes each for a total of 108—an average of slightly less than 1.8 dishes per guest, as compared to 2.4 in the first menu.[19]

This call for restraint was heard throughout the century, but to moderate effect for a long time. In 1821 Archambault, who had witnessed the lavishness of former times, feels only a slight twinge of remorse after proposing 78 dishes—including 28 dessert selections—in a menu for twenty-five: "Two or even four of the 12 entrées can be omitted and replaced by eight substantial entrées, plus four hot hors d'oeuvres such as small pasties, kidneys, blood puddings, sausages, etc."[20] A quarter of a century later, in 1856, the French-service menus of Urbain Dubois and Émile Bernard still number 20 to 44 different dishes, excluding desserts; only for Russian-service meals does the number of dishes drop to 10 or 20, not counting the desserts.

Note also that there is no longer a clear connection in either style of service between the number of different dishes and the number of guests, because convenience led to the custom of multiplying the highlight dishes as

DINNER FOR SIXTY SERVED RUSSIAN STYLE "BY FIVES"

Spring soup
Soup of puréed green peas
5 Ortolan canapés
5 Salmon steaks à l'Impériale
5 Veal loins à la Jardinière
5 Chicken galantines à l'Anglaise (table display)
5 Partridge salmi in crust
5 Macaroni timbales à la Parisienne
5 Hen gizzards à la Périgueux
5 Foie gras aspics en belle vue

PUNCH À LA ROMAINE
5 Roast ducklings and truffled quail
5 Twin horns of plenty filled with glazed fruits (table display)
5 Artichoke hearts and peas
5 Charlottes à la Sicilienne
5 Jellied strawberry sultanas
5 Parisienne charlottes with nuts and dried fruits

———

FIGURE 14. Dinner for sixty served Russian style "by fives." Urbain Dubois and Émile Bernard, *La Cuisine classique* (1856), p. 7.

necessary. It was, for example, acceptable at a table for sixty to offer only 16 different dishes, served in the Russian style "by fives"—that is, with five platters of twelve portions for each dish (figure 14).[21]

This reduction in the number of dishes, compared to Grimod de La Reynière's menu of 108 dishes for the same number of guests, continued throughout the century and beyond. Menus from the 1890s feature about ten. See, for example, as reproduced in *La Cuisine française et étrangère,* the menu for an "Intimate dinner" given on Friday 22 June 1894 for 160 guests by the Paris restaurateur Margery (figure 15).

Soups and Hors d'oeuvres

Soups, which began all seventeenth- and eighteenth-century meals, sometimes relinquished this first position during the nineteenth century. Cold hors d'oeuvres came before them in a number of menus of that period, including the menus of Dugléré at the Café anglais, eight of which were pub-

"INTIMATE DINNER" FOR 160 GUESTS

SOUPS
Creamed asparagus and bisque

HORS-D'ŒUVRE
Melon, butter, shrimp

RELEVÉ
Salmon trout, Venetian sauce, and shrimp

ENTRÉES
Saddle of pré-salé lamb with new flageolets
Truffled hen à la Lucullus
Fine champagne granité

ROAST
Young ducklings in blood sauce
Romaine salad
Chaud-froid of ortolans
Crawfish à la Vosgienne

ENTREMETS
Bombe Nabah and bombe Phryné

WAFFLES
Cheeses, various fruits, dessert

WINES
Carafes of vintage Médoc Beaune Hospices 1878
Musigny blanc 1878 Château Yquem 1871
Château Grand-Puy 1874 Champagne J. Mumm
Champagne Heidsieck monopole

———

FIGURE 15. Dinner menu by the Paris restaurateur Margery on 22 June 1894, from *La Cuisine française et étrangère.*

lished at the back of *Le Grand Dictionnaire de cuisine* by Alexandre Dumas.[22] I do not believe this inversion is any longer a matter of page lay-out—as was the case in eighteenth-century menus—but rather a difference in order of consumption. In a sense, this type of menu represents a return to the sixteenth-century sequence or, even more, to that of the fourteenth. In the sixteenth century, the table entrée (whose function was similar to that of nineteenth-century hors d'oeuvres) was always still mentioned and probably eaten before the soups, while in the nineteenth century, as in the fourteenth, soups were not always preceded by this first course and often remained the first to be eaten.

Other nineteenth-century menus mention hors d'oeuvres after the soups. But these are hot hors d'oeuvres, not cold as in the previous case. Take, for example, the "Dinner menu for 15" organized by Verdier of La Maison dorée, and the "Dinner menu for 24."[23] But even those who followed this custom sometimes preceded soups with oysters, which I would hesitate to consider a cold hors d'oeuvre. Examples include the "Menu of a dinner for 12 offered by Alexandre Dumas on 15 January" at La Maison dorée; the "Dinner served at the Dresden court" to the "Saxe royal family," published in Dubois and Bernard's *Cuisine classique;* the menu for a "Dinner for 20 served at the Darmstadt court on 15 October 1868"; and the "Dinner served at the Karlsruhe court."[24] These oysters could even precede cold hors d'oeuvres, as in a "Supper for 12" by Verdier.[25] There were also occasions when the oysters followed the soup, as for instance at a dinner served at the Saxe-Weimar court and another at the Stuttgart court.[26] While it is true that these meals took place outside France, they were otherwise very French.

The contrast between hot and cold, however, is not the only possible explanation for these different sequences within the course. According to Dubois and Bernard, customs had not rigidly defined the right moment for cold dishes: "By preserving the serving sequence we used in various countries in keeping with local high-society practices, we wanted to show that the rule is not inflexible and can be modified depending on the circumstances. Serving a cold selection before fish, immediately after the relevés, instead of after the soup or the hors d'oeuvres, is simply a matter of preference with no great influence on the order or outcome of a dinner as long as one is aware of it."[27]

Number of Relevés and Displacement of Entrées

Prior to the nineteenth century, the number of relevés and soups was always equal, but not subsequently. For example, in a dinner for forty given by Vuillemot at the restaurant La Tête noire in Saint-Cloud, the only soup is a "Crayfish bisque tapioca," but there are nevertheless four relevés: a "Salmon trout *sauce Génoise,*" followed by "Turbot à la hollandaise," "Beef filet à la régence," and finally, "Deer quarter sauce poivrade."[28] Similarly, in the tenth of the royal menus noted by Dubois and Bernard (for the imperial family of Austria), there is just one soup—"Spring consommé with poultry quenelles"—for two relevés, one a "Salmon sauce Genevoise et hollandaise" and the other a "Beef filet à la financière."[29] It does appear that by the years 1867–1868 the original meaning of the term *relevé* was forgotten. The book by Philippe Mordacq even contains in the margin a menu for a "Lunch for 16 October 1867," which includes no soup but starts directly with two relevés—"Salmon sauce Genevoise" and "Beef filet à la Podard"—followed by four entrées, two roasts, etc.[30]

Remember that according to Grimod de La Reynière, "the entrées, eaten after the boiled food, leave time to apportion the relevés that have replaced the soups." Or at least, this is when these entrées were eaten in the eighteenth and early nineteenth centuries. But did this still hold after the middle of the century? I have my doubts, because after centuries of being relegated to later and later in the meal, entrées were by this time systematically mentioned after the hors d'oeuvres, after the soups, and often after the relevés, at the very end of the first "course"—insofar as one could still refer to it as such. By then the original meaning of *entrée* had manifestly fallen into even deeper oblivion than that of *relevé*.

We have already seen that in the seventeenth century, entrées had been shifted to follow the soups. Entrées came even later in the meal during the eighteenth and nineteenth centuries with the creation of hors d'oeuvres and relevés, which ultimately preceded them in most cases. We have just seen that in eighteenth-century menus the relevés sometimes appeared before the entrées and sometimes well after them—and were most likely eaten afterward. But in the nineteenth century they were most often mentioned before the entrées, along with cold or hot hors d'oeuvres, and the timing of their consumption more accurately corresponded to their menu placement. As a result, entrées appeared after the oysters or cold hors d'oeuvres, the soups, the hot hors d'oeuvres, and the relevés or "major features," in other words in fourth or fifth place, just before the "midway pause."[31]

FROM SINGULAR TO PLURAL

From Roast to Roasts

I have mentioned that the seventeenth-century practice of consolidating the roasts into a single roast course continued in subsequent centuries. But something changed in this regard during the nineteenth and twentieth centuries: this type of dish came to be referred to in the plural rather than the singular.

We saw that in the "Table for three platters" from *Le Nouveau et Parfait*

Maistre d'hostel royal by Pierre de Lune (1662), seven types of roasted animals presented as three dishes comprised the "roast," in the singular; in the royal menu of 21 June 1751 we also saw that six or seven types of roasted animals presented as six dishes made up the "roast," also in the singular. Likewise (or nearly), the center of the second course [in the menu titled "Service for 25"] in the 1821 *Cuisinier économe* by Archambault is dominated by "Four dishes of roast"—two of which, incidentally, were fishes, probably poached.[32]

Things changed in the latter half of the century. For example, in the spring "Menu for 15" at the Café anglais, a plural—"roasts"—collectively refers to "Chickens flanked by ortolans" and "Studded American guinea hens" accompanied by "Two salads." In the menu for a "Dinner for 15 offered by Alexandre Dumas at La Maison dorée on 10 November," a plural "roasts" designates not only a dish of assorted roasted quail, partridges, and ortolans, but also other dishes of "Sautéed green beans" and "Gelée noyaux with apricot garnish," in other words, a single dish of roasted fowl accompanied by a dish of vegetables and a sweet entremets.[33] In the "Dinner for 12" also offered by Alexandre Dumas at the same restaurant on 15 January of the following year, the plural "two roasts," designating a dish of "Truffled turkey" and another of "Ardennes woodcock," indicates even more explicitly that the collective singular that had ruled until the mid-1800s had fallen into disuse. In contrast to the previous century's political transition from "liberties" to Liberty, here we see a shift from the abstract to the concrete—a phenomenon I would hesitate to interpret, but that cannot escape notice.

From Dessert to Desserts

This trend from singular to plural held not only for the roast—the central component of the menu—but also for the meal's final course, whether called "dessert" or "fruit."

I have mentioned that in the eighteenth century, *fruit* was the aristocratic term and *dessert* the bourgeois term. The first and last of the three menus of *La Cuisinière bourgeoise,* for instance, use the word *dessert,* while the second menu ends with a "fruit," consisting of "Seven plates of fruits." But it should not be surprising that in 1821, after the bourgeois revolution and despite ongoing political restoration, Archambault adopted *dessert* and discarded *fruit.* When the word *fruit* reappeared in menus during the last decades of the nineteenth century, it did not designate a course, but fruits, and was therefore in the plural—like the roasts of the second dinner of

Alexandre Dumas. For example, the menu for a meal served to Sadi Carnot, president of the Republic in 1888, to inaugurate the first railway dining car, ends with "Ices and pastries, Cheeses, and Fruits."

As for the term *dessert,* which prevailed for so many centuries, note first that it was properly in the singular because it referred not to a collection of dishes, as in the case of roasts, soups, entrées, and hors d'oeuvres, but to the course that came after the table was cleared *(desservi)* for the first time since the start of the meal. Up to that point, dishes from the preceding course were simply removed *(relevé),* that is, replaced one at a time by the dishes of the next course, the table never being left bare. For this last stage, all dishes were cleared from the previous course. It was long the practice even to take away the top tablecloth as well, the dessert dishes then being set on the second tablecloth underneath.

But then, at the onset of the twentieth century, usage evolved to the plural *desserts,* just as it already had for soups, entrées, hors d'oeuvres, roasts, and entremets. The singular form no longer referred to the course itself but to each dessert selection. This change dates from the last few decades of the nineteenth century, the first plural perhaps being the one that appears on an 1870–1871 menu for an outlandish "Grand Parisian Dinner" featuring wildly fanciful dishes to which the guests were allegedly subjected. But the date of this menu—and the evidence it might offer—may not be any more reliable than its contents.[34] Philippe Mordacq's book *Le Menu* documents plural usage in two menus from 1883—one Italian and the other French— as well as in one menu from 1892, one from 1894, three from 1895, one from 1896, two from 1899, two from 1900, two from 1901, one from 1904, one from 1906, and one from 1912. We should not conclude, however, that plural became the rule as of 1871 or even 1883, because other menus used the singular *dessert.*[35] Some of these historical menus, it is true, are foreign; and research to date reveals other foreign menus as early as 1883 that use the plural, in other words as early as in France.

During those years and throughout the twentieth century, the trend toward the concrete can be seen in menus as the collective *dessert* was replaced by the specific components of the course. Early examples suggest that this trend may have come from abroad. On 20 December 1889, a "Closing dinner of the Commercial Conference of the Union of South American countries and the United States," served at Delmonico's in New York, concluded with "SWEET ENTREMETS. Savarin. Montmorency. Tiered pastries. Sloe jelly. Cream meringues. Fantasy ices. LIQUEURS. Fruits. Petits fours. Coffee." There is no mention of dessert.[36] French examples also abound, albeit somewhat later. These include a first communion meal on 20 April 1902 in Épernay, which proceeded from a "Romaine salad" to a final series of pastries: "Charlotte russe, Tiered pastries, Nougat duchesse, Regent cake, Petits fours, Coffee, and Cognac."[37]

IN CONCLUSION

To sum up this chapter on nineteenth-century changes in the sequence of dishes, it should be noted that a great many of them occurred at all levels. Most obvious is the replacement of French service with the Russian style. This was accompanied—however slowly—by a clear reduction in the number of dishes served throughout the meal, but with no marked impact on their order of presentation or consumption.

The previous chapter showed the migration of sweet flavors toward the last two courses of the meal, the entremets and dessert. Although this was a much more important development in the history of gastronomy, it seems to have left a less vivid impression, perhaps because our memory of sensory evolution in this respect is more irretrievably lost. To be sure, the separation of salty and sweet, which seems essentially to have taken shape within a few years near the end of the seventeenth century, had already begun in the sixteenth century and continued until salty cheeses—often overpoweringly pungent—were ultimately banished from dessert. This occurred only after the turn of the twentieth century, as will be discussed further on.

What took place right after the Revolution was a proliferation of fish dishes: they appear in just about all upper- and middle-class menus along with meat dishes, as if the distinction between meat and meatless no longer applied. Closer study reveals that this distinction did not disappear, but became much more discreet than previously, and was articulated in only a very small number of menus.

Lastly, course names changed during the nineteenth century from singular to plural: roasts instead of roast; fruits or desserts (or their components) instead of fruit or dessert. This plural form for the last courses brought them into line with the earlier courses of the meal: soups, hors d'oeuvres, entrées, relevés, and entremets.[38]

NINE

Hidden Changes
in the Twentieth Century

NOTHING APPEARS TO HAVE CHANGED during the twentieth century: throughout this period, the soup, hors d'oeuvres, and entrées were always served at the beginning of the meal, roasts and vegetables in the middle, the salad next, and the cheeses and desserts at the end. In another way, however, everything changed in the sequence of dishes and in the association or succession of flavors. This upheaval took place over the course of the century without fanfare, for reasons erroneously considered obvious, which are further examined in the last section of this book.

Continuing the nineteenth-century trend already mentioned, the number of courses and dishes further declined throughout the twentieth century. Compare, for example, the menu of a dinner for the Association of Editors on 22 December 1902 with a menu offered by Giscard d'Estaing, president of France, in 1978 (figure 16).

Ten dishes—not counting coffee and liqueurs—appear in the 1902 menu, compared to only six in 1978. The two soups in 1902 could have been replaced by just one, but all of the other dishes were still requisite.

At the time of his death, Flandrin had completed the first eight chapters of this book. He left only an outline of chapter 9, which we reproduce here.

ASSOCIATION OF EDITORS' DINNER, 22 DECEMBER 1902

Reine Margot soup
Spring consommé
Lake Balaton fogas à la Boitel
Roasted baron of Chezelles beef
Potato croquettes Parisienne
Fowl terrine Sémiramis
Salad Ninette
Bombe Praline
Waffles
Fruits
Coffee
Liqueurs
Graves. Carafe of Médoc. Chilled Champagne.

———

BANQUET OFFERED BY PRESIDENT GISCARD D'ESTAING FOR BOCUSE'S LEGION OF HONOR IN 1978

Truffle soup (Bocuse) *Montrachet 1970*
Salmon filet in sorrel (Troisgros)
Duck (Guérard) *Château-Margaux 1926*
Little Moulin salads (Vergé)
Cheeses *Morey-Saint-Denis 1969*
Paul Bocuse's desserts
Champagne Roederer 1926

———

FIGURE 16. Two twentieth-century menus, 1902 and 1978.

COLD DISHES

Cold dishes, banished from the beginning of the meal in the seventeenth century, reappeared in the twentieth as entremets (in the provinces) and as hors d'oeuvres. Salads also variously appeared as entremets (Paris) and hors d'oeuvres (provinces), while cold shellfish migrated from after the meat-day roast to the position of an hors d'oeuvre. Fried foods also now tended to come first. Fish, eaten after the meat roast until the nineteenth century, has since been eaten before it. Although vegetables lost their description as entremets, they essentially retained their position after or increasingly along with the roast, which tended to become a garnished meat dish, and not necessarily a roasted one.

Sweet entremets kept their name but—as all sweet dishes did—migrated to dessert, after the cheeses. Nothing salted remained in the dessert course. Fruits eaten with salt tended to lose their description as "fruits" (e.g., tomatoes, green peas, and artichokes), except for some sweet ones like melon, which could also be eaten for dessert.

Cheeses were no longer served at dessert but just before it—with some hesitation and a few uncertainties. Sugared fresh cheeses were not banished outright, and goat cheeses eaten with salads were assigned various positions (hors d'oeuvre or salad).

CONCLUSION

Do these changes represent a modernization of table customs in all Western countries?

Serving woman bringing all the dishes of each course at the same time. *De raison et de mesure.* Manuscript of *Les Dits de Watriquet de Couvin,* fourteenth century. (Bibliothèque nationale de France)

Meat and meatless dishes coexisting. Later, the church would forbid the combination of fish and meat in the same meal, clearly separating meat and meatless meals. Manuscript of *Les Trois Dames de Paris,* fourteenth century. (Bibliothèque nationale de France)

Jean, duc de Berry, at table; detail showing the multiplicity and diversity of dishes in a single course. *Très riches heures du duc de Berry* (month of January). Miniature by Paul de Limbourg, before 1416. Musée Condé, Chantilly. (Giraudon/The Bridgeman Art Library)

Etching by the famous French engraver Abraham Bosse (seventeenth century) representing a banquet offered on 16 May 1633 at Fontainebleau by Louis XIII to the knights after their nomination (detail). Note the multiplicity and diversity of dishes in this course, as well as the aesthetic disposition of the round plates. Musée Carnavalet, Paris. (Photothèque des musées de la Ville de Paris; photo Degrâces)

Marriage of Louis XIV. Etching (detail). Note the various types and sizes of platters. (Bibliothèque nationale de France)

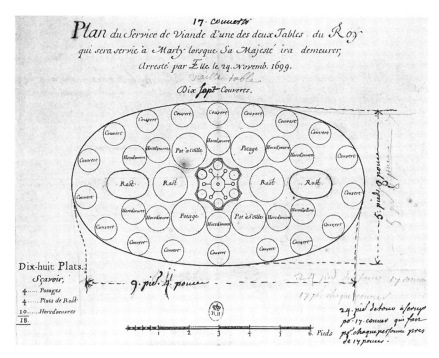

Layout for serving the "meats"—in other words, the dishes—at one of the two royal tables in Marly on 24 November 1699. There are 18 dishes total: 4 soups, 4 roasts, and 10 hors d'oeuvres. (Bibliothèque nationale de France)

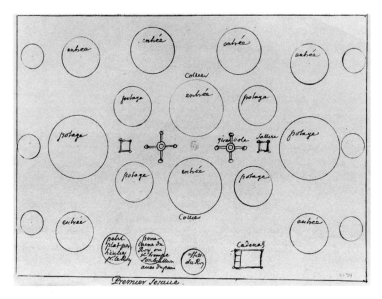

First-course layout for the Grand Table Setting at Versailles, Office de la Bouche du Roi, 1702. (Nationalmuseum, Stockholm)

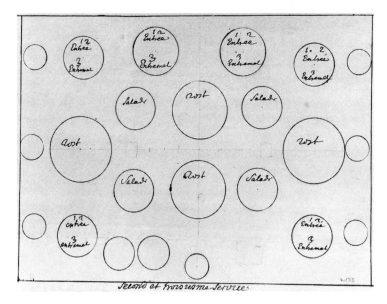

Layout for the first, second, and third courses of the Grand Table Setting at Versailles. Office de la Bouche du Roi, 1702. (Nationalmuseum, Stockholm)

Banquet offered in Paris by the duke of Alba for the birth of the prince of Asturias (detail). Engraving by Scottin after Desmaretz, 1707. Note the size of the centerpieces and the pyramidal arrangements on certain platters. (Bibliothèque nationale de France)

A "little supper" for the regent, Philippe d'Orléans, first quarter of the eighteenth century. Contemporary engraving (detail). An intimate meal with a small number of dishes; diverse dishes are intentionally served together for this course. (Bibliothèque nationale de France)

Meal offered by City Hall to Louis XV on the birth of the crown prince in 1729. 1730 Almanac (detail). Note the abundance and diversity of dishes and the graceful circular design. (Bibliothèque nationale de France)

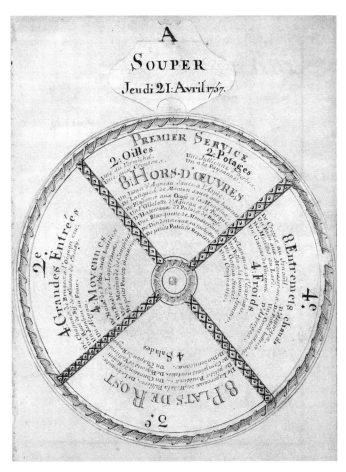

Menu for one of Louis XV's meals: Thursday 21 April 1757 supper at Choisy. The round menu revolves behind a cutout successively displaying each course and its dishes. From *Voyage du Roy au Château de Choisy, avec les logements de la cour et les menus de la table de Sa Majesté,* by F.-P. Brain de Sainte-Marie, 1757. Châteaux de Versailles et de Trianon, Versailles, France. (Réunion des musées nationaux/Art Resource, NY; photo Gérard Blot)

Souper du prince de Conti au palais du Temple à Paris, by Michel Barthélemy Ollivier (1766; detail). The number of dishes per course decreases in the intimate meals of the eighteenth century, but care was taken to preserve their diversity. Châteaux de Versailles et de Trianon, Versailles, France. (Réunion des musées nationaux/Art Resource, NY)

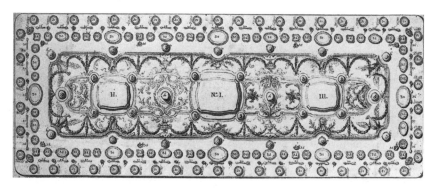

Design for a table with fifty place settings. France, circa 1770. Each dish in this table diagram is numbered to serve as a course guide, and each number refers to a different recipe. (Musée des arts décoratifs, Paris; photo Laurent Sully Jaulmes, all rights reserved)

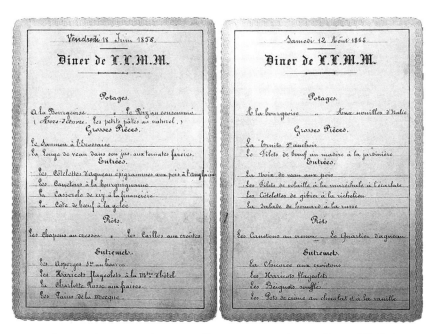

Menus for Napoléon III and Empress Eugénie, 1858 and 1865. (Roger-Viollet)

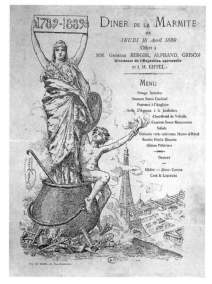

Banquet menus from the late nineteenth century. *Left:* Hôtel Continental menu, 24 May 1888, for the Second Annual Meeting of the Académie des Sciences, presided over by Mr. Janssen. *Right:* Menu for the "Dîner de la Marmite" on Thursday 18 April 1889, offered to Messrs. Georges Berger, Alphand, and Grison, directors of the Exposition Universelle, and to Mr. Eiffel. Bibliothèque des arts décoratifs, Paris, France; photos Bulloz. (Réunion des musées nationaux/Art Resource, NY)

Menu for the French mayors' banquet, 1900. Dishes are served one after the other. Russian service has replaced the French style. (Roger-Viollet)

Russian-style service prevails; these tables resemble ours today. City Hall banquet for Franco-Russian celebrations (detail), by Hoffbauer. Musée Carnavalet, Paris. (Photothèque des musées de la Ville de Paris; photo Giet)

PART THREE

Other Countries, Other Sequences

Jean-Louis Flandrin had planned a comparative part three to this book, with the following outline:

He had already published two essays pertinent to the above. The first, "Structure of Aristocratic French and English Menus in the Fourteenth and Fifteenth Centuries," appeared in Du manuscrit à la table, *edited by Carole Lambert (Paris: Champion; Montreal: Presses de l'Université de Montréal, 1992), pp. 173–192. The third part of that essay corresponds to Flandrin's planned section A of chapter 12, as listed above, and is reproduced in the present book as* **chapter 10** *(pp. 111–117). The second, "Western Views of Poland's Banquets in the Sixteenth, Seventeenth, and Eighteenth Centuries," coauthored with Maria*

Flandrin, was published in Między polityką a kulturą (Mélanges Andrzej Wyczański), *ed. Cezary Kuklo (Warszaw: Państwowe Wydawnictwo Naukowe, 1999), pp. 307–317. The second and third parts of that essay clearly provide the material for Flandrin's planned chapter 13 and are included here as* **chapter 11** *(pp. 118–125).*

TEN

English Menu Sequences

AT FIRST GLANCE, THE TWO- or three-course structure of medieval English menus seems much simpler than that of French menus. But French courses were distinguished by the different types of dishes served in each. Trying to read English menus the same way only creates confusion.

When seeking the logic of a foreign menu, people naturally look for familiar indicators: which course contains the soup, which the roast, which the entremets. Just such an approach led Montaigne to note that the Germans sometimes serve soup first, like the French, and sometimes present it all "backwards."[1] A survey of English menus soon suggests that soups, entremets, and roasts were all served in every course, although certain dishes were systematically linked with particular courses, just as in a French menu.[2]

DISTRIBUTION OF DISHES AMONG COURSES

In the 13 menus published by Thomas Austin from a fifteenth-century manuscript (British Library MS Harley 279),[3] capon, roasted or not, is served 7 times out of 7 in the first course, as are all 8 salted eel, herring, and other salt fish; all 5 swan; all 4 pike; and so on. Roast venison is never featured in the first course but 8 out of 10 times in the second, as are all 6 coneys, all 3 suckling pigs, and both hake and halibut. All 6 almond creams are presented in the last course as are all 5 quail, all 4 perch, and 5 out of 7 pigeons. English "courses," like French ones, were thus not equivalent to each other, but considered more or less appropriate for presenting certain dishes.

Yet the functions of these English courses are even more difficult to define than those of French ones. A few specific dishes can be linked to particular courses, but categories of dishes usually cannot. We saw the exception of salt fish, presented 8 times out of 8 in the first course. The same holds for fruits, presented 8 times out of 9 in the last course. No other category of foods, however, was associated with a specific course—not vegetables (which did not even exist as a category), not eggs (practically nonexistent), nor butcher's meat, venison, domestic or wild fowl, nor saltwater or freshwater fish.[4] All told, fish as well as fowl and meat were fairly evenly distributed among the meal's two or three courses. This should not be surprising: since at that time the British served fish only on meatless days, it thus naturally appeared in all courses. As we have seen, fish was also served in a wide variety of courses in France, albeit on meat days as well as meatless ones.

Cooking methods provide somewhat more relevant categories. As noted above, Austin's menus associate roasts most strongly with the second course. Boiled preparations belonged more clearly in the first, as did dishes served in sauce, pasties, croustades, and pies.[5] Other oven-baked dishes were slightly more likely to appear in the second course, while fried preparations were more clearly third-course selections.[6]

Lastly, just as in France, the first course favored boiled dishes, salt-cured foods—which were probably also boiled—sauced dishes, and pasties; the second course, roasts and oven-baked dishes; and the third, fried specialties. But this distribution of dishes among courses is much less clear and less significant for understanding English menus than French ones. The essence of the English menu resides instead in the order in which dishes were presented within each course.

SOME CURIOUS POSITIONING FREQUENCIES

Oven-Baked Dishes

Let us again consider the category of oven-baked dishes, but from the perspective of their order of presentation within the course: of the 17 listed by Richard Warner in *Antiquitates Culinariæ*,[7] 10 fall between the tenth and twelfth positions, including 6 in eleventh place. They emerge even more tightly clustered when their position is counted from the end of the course [indicated by a minus sign], all falling between position –1 and –4, with a concentration of 8 out of 17 in position –3. Can this rationally be ascribed to chance? The menus published by Warner reveal equally striking position patterns for dishes that are fried, roasted, sauced, jellied, and served "en feuille" (possibly meaning covered with gold or silver leaf).

Let us set aside the 8 menus published by Warner, however, because they concern just two meals. Despite clear differences in what was eaten at each table, the menus may contain similarities that would skew results on this point.

Since the 13 menus published by Austin involve seven different meals, such skewing (if any) will be negligible. Yet these menus also reveal obvious positioning. Out of 15 oven-baked or crust-covered dishes, 13 are grouped in the last (6), penultimate (4), and antepenultimate (3) positions. Of 18 fried selections, 11 are grouped in the penultimate (4) and antepenultimate (7) positions. Roasts, listed as such 29 times, are served 20 times between the fifth and seventh positions. At least two dishes are always mentioned before them and at least one afterward.

The position of fattened roast capon is especially striking. It appears in 5 instances: 4 times in fifth position and once in sixth. Swan, mentioned 6 times, is always served between the fourth and sixth positions, as are pigeons, though only 5 times out of 7. Chicken appears 4 times out of 5 between the fifth and seventh positions, as does pheasant 5 times out of 6, partridge 5 times out of 7, and so on. It is as if a place were reserved for fowl in the middle of each course—with the preceding and following positions saved for other types of dishes. The same holds true for fish in meatless menus.

Which dishes are systematically mentioned at the start and the end of a course? The 24 dishes that appear to be sweet or savory pastries appear in any course but always near its end in the last (7), penultimate (9), or positions –2 or –3 (5 and 3 times, respectively). Likewise for fried dishes (among which 8 out of 9 fit between positions –1 and –3) and for the 19 "Leche," always mentioned between last position (2 times) and position –4 (3 times), but particularly in position –2 (7 times).

Course openers feature jellied dishes and cream custards. Jellied dishes are mentioned 4 times in first position, 3 times in second position (and, exceptionally, once in last position). Cream custards appear twice out of 6 times in first position and 4 times in second. Note that creams and jellies always appear in the last course.

"Vyands" [victuals, provisions], which have nothing to do with what we today call meats, are distributed among all courses but always as openers (with one exception): 2 times in first position and 9 times in second.

The 7 frumenties, always in connection with venison or porpoise, could be presented in the first or the second course but always before other dishes. The 7 "Mammenye" [minced chicken with a sauce made of wine or almond milk] are also listed 5 times in first position and 2 times in second.

Soups and Entremets

All dishes presented in the first two positions could in fact be classified as soups, and many of those presented in last place as entremets.

As an initial observation, seven of the dishes presented as course openers in the Austin menus are soups: "Venyson with furmente," "Vyaund Ryal," "Perrey fyn," "Rapeye," "Brode canelle," "Blandyssorye," and "Compost." All of these soups are mentioned in the first or second position. Closer examination reveals that they are in the second position only when another soup occupies the first. Does this priority apply to a dish only when it is described as a soup, or also when not explicitly labeled as such? The answer is clear: the seven dishes labeled as soup in at least one occurrence are mentioned in first or second position wherever they appear in our 13 menus (16 instances). This suggests that they were consistently considered soups, even in courses where this is not specified. Furthermore, if a dish can be a soup without being explicitly named as such, there may well be several dishes never called soup in our 13 menus but viewed as such and serving that function.[8]

We can thus assume that all of the dishes systematically presented at the start of a course (frumenty, "Mammeny," "Vyand," etc.) were all considered soups, including those we would not think of calling by that name, such as jellies or creams. This category should also include a few other dishes I have not yet discussed because they are rarely mentioned and sometimes do not sound much like soups: two "Mortrewys" (a ground meat dish probably comparable to the French *mortereul*); one "Braun en peverade" (possibly capon breast in pepper sauce); two dishes of blancmange; one dish of "Brewys"; one *chaudeau* called "Caudel Ferry"; one dish of boiled chicken ("Chykonys y-boylid"); one dish of date preserves ("Datys in comfyte") and another of quince ("Quyncys in comfyte"); one dish of eels "in sorry"; galantines of lamprey and of filets; one dish of deer "nombles" ([spiced-tripe humble pie], "Nomblys de Roo"); two dishes of pears in syrup ("Perys in syrippe"); a stewed deer ("Ro Styuyd"); one rice dish called "Rys Moleynz"; a "Sew lumbarde" (Lombard steamed dish?); and two dishes of venison in broth.

Just like cinnamon brewet, "râpée," and "porrée," several of these dishes resemble such French "soups" of the period as *chaudeau,* meat or fish *en galantine,* and venison in broth. In fact, some are labeled as soups in the Warner menus: "Blank desire," "viante Cipre," "Rice molens," frumenty, and "Mammonie." Others are totally foreign to our concept of a soup: for example, jellies, pears in syrup, stewed fruits, or date and quince preserves. But as we have seen, the "Compost" is explicitly called a soup in the menu that lists it. Selections presented as soup in Warner's menus in fact include several types of jellies and even a "Joly Ipocras Tart," which strikes me as even stranger than preserves or pears in syrup. In addition, with very few exceptions, these dishes always occur in the first or second position whenever they appear.

In conclusion, all of the dishes explicitly described as soups occupy the first or second position in various courses, and it does seem that every first and possibly second position of every course is filled by a soup in all of the menus analyzed. Some of the dishes occupying these positions are labeled as such in the Warner menus, and none ever occupies any position other than first or second in any of the menus examined.

The position of another type of dish, the "sotelte" or entremcts, is just as systematic, or nearly, in the last position of each course. There are few exceptions. The Austin menus feature entremets 18 times, always in last position, with one exception that actually confirms the rule.[9] In the Warner menus, the entremets are not as uniformly positioned, some appearing at the start of a course that in fact includes two other entremets in the last two positions. This does not mean that the Warner menus are less sophisticated than the Austin ones, quite the contrary: it seems that Warner maneuvered the number and position of entremets to achieve nuanced distinctions of status among different tables at important feasts.

Entremets do not appear in all of the menus—only in 6 of Austin's 13 and 4 of Warner's 8. Austin includes them only in three-course menus (which I am inclined to believe was the norm), where they unfailingly come at the end of each course. But they do appear in 1 of the two-course Warner menus. One three-course menu (menu 2) features 6 of them. Another, menu 6, includes only 2 in a very curious meal where the third course is merely a sort of sendoff, called "the thirde course Plate," which followed the actual meal and seems to have included several entremets. But aside from these divergences, the entremets appears to have been a characteristic component of all major feasts, appearing normally at the end of each of the three courses.

Just as in France, the contents of these entremets vary significantly. Many represent personalities or events: Saint André, Saint George, Samson; the king presenting the archbishop of Canterbury to Notre Dame. Some simply portray figures: an eagle, a deer, a tree, a man, a jurist, an Agnus Dei, and so on. Other dishes labeled as entremets include "Great custard planted," "Cheston ryall," "Chamblet viander," "Leche Damaske," "a Tart," and the like.

Most of the less spectacular dishes are mentioned "as a suttletie," while others are served along with or just before the entremets, as for example at the end of the last course in Warner's menu 2: "Leche Lumbart gylt, partie gelly and a suttletie of Saint William, with his coate armour betwixt his handes." It thus becomes unclear whether to consider these "leche" [honey and egg loaves with sweet wine syrup], fried foods, pastries, and other oven-baked dishes as entremets, or simply as treats offered near the end of a course before the entremets if there is one (or instead of it if there is not). These dishes are too seldom labeled as entremets and their assigned position too inconsistent to justify the same reasoning as for soups.

Significance of Position

The significance of position in medieval menus remains to be elucidated. Were positions just a convention of form, or do they provide insight into the deeper structure of the meal?

Position probably did not hold the same meaning in France and in England. In France, the roast was mentioned before accompanying dishes to indicate that it constituted the main component of the course. The frumenty and venison in subsequent courses were surely mentioned first for the same reason. Frumenty and venison, incidentally, were almost as essential to the feast as the roast: they appear 14 times in the 18 meat-day dinners of *Le Ménagier de Paris,* while meat roasts appear 16 times.

In England, every category of dishes had its position, which indicates that each course of the meal had a beginning, a middle, and an end. English service unfolded over time, it was dynamic—as the term "course" suggests—whereas French-style service was static, as indicated by the word *assiette* ("service platter").

Does this mean that English service at the end of the Middle Ages brought one dish after another to the table, like the Russian service that replaced the French style in France in the nineteenth century? Or were they all set on the table at once and then consumed in a prescribed order? I am reluctant to accept the first of these theories, which runs counter to accepted ideas. Yet the second hypothesis is inconceivable in practice. Guests could not possibly eat helpings of all of the dishes listed in the menus, from soups to entremets. And I cannot imagine the spectacular entremets being set on the table at the same time as all the other dishes.

The truth may lie somewhere in the middle, the dishes of one "course" not being brought to the table either one at a time or all at once, but grouped into several stages: perhaps first the soups, then the boiled or roasted butcher's meats, then the roast fowl, then the pastries, fried dishes, and other treats, and finally the entremets. But this is merely conjecture, with no corroborating evidence in the menus examined.

CONCLUSION

Dishes were not brought to the table and eaten in just any order in fourteenth- and fifteenth-century England any more than they were in France. Quite the contrary, service in both countries adhered to specific rules. Those governing the distribution of dishes among different courses *(assiettes)* were essential in France and remained so in the so-called French service.

English rules focused on the succession of dishes within each course. These rules need to be more precisely reconstructed than I have been able to do here, and their significance better understood. But already they suggest that the structure of English banquets was quite different from what has until now been assumed, English menus having been excessively viewed through the lens of the French model.

ELEVEN

Polish Banquets in the Sixteenth, Seventeenth, and Eighteenth Centuries

THE POLISH ARISTOCRACY OF the sixteenth, seventeenth, and eighteenth centuries enjoyed banquets and devoted a great deal of time to eating and drinking. According to Jędrzej Kitowicz [c. 1727–1804], who chronicled their customs during the reign of Augustus III, "at home and in public houses, the nobles liked to sit down at table, regaling each other with dinners and suppers; they invited their friends, ordinary citizens, military men, and their neighbors; a day without guests was quite unusual; these meals were accompanied by dancing and hearty drinking."[1]

My objective is to single out what surprised foreign, and particularly French, travelers about these banquets and what struck them as typically Polish manners.

DISHES AND THEIR ORDER OF PRESENTATION

To quote Hauteville first, concerning food: "Poles eat a great deal of meat and very little bread, even though Poland grows plenty of grains, mainly rye, which is better than France's."[2] Werdum also noted that "in general with all dishes, they eat very little bread."[3]

Before turning to the typical dishes of the Polish table, we should note one element that struck all French travelers: the absence of any soup. In France (from the seventeenth century in any case), meals usually started with a soup. They might not proceed any further—particularly for poor peasants—but a real meal without soup was inconceivable. Thus the absence of soup in Poland seemed very strange to them. Charles Ogier, describing a wedding feast in Gdansk in 1635, was the first to document this fact: "There were enormous amounts of meat to eat but no soup or potage."[4] Hauteville also wrote, "The Poles do not serve soup. But when French cooks prepare it, they eat it willingly and find it very good."[5] In his account, Beauplan first enumerates the meats of the first course, then continues, "All these meats . . . are cut into ball-size pieces so that everyone can help himself according to his appetite, which does not lean toward soups; these are never served at table because the meats are presented in their broth."

The issue is not that seventeenth-century Poles found soup distasteful, or that their food included nothing that resembled soup, since these meats bathed in broth certainly did. Besides, according to Hauteville, they drank a sort of beer soup *(polewka piwna)* in the morning: "Every morning, men and women drink primarily a hot beer broth with ginger, egg yolks, and sugar." What the French found disturbing in seventeenth-century Poland was that neither dinner nor supper systematically started with soups.

It should also be noted that a late-eighteenth-century Polish cookbook, the *Stół obojetny,* gives recipes for ten soups, five broths, one *Kontuza,* four borscht, and eleven *polewka.*[6]

Foremost among the Polish specialties that impressed the French were sauces, particularly fruit sauces such as existed in Germany and a few other European countries but not at all in France. As Hauteville noted, "Their sauces are also extremely different from ours. They make a yellow one with saffron, a white one with cream, a gray one with onions, and a black one with prune juice, and all them contain a lot of sugar, pepper, cinnamon, ginger, cloves, nutmeg, olives, capers, pine nuts, and currants."[7] These sauces were generally intended for first-course meats—presumably boiled—but were interchangeable, not specific to a particular meat. Beauplan tells us that no sooner were they seated than the guests were regaled with dishes brought to the table in advance, "prepared and seasoned as was their custom, that is, some with saffron, for a yellow sauce, others with cherry juice for red sauce, or with prune mash and juice for black sauce, and finally a gray sauce that they call *gonche [gaszcz],* made from cooked and sieved onion juices . . . each guest chooses the one he likes among these sauces, which never number more than four."[8] These four sauces differ slightly from Hauteville's, since instead of the white cream sauce, Beauplan mentions a red cherry sauce. He also lists a horseradish sauce that was very typical and is still quite common in Poland. He comments that it is a sauce "that they make from a root they call *Cresen [chrzan],* grated and soaked in vinegar, with a very tasty and excellent mustard flavor, good to eat with fresh or salt beef and all sorts of fish."[9]

Among other distinctive first-course preparations, Beauplan mentions dishes "of salted cabbage with a piece of salt pork, or millet, or a boiled dough, which they eat as great delicacies." These were probably *kluski,* which Hauteville described as "dough fricasseed with butter, shaped like cheese-filled macaroons," but served at the end of the second course, with other pasta doughs and all kinds of kasha.[10]

Beauplan relates that, as in France, the second course was apparently composed of various roasted meats with salad garnishes: "This first course being finished and the plates empty . . . it is cleared along with the first platters. They then serve the second course, consisting entirely of roasted meats like veal, mutton, and beef, carved into portions larger than half a quarter of said kind, capons, chickens, hens, goslings, ducks, hares, deer and doe, roe deer, boar, etc., and all sorts of other game like partridge, swallow, quail, and other small game birds that are plentiful . . . all of which are served indiscriminately, mixed with each other and assorted salads for variety."[11] (These large bowls piled with various roasts were also used in France until the end of the seventeenth century, as can be seen in figure 17.)

At the end of this course comes what our observer takes to be an entremets—for in France this would be the right place for the entremets course, which, among other things, included all vegetable dishes: "This second course is followed by an entremets consisting of several assorted fricassees of mashed peas with a large piece of salt pork from which the guests each cut a piece, dicing and spooning it in their puréed peas, a dish that they prize and swallow without chewing, so highly valued that they feel they have not been well received if it has not been offered, and if they have not had it to eat by the end of their meal."[12] This purée of peas caught the attention of all travelers, German as well as French. Werdum wrote, "They like to eat fat food. We were given a taste of fresh cheese fried in butter, and split peas thickly mixed with diced lard."[13] Similarly, Hauteville commented that "the most noble lords seldom dine without a dish of peas and lard, but with slices of yellow lard placed on top."[14]

The French also noted the Polish fondness for wild mushrooms—including some that were considered poisonous in France—and for equally suspect poppy seeds: "They eat all sorts of mushrooms that sprout in the

FIGURE 17. Seventeenth-century French print: Louis XIV and the royal family seated at a lavish banquet offered in 1687 at the Paris City Hall (detail). The dishes for this course are brought in all at once by the stewards. (Bibliothèque nationale de France)

forest and even some that grow against tree trunks, gathering and drying them. One would not dare eat those kinds of mushrooms in France, for fear of poisoning. It may be that they are poisonous in France but not in Poland, just like poppy seeds, which everyone there eats as if they were millet."[15]

At the time, the French were apparently less surprised by the countless grain-based specialties, which today seem more ethnic to us than puréed peas. Beauplan documented a whole list of them: "millet with butter, hulled barley seasoned likewise and called *cacha,* or *gru* in Holland, fricasseed buttered dough shaped like cheese-filled macaroons, and other buckwheat batters made into very thin pancakes flavored with white poppy seed juice, all of which they eat, I suppose, because it is very filling and helps them sleep."[16] This account is corroborated by Hauteville: "They eat a lot of root vegetables that they prepare very well, and *cachat,* a sort of gruel from grain like barley, millet, and oatmeal, and even a small grain they call *manna.* These *cachats* are very good when well prepared. On meat days they eat them with milk and butter. On meatless days, they are eaten only with oil."[17] Note that French fourteenth- and fifteenth-century aristocratic tables featured somewhat different grain dishes—frumenties, millet mash [*millot*], oats [*avenat*], pearl barley, and the like—at the same point in the meal. But they had practically vanished from the modern table.

Then came dessert, as in France. But while French dessert consisted of all kinds of fruit—raw and cooked, stewed or preserved into soft or thick jams, in coulis, juices, and sorbets—the Polish dessert apparently consisted mostly of cakes, custards, and dairy selections that did not much appeal to French travelers. Beauplan has only this to say: "After this second course is cleared, . . . dessert is presented as the season and the occasion allow, such as cream, cheese, and other things that I cannot recall at this time."[18] Fortunately, many of these desserts are known from the 1784 cookbook *Stół obojetny*.

TABLE SERVICE

Our seventeenth-century French travelers did not note great differences in serving style. Just the same, it needs to be considered here. In nineteenth-century France, the history of meals was dominated by the switch from traditional French table service to Russian table service. Russian service is what specialists call the current manner of presenting dishes one after another, with each dish being offered by servants to each of the guests. The latter are expected to partake of every one of those dishes, which thus should not be too numerous.

Until the first half of the nineteenth century, French service divided the meal into three or four sequences, each of these "courses" containing numerous dishes. The dishes were not presented to each guest, and it was not expected that everyone eat from every dish. Everything was placed on the table and guests helped themselves according to their fancy, just as in today's buffets. French commentators generally maintained that this method was more luxurious than the much more costly Russian service, and that it was the only way to accommodate the guests' range of tastes, long believed to depend on personal temperament and physiological requirements.

But French service also had its drawbacks. For Grimod de La Reynière, in 1805, "A glance at this multitude of dishes satiates rather than tempts; and . . . the overabundance of choice is so confusing that the appetite wanes and the dinner gets cold before one can make up one's mind. We have seen . . . how detrimental symmetry is to fine dining. But formal dinners force the sacrifice of one for the other, and there is no way to serve a forty-place table one dish at a time."[19]

Some twenty years earlier, Sébastien Mercier was already criticizing the way beverages were served at big French-service dinners: "I would not advise a gentleman without a footman to attend a dinner in a grand home.

Only at the discretion of the servants can you drink there. Make a modest request, and they will turn on their heel and run to fetch a drink from the sideboard for some other guest. Soon your throat will be too parched to raise your voice: your pleading glances will receive no better reaction than your requests. Your palate will be burning, and you will no longer be able to taste any of the food on the table. You will have to wait until the end of the meal for a big glass of water to finally dampen your mouth. This system was conceived as a way to exclude people who have no domestic staff: this is how the wealthy protect their table from overcrowding."[20] Perhaps. Rousseau made the same complaint. But there were other reasons for the lack of glasses and bottles on French-service tables. In 1560, Calviac explains that "one could hardly keep the glass on the table without interfering with someone trying to reach a dish or otherwise inconveniencing him."[21] There was of course less risk of upsetting glasses or bottles in countries where the table was less cluttered than in France, and where servants passed the serving plates around after carving the meats on them. Also, as we shall see, it was not the custom in those countries to drink much while eating.

Yet the Russian writer Denis Fonvizin, during a stay in Montpellier in 1777–1778, concurred with Mercier even more vehemently: "Each guest has his footman standing by behind his chair. The unfortunate soul who has no footman risks dying of hunger and thirst. There is no alternative because according to French custom, the dishes are not sent around the table. You eye the one you like and tell your footman to serve you. Nor are the wines set before each plate. When you are thirsty, you send your footman to get some from the pantry. Think of the result if you have no footman to serve you and change your plate. Your neighbor's footman will not serve you; plead all you like, he will answer, 'I serve only my master.'" This may be a somewhat jaded account, because all the manuals of good manners allowed one to ask neighbors at the table to pass dishes one wished to taste. But Fonvizin was shocked that there were no servants to present serving platters to each guest, as there would be in Russia. He concludes, "In all fairness, French cuisine is excellent, but the service is abominable as you can see. When I dine in town . . . I am often famished when I rise from the table: in front of me is a dish of something I do not eat, and I am so nearsighted that I cannot see what is at the other end. The Russian way of serving the platter all around is most rational. In Poland and Germany, they serve as we do."[22]

Were meals really served in the Russian style in Germany and Poland? Certain documents suggest that service dish-by-dish was customary in Germany among the common people. In Swiss and German inns, according to Montaigne, one servant was sufficient for a large table: he would bring dishes two at a time, up to six or seven times in a row, with the result that "the least little meal lasts three or four hours."[23] But at princely banquets, according to Marx Rumpolt, author of the major German cookbook of the sixteenth century, there were only a few courses, each with a great many dishes, just as in France.[24] The difference was that the guests were not supposed to serve themselves: the servants of the household presented the dishes one at a time, as in Russia.

Accounts regarding Poland are also somewhat ambiguous. According to Werdum, the Poles "bring dishes to the table one at a time rather than all at once, and since there are 10, 15, or 20 dishes and they help themselves to each, meals last for long hours."[25] This is clearly Russian service, and surprisingly, he talks about it as if things were done differently in Germany. But another German, Johann-Joseph Kausch, definitely seems to describe French service at a small eastern country estate in the eighteenth century: "Let us enter . . . the dining room where our foreign visitor finds six dishes already set on the table as a first course. He is surprised because he sees signs of poverty at every corner. He will be even more surprised to see at least twenty-three dishes for the second course."[26]

But in fact, there is no discrepancy. Beauplan, who resided in Poland between 1630 and 1651, gives very detailed descriptions of aristocratic feasts that reconcile the two accounts just cited. As in France the meal was usually divided into three courses (he uses the term *mets*, as in the Middle Ages), each course composed of multiple dishes placed simultaneously on the table: "Then the lords are ushered into the hall. . . . This first course being finished and the plates empty . . . it is cleared along with the first platters; the second course is then served. . . . This second course removed the same manner as the first, dessert is brought in."[27] Again, as in France, the guests were assisted by their personal footmen, who brought their drinks and cleared their plates. But there were carving stewards to serve them, a characteristic of Russian service: "Seated and arranged in that fashion, they are served by carving stewards, who number three at each table."[28]

Beauplan's observations are confirmed at the end of the eighteenth century by those of another Frenchman, Hubert Vautrin. If Fonvizin was upset by French service, Vautrin is even more enraged about Russian service ("German service," as he calls it): "Service is in the German style, which springs from vainglory combined with gluttony. The master of the house is served first so that he gets his choice of the morsels, and nobody touches a dish before he does. The table starts out covered with all of the dishes. Once the guests are all seated after the master according to their social standing, the *maître d'hôtel* removes the first dish for carving, then presents it to the masters of the house, followed by the guest held in next highest esteem, always going from most to least worthy, such that the order in which each compatriot or foreign guest is served heralds his rank. Even if you are starving or turn down a dish, you will still have to wait until the footman charged with assessing your standing, or guessing his master's opinion of it, has presented the dish you want to those he ranks above you. If [those guests] deign to take notice, they may go ahead and partake from the platter even before they are ready so that it reaches you sooner; if not, you wait your turn or do without, as the platter is very often empty before it makes it around the table."[29] French and Russian service each had drawbacks. But there is pointed irony in finding that Poland, the most politically democratic country, was the least egalitarian at table, while France, which was politically autocratic, was the most egalitarian at meals.

POSTSCRIPT

In addition to the four chapters that were to make up part three (see outline on p. 109), Flandrin had also planned an analytical part four titled "In Search of Explanations," which was to contain two chapters.

The first (chapter 14 of the projected book) was to be called "Dietary Concerns." In it, Flandrin intended to develop the following topics:

A. Implausibility: European dietetics were essentially the same in all countries, while the sequence in which dishes were presented was very different
B. Dietetic principles and the reality of meal service:
Heavy food and light food
Cooking methods: boiling and roasting
Flavors: sweet, sour, and bitter

Chapter 15, "Gastronomic Concerns," was to cover the following ideas:

A remark by Cardinal Carafa's *maître d'hôtel* to Montaigne in the sixteenth century already hints at gastronomic considerations in the organization of meals: "I asked him about his duties. He discoursed about the science of eating with masterly gravity and bearing, as if discussing some major point of theology. He distinguished different sorts of appetite for me: when fasting, after the second course, after the third; the ways to just satisfy it, or to awaken and stimulate it; the guiding principles about sauces in general, then in terms of specific attributes and effects of ingredients; the differences between salads according to season, those that should be warmed, those that should be served cold, how to garnish and enhance them to make them even more pleasing to the eye. Next, he expounded on the sequence of a meal, with many interesting and important considerations. Even the Greeks, for instance, highly praised the order and disposition adopted by Paulus Aemilius for the feast he gave them on their return from Macedonia" (*Essais*, 1.52, pp. 343–344).

A. Salty and sweet are separated starting in the seventeenth century and increasingly ever since.

B. Sequence of dishes and of wines: essentially in the twentieth century. Proper pairing became a concern mainly in the twentieth century, but appeared as far back as the sixteenth century, not in France or Italy, but in the cookbook by Rumpolt, the premier German chef of the period, who emphasized striving for such harmony.

C. Is diversity more compatible with gastronomic considerations than with dietetic concerns?

CONCLUSION

Here are the few lines of conclusion that Jean-Louis Flandrin had included in his outline for the book:

Many changes in meal sequence in France.

Great diversity of meal sequence in Europe.

A sense of natural order reigns always and everywhere in spite of diversity and changes.

Historically, order explained mainly in terms of dietetics throughout Europe, despite diversity.

Today, order explained mainly in terms of gastronomic considerations; but these explanations raise questions as well.

International influences exist, but they do not explain everything.

APPENDIXES

Flandrin had asked Jeanne Allarde to provide him with material on the sequence of dishes in Spain. These notes can be found in appendix A.

He devoted a session of his seminar at l'École des Hautes Études en Sciences Sociales to the topic of the first chapter of his projected part four. In appendix B we have printed his notes for that lecture, albeit in a different order: (1) Flavors and fruits; (2) Heaviness and lightness of food; (3) Cooking methods.

We have included as appendix C Flandrin's notes for a paper he gave in Brus-

sels on 28 October 2000 at the Symposium on the Renaissance and the Art of the Table, organized by the Institut Cooremans. Titled "The Cuisine of the Renaissance," this paper compares the sequence of dishes in France, the Netherlands, England, and Italy.

Lastly, appendix D is Flandrin's list of sources, most of which are not cited in the book. (We provide a list of works cited following the notes.)

Additional Material for Part Three

In the chapter of his *Libro de cozina* (first Spanish ed., 1525) titled "How to present dishes at the table," Roberto de Nola states,

> It is also customary to provide a napkin with each soup, and to offer the courses progressively, starting with fruit, then soup, and then the roast; then another soup, followed by a boiled dish, unless the soup is a *blanc-manger*, which is usually served at the beginning, after the fruit. Some nobles start with the boiled dish followed by the roast; if there are fritters, they should be served at the end, followed by the other fruit, and such is the form and manner of serving according to custom at the court of my lord the king. And there being so many novelties each day in the ways of table service, I shall end here.

TWO MENUS FROM SPAIN

Figure A1 reproduces a menu for the midday meal offered by Juan de Ribera, archbishop of Valencia and viceroy, for Felipe II in 1586. The king was accompanied by the eight-year-old crown prince, the twenty-year-old infanta, and court attendants.

The starters are the same for king, prince, and infanta: radishes, sliced fruit, grapes, melons, prunes, sweet oranges. For the ladies-in-waiting, the grand commander, the chamberlains, the majordomos, and the royal dining staff: creams, sliced fruit, grapes, melons, pomegranates, and cooked hams. For the assistant chamberlains and comptrollers: grapes, melons, sweet oranges, and ham.

THE KING'S TABLE

FIRST COURSE
Roast francolins, capons
Cooked suckling pig, kid, and another capon
Flaky pastries

SECOND COURSE
Roast capons, pigeons
Cooked veal, mutton + blancmange

DESSERTS
Honeyed Jordan almonds, citron morsels, glazed orange flower
morsels, nougats, quartered quinces in syrup, marmalade, pomegranate
jelly, biscuits, pears, apples, Seville olives, Tronchon cheese

THE PRINCE'S TABLE

Roast francolins, veal, turkey, capon, partridge
Cooked veal, capon, mutton

DESSERTS
Same as the king's

THE INFANTA'S TABLE

FIRST COURSE
Roast francolins, turkey, suckling pig, veal
Cooked veal, capons

SECOND COURSE
Roast partridge, veal, capon, pigeons
Cooked mutton, veal empanada, couscous

DESSERTS
Same as the king's plus cheese fritters and marzipan

THE LADIES' TABLE

FIRST COURSE
Roast partridge, turkey, suckling pig, veal
Cooked veal, capon

SECOND COURSE
Roast veal, capon, rabbits, pigeons
Cooked chickens, kid, mutton

Apples, pears, olives, cheese, Jordan almonds, nougat, biscuits,
cheese fritters

THE GRAND COMMANDER'S TABLE

FIRST COURSE
Roast turkey, suckling pig, partridge, young rabbits
Cooked veal, capon, mutton

SECOND COURSE
Roast capon, veal, rabbit, mutton
Cooked mutton + blancmange

DESSERTS
Same as the ladies'

THE MAJORDOMOS' AND ROYAL DINING STAFF'S TABLE

FIRST COURSE
Roast turkeys, suckling pigs, partridge, pullets
Cooked veal, capons, kid

SECOND COURSE
Roast capons, veal, rabbits, mutton
Cooked mutton

DESSERTS
Same as the grand commander's

THE ASSISTANT CHAMBERLAINS' TABLE

Roast turkey, veal, partridge, rabbits
Cooked suckling pigs, mutton, capons

DESSERTS
Pears, apples, Jordan almonds, cheese, olives, nougat, and wafers

THE COMPTROLLERS' TABLE

Roast capon, veal, partridge, rabbits
Cooked kid, chickens, mutton + blancmange

DESSERTS
Same as the chamberlains'

———

FIGURE A1. Menu for a 1586 banquet for Felipe II in Valencia.

MIDDAY MEAL FOR THE MONTH OF MAY

FIRST COURSE
Ham and starters
Roast capons
Cooked mutton, fowl, and ham stewpot
Flaky pastries
Cooked chicken and fava beans
Cooked trout
Chopped roast leg of mutton
Roast bacon and mutton testicles
Baked cream pots
Skewers of veal paupiettes and lettuce
Bacon empanadas in sweet crust
Fowl cooked and crusted
Cooked artichokes with hocks

SECOND COURSE
Roast young rabbits
Cooked white boudin sausages on biscuit and cream soups
Veal and marrow and pigeon and truffle pâtés
Chopped roast veal
Empanadas of young pigeons with mutton testicles and marrow
English empanadas of veal breast and beef tongues
Stuffed flaky pastry
Marrow fritters
Roast stuffed pullets on glazed soups
Venison empanadas
Small pâtés of preserves and shirred eggs

THIRD COURSE
Fresh salmon
Roast pullets on rich rice
Roast pigeons on crêpes
Brown sauce pâtés
Roast and larded kid
Ladies' pies
Cooked sausage of suckling pig
Cold empanadas
Mullets fried in lard and bread croutons
Blancmange
Pineapple fritters
Baked eggs maymone

FIGURE A2. Menu from Martínez Montiño's *Arte de cocina, pastelería, vizcochería, y conservería* (1611).

Figure A2 gives the menu for a midday meal for the month of May by the royal chef Francisco Martínez Montiño in 1611. "The meal must close with all available fruits and with *requesones*" (a type of ricotta cheese made from milk curds).

APPENDIX B

Dietetics and Meal Sequences

We have seen that French meal sequences evolved significantly between the fourteenth century and our own times. The present sequence appears to arise essentially from gastronomic considerations: succession of flavors, food and wine pairing, and so on. By contrast, the former order seems to have been based largely if not entirely on antiquated dietetic considerations that obviously no longer hold sway. Those considerations revolved around several older criteria.

FLAVORS AND FRUITS

Dietetic Principles

Today, meals in France and many other European countries are organized around flavors, or more specifically two flavors (salty and sweet), on the principle that the two should not be mixed but should succeed each other, salty foods being eaten first and sweet dishes afterward.

BFlavor distinctions also seem to be an essential criterion of meal organization in various Eastern cultures:

- In the medieval Arab world, as we saw last year at our "L'Anonyme andalou" banquet. Vinegar-flavored dishes were preceded by *murrī*-seasoned ones and followed by honeyed or sugared dishes.

Seminar of 10 December 1999.

- Perhaps in Chinese culture; Françoise Sabban's article *Tables d'hier, tables d'ailleurs* (p. 379) remains elusive on this point: "Then come successive series of hot dishes, large and small, which alternate and combine various cooking methods, flavors, textures and aromas."
- And in Vedic Indian culture, if I recall correctly a presentation by Guy Mazars at the 1990 "Alimentation et médecine" seminar in Brussels, the proceedings of which appeared in 1993.

There were also instances of organization by flavor during the Middle Ages and the Renaissance, but only insofar as flavors had dietetic significance. Western dietitians of those times referred mainly to three flavors:

- bitter
- acidic (or sour)
- sweet

This is especially true for Italians. Take, for example, what Platina wrote about cherries in *De honesta voluptate et valetudine* (Venice, 1475):

> You should know that there are three sorts of cherries: sour, bitter, and sweet. First, the bitter ones, black and firm-fleshed, harden the belly and spoil the stomach, and should be reserved for the third table, since their bitterness tightens the stomach's orifice; that closed orifice improves and lightens digestion. The sour ones break up phlegm and repress yellow bile, calm the thirst, promote good blood, [and] conveniently stimulate the appetite for eating at the first table. The sweet ones, however, are bad for the stomach, engender worms, bad humors within the body, and give little nourishment eaten in the morning. (fols. XVII–XVII)

More generally, Platina advocated eating acidic and sweet dishes for the first course: "At the first table one offers . . . apples and some sweet pears, . . . [and] all kinds of cooked and raw meats eaten with oil and vinegar, . . . and some marmalades like *pinhonat* preserved in honey or sugar" (fol. XVII); and reserving the last course for bitter dishes—which were referred to as "austere," "styptic," or "astringent":

> For the third and final table it is appropriate to offer apples or pears, mainly sour and styptic, to repel the exhalations and vapors rising to the head and the brain. . . . The sweet apples and pears such as mentioned in their own chapter and section are so much better suited to the first table and not appropriate for serving here. (fols. CCLV–CCLVI)

Further down he writes, "In addition to the above, all quince and *migrannes*, mainly sour ones, and generally all things styptic and restrictive, are compatible and appropriate for the third table" (fols. CCLV–CCLVI).

In *Il Thesoro della sanità* (1632 ed.), Castor Durante draws a vague contrast between "slippery" *(le lubriche)* and "astringent" *(all'astringenti)* foods—but this has less to do with flavor than with effects on the digestive tract. Gieronimo De' Manfredi, in his *Libro intitolato il perche* (Venice, 1622?), develops this theme further:

> So it is good to finish the meal with styptic foods like preserved quince, pomegranates, or a little cheese. All things that push the foods to the bottom of the stomach [and] prevent them from floating there, improve digestion. Because the bottom of the stomach is hotter and stronger for digestion than the upper part, so that vapors from food floating low in the stomach do not rise to your head. Therefore the things mentioned here are good after meals for the two reasons given.

While acknowledging the principle of astringent foods at the end of meals, Ugo Benzo, in his *Regole della sanità et natura dei cibi* (Turin, 1620), stresses the reasons for eating them at the beginning:

> *Astringents, when appropriate.*
>
> . . . if perchance a tired stomach allows food to descend faster than necessary, then start the meal with astringents, which strengthen the stomach; for they help complete the digestion of food because styptics and astringents absorbed [?] before the meal tighten the body [?] and retain the food in the stomach as long as it has not been [?] digested; and when absorbed [?] after the meal, because of the compression they exert on the body, render it slippery and fluid [?]; nevertheless, to seal the stomach at the end of the meal one can (in small quantity) sometimes take some astringent food, like quince, cooked pears, coriander, or even a bit of cheese, because their sealing effect strengthens the orifice of the stomach, and the natural heat needed [?] for digestion does not allow too many vapors to rise [?] to the head.

Realities of Table Service

In France, menus from the fourteenth, fifteenth, and sixteenth centuries (namely, the twenty-seven menus from *Le Ménagier de Paris*, the six from the published edition of *Le Viandier de Taillevent*, and the twelve from *Le Livre fort excellent de cuysine*) demonstrate the following points with regard to acidity and fruits.

In the sixteenth-century menus—though not in those of the fourteenth and fifteenth centuries—acid flavor is represented by salads. In *Le Livre fort excellent de cuysine*, these usually appear to be served as entrées. This is the case for 9 salads in six menus, namely, 2 of [bitter] orange, 1 of lemon, 1 of greens, 1 of herbs, 1 of chicory, 1 entremets [?] salad, and 2 salads of parsnips. There do exist 9 others apparently presented in other courses (1 lemon salad, 1 of pomegranates, 2 of pears, 1 of lettuce, 1 green salad, 2 white salads, and 1 of hops). But these particular salads appear in a single list of dishes that does not really constitute a menu.

Fruits appear to have almost always been served as doctors recommend:

Very acidic fruits—oranges, lemons, limes—were presented as entrées, usually in the guise of salads.

Cherries were served as table entrées in every instance (2/2). We are not told if they were sweet, sour, or styptic, but on one of those two occasions they were served with sugar.

In the nineteen menus mentioning them, pears were served at the end of the meal, whether raw or cooked, sugared or not. Nothing indicates whether they were bitter or sweet, crisp or tender, since their varieties are never mentioned, except for the "two-headed pears," which are unfamiliar to me (and which could just as well refer to a dish as to a variety).

Apples could be served at the beginning or at the end of the meal. They appear:

4 times as a table entrée,

7 times at the end.

But of course nothing says whether the former were sweet and the latter bitter or acidic. We simply know that the four served as entrées were "cooked" or "baked," while those at the end of the meal were either raw or prepared more elaborately: two "Papillons," one "baudrier," one tart, and baked "Rouvel apples topped with a white dragée."

Matters are clearer for other fruits: we generally find that, as prescribed by most doctors, the sweet, juicy, most perishable fruit was eaten at the start of the meal, while bitter and also dried fruit was consumed at the end:

Perishable fruits
  Figs: 4 at the start and 3 at the end
  Grapes: 1 at the start (1545) and 3 at the end (1393: raisins?)
  Plums: 5 at the start (1545 and 1486) and 1 at the end (1486: preserved)
  Apricots (1545): 1 at the start
  Peaches (1545): 2 at the start (with grapes and plums), 1 at the end (with pears)
Bitter fruits
  Medlars: 3 at the end (1393)
  Quince: 1 at the end
  Verjuice (pie): 1 at the end (1545)
Dried fruits
  Almonds: 8 at the end
  Dried walnuts and green walnut meat: 7 at the end
  Hazelnuts: 1 at the end
  Wild filberts: 1 at the end

Evidently the flavor criterion was decisive only for bitter fruits (medlars, quinces, and verjuice). At the time, dried fruits were considered to have a smooth *[grasse]* flavor, which did not enter into instructions on placement within the meal sequence. But juicy, perishable fruits are all somewhat acidic and somewhat sweet, a mix of the two flavors that Platina recommended serving at the start of a meal.

National Variations

While French and Italian dietitians generally agreed on the point in the meal at which various fruits should be served, the Italians tended to base this placement on flavor and the French on how firm or fragile, how light or heavy the fruit. The frequent recommendations that pears, quinces, medlars, and ripened cheeses be served at the end of the meal refer to their substance or solidity, often without reference to flavor, and recommendations on entrée fruits stress their lightness, coolness, and tendency to spoil rather than their sweet or acidic taste.

For example, Guy Patin, in his *Traité de la conservation de la santé* (1632 ed.), recommends that "solid and astringent" fruit be eaten at the end of the meal and "moister" ones at the start because "they spoil easily." His list of end-of-meal fruits includes "pears, quinces, medlars, cornel berries, and Whitty pears [the fruit of the service tree]" whose "astringent properties" compress "the ventricle and thus promote digestion." The astringency referred to here seems to me a property more than a flavor; it describes a tightening effect rather than a bitter taste.

Only Italian dietitians recommended that sweets be served at the beginning of the meal, and Italian menus are in fact the ones that show confectioneries, such as pine nut nougat, being served first. Thus far, the only quote I have found to this effect is by Platina. But I doubt he was the only one, since Italian banquets in fact held to this principle. At least in the sixteenth and seventeenth centuries, they started with sweets, which was much less true of French meals.

See, for instance, the menus published by Vittorio Lancellotti in *Lo Scalco prattico*. The "Primo Servitio fredo" (first course) of a banquet on 1 January 1611 includes not just jellied cold roast or fowl and pasties, but an equal number of sweet pastries and confectioneries:

- Cinnamon blancmange with a domed center, surrounded by pistachio-paste stars separated by sugar-paste rastelli [Biancomagnare cannellato di mezo rilievo, servito con stelle di pasta di pistacchiata intorno, tramezate di rastelli di pasta di zuccaro]
- *Sommate*, frozen as marzipan and served with slices of sponge cake [Sommate, agghiacciate a modo di marzapane, e servite con fette di pane di Spagna]
- Rosettes of flaky pastry [?] filled with marzipan paste and Api apples with syrup, sugar, and cinnamon [Rosoni di pasta di sfoglio, ripieni di pas di marzapane, e mel'appie siroppate, zuccaro, e canella]
- Blancmange timbales and small pumpkins coated with sugar as marzipan glaze, served with preserved citron [Crostate di bianco magnare, e cucuzzata,

agghiacciate di zuccaro, a modo di lustro di marzapane, servite con un cedro condito]

Royal slices of blancmange [Biancomagnare in fette Reali]

Out of twelve sixteenth-century [French] menus I did find one that starts with sugared selections (white *hypocras* and marzipan in menu 10). But it is the only instance I have found from this period when the separation between sweet and salty had not yet been established and when Italy was greatly influential in gastronomy and other domains. Conversely, in seventeenth-century France, it became the norm for sweet pastries and confectioneries to be served at the end of the meal (entremets and dessert).

As we have seen, salads and acidic flavors were presented at the start of the meal in Italy and in sixteenth-century French menus. In the seventeenth century, this remained the order of menus in Italy, but not in France. Furthermore, it became one of the characteristic differences between French and Spanish eating customs. According to *La Oposición y conjunción de los 2 grandes luminares de la tierra, o la antipatía de Franceses y Españoles,* by Carlos García (1617): "Spaniards eat salad only at supper and as a table entrée, the French, at all meals and at their conclusion." This is somewhat overstated given that in France the salad was eaten with the roast at the midpoint of the meal rather than at the end. Also, it is not clear that all French people necessarily ate salad in the same manner as Parisians and courtiers.

Aside from these nuances, I believe that this point did constitute a contrast between eating habits in France and those in neighboring countries.

HEAVINESS AND LIGHTNESS OF FOOD

Dietetic Principles

In both France and Italy, the main criterion for the order in which dishes were consumed was their heaviness or lightness. All dietitians discussed it. See, for example, Aldebrandin of Siena, in 1256: "It is proper to eat light foods first and heavy ones afterward"; Platina in Latin (1475) as well as French (1505): "At the first table are served all things laxative, light, appetizing, and not very filling"; and Nicolas Abraham, Sire de La Framboisière, in 1613: "Let foods that are light, easily digested, easily dissolved, and known to loosen the stomach always be eaten first; and the large, hard, astringent ones, last."

For dietitians, what mattered was not the flavor of the food but its consistency, its weight, its digestibility. Why? Guy Patin explains in 1632:

First partake of those things that soften and loosen the belly, that are not so succulent, that easily cook and descend from the ventricle to where they can more easily be decomposed; next, have what can stop the belly, is harder to digest, does not leave the stomach so soon, and is more succulent and more worthy as nourishment.

For if this order is not observed[,] and things that loosen the belly are eaten at the end of the meal, the fibers of the upper orifice of the ventricle will loosen, possibly resulting in nausea, vomiting, and other mishaps that will prevent digestion and upset the entire natural cycle.

And if the meal starts with things that are harder to digest, what is eaten afterward will remain longer in the stomach, where it will spoil, spreading this decay to the other foods.

And Castor Durante remarks: "Foods that descend more easily and are more tender, if eaten later, will float above [the others] and decay."

Several types of foods were considered light and easily digested:

· Liquids such as broths and other soups
· Most juicy fruits
· Greens

Of liquids, Guy Patin wrote, again in 1632,

Liquids must be taken first so that they will be digested first and distributed more easily. Moreover, the digestion of the meat occurs in our stomach as raw meat is cooked in a kettle (hence Aristotle's comparison of the first digestion to stewing); as water goes in the pot before the meat, so, too, one must drink first, then eat. Authors of the Salerno school agree: *V^e vites poenam, de potibus incipe cœnam* [to avoid pain, start the meal with drinks]. . . . As for me, I feel one should always start with broth when there is any, then eat a bit of solid food.

And of fruits, he wrote: "Among fruits that do not keep and that spoil easily, take the most humid and eat them as table entrées, such as plums, cherries, blackberries, peaches and grapes." But there is no need to dwell on fruits, which I have already sufficiently discussed.

In the thirteenth century, Aldebrandin of Siena writes that "light foods" included "cabbage, lettuce, porcelaine [= purslane], and other similar greens, and all fruits save heavy ones like pears, quince, chestnuts."

Greens were also mentioned in many medical texts. The 1630 *Art de vivre longuement sous le nom de Médée,* for example, states,

The greens appear first in this treatise, just as at table they are served in the first courses. We are referring to edible plants, not medicinal ones. They are also called *hortailles.* They are often used for meals. . . . Some have a warming effect and others are refreshing; the latter include lettuce, purslane, chicory, shallots, leeks, spinach, *responses,* and various kinds of sorrel. Such plants are suitable in the hot season, either as salads or as *chaudeaux,* inasmuch as they temper the stomach, favor digestion, increase appetite, loosen the belly; but for reasons argued elsewhere, take care to use them at the beginning of the meal and not at the end, as was the custom of the Ancients, as Martial says: *Claudere quœ cœnas lactuca solebat avorum, / Dic mihi cur nostras inchoat illa dapes?* [The lettuce that used to conclude the meals of our ancestors, tell me why it is at the beginning of our banquets.]

Castor Durante concurs: "L'herbe si devono mangiare nel principio della mensa."

Note that not all edible plants were considered light. Legumes, for instance, were rather heavy and not to be served as entrées. As Durante explains, "Però usandesi alcuna volta, si prendano in mezo degl'altri cibi, che in questo modo temperarassi la malitia loro." [However, if occasionally used, they are taken with other foods, which thus temper their ill effects.]

Some meats were deemed heavy and some light. As examples of "light flesh," Aldebrandin cites "pullets, kid, Geline chickens and others." Also eaten at the start of the meal were certain parts of quadrupeds used for large cuts of meat such as beef and pork. Thus, according to Aldebrandin, "Brains are cold and moist, and because they are viscous they produce discomfort and slightly [= easily] spoil in the stomach, which is why those who want to eat them should do so before any meats."

Conformity between Theory and Practice

Generally speaking, French meal sequences conformed fairly well, but not totally, to this dialectic of heavy and light.

LIQUID FOOD BEFORE SOLID   If liquid before solid meant drinking before eating—as some physicians understood it—this rule does not seem to have been followed in common practice.

But if it meant eating liquid dishes before solid ones, this was indeed the practice:

· Soups were part of the first course, especially starting in the seventeenth century, when they were eaten before the entrées
· Earlier, the juicy fruits eaten as entrées could be considered succulent and therefore full of liquid

I am not so sure, however, that seventeenth-century soups were all that liquid: they had substantial garnishes, and bread was always soaking in the broth. In the eighteenth century, the garnishes became more discreet, but wasn't bread still simmered in the broth?

Note that broths and very liquid soups seem to have been especially important in France. They were considered essential to health (cf. *La Princesse Palatine*) and restorative against fatigue (hence the term *restaurant*)—just as the English feel about their "nice cup of tea."

FRUITS   This has been amply covered and need not be examined again.

GREENS AND OTHER CROPS   In La Varenne [*Le Cuisinier françois* (1651)]:

· Greens: 13 soups + 1 entrée (pie of greens) → all as starters
· Green vegetables: 15 soups + 4 entrées + 2 entrées or entremets + 3 entremets → 20 to 22 at the start and 3 to 5 at the end

But our data are flawed in that French menus did not usually mention the salads, which, as we know, were served at mid-meal along with the roast.

Problems and Obscure Points

Plant-derived foods
  Grains
    In M.P. *[Le Ménagier de Paris],* always a third or fourth course (frumenty).
  Legumes
    In the Middle Ages
      Peas: 13 soups + 10 first-course + 1 second-course (M.P. menu 1: with table platter before the soups) → 24/24 as starters
      Chickpeas: (Chiquart *[Du fait de cuisine]*) 2 dishes for invalids
      Fava beans: 20 soups + 2 first courses + 1 second course → 22/23 as starters in early sixteenth century
      Legumes: 2 soups → 2/2 as starters in early seventeenth century
    In La Varenne
      Lentils: 1 soup + 1 entrée → 2/2 as starters
      Peas: 9 soups + 3 entrées + 2 entrées or entremets + 1 entremet → 12 to 14/15 as starters
    In Pierre de Lune
      Peas: 3 soups + 2 entrées de V.S. and 3 entremets → 5/8 as starters
      Fava beans: 2 entremets → 2/2 at the end
      Lentils: 1 V.S. soup + 2 V.S. entrée → 2/2 as starters
  Meats
    In the Middle Ages
      Beef: 3 first courses (Chiquart) + 2 soups (TVt. Vat. 1) → 5/5 starters
      Pork: 6 roasts + 1 entremets *(chaudun)* and 7 soups (4 *chaudun* + 3 hams) + 2 first courses (loin)
      Suckling pig: 7 roasts + 7 entremets (6 *soux* + 1 fire-breathing, golden brown suckling pig)
      Veal: 15 roasts + 1 second course and 4 soups + 2 first courses → 6 starters and 16 middle
      Sheep: 6 roasts + 3 entremets and 4 first courses + 1 soup → 5 starters and 9 middle
      Lamb: 6 roasts
      Kid: 5 roasts + 2 second courses [= roasts] and 1 first (caul) and 1 third course (after the first roast)
      Fowl: 106 roasts + 18 entremets [+ 4] and 41 soups + 23 first courses + 39 second courses
    Thus, in sum:

Beef at the beginning.

Pork equally distributed between beginning and middle.

Sheep and veal mostly toward the middle.

Lighter meats (veal, suckling pig, lamb, kid, and poultry) mostly but not exclusively for roasts and entremets.

And there is the rub: in actual practice, the lightest meats were more often served in the second course and the heavy meats as entrées in the first course. There may be several explanations for this.

Dietitians conceded that very heated stomachs needed the heavy meats first to dampen the excessive heat. In the thirteenth century, for instance, Aldebrandin wrote in his *Régime du corps,*

> Li estomacs caus cuist plus legierement les grosses viandes que les soutix, si com char de buef, oès, awes, et assés d'autres; les soutiul viandes, si com char de poucin, lait, chievrel et autres assés ardent et corrunpent, et por ce, cil ki a l'estomac de tel complexion doit avant mengier les grosses viandes ke les legieres, et se doit garder de mengier aus, et poivre, et totes coses caudes, et boire vin fort, se che n'est vin verdelès foibles.

In *The Haven of Health,* Thomas Cogan even applied this rule to all Englishmen, most of whom were reputed to have a hot stomach: "For asmuch as our stomackes in England most commonly be boate [= hot] and cholericke, that grosse meats be most convenient to be eaten first: for in a heate stomacke fine meats if they were first taken would be burned before the grosse meates were digested."

Note that entrée meats in fact generally included some delicate and light ones as well as large and heavy ones. Sixteenth-century examples can be seen in the two menus of figure B1.

The concept of light foods included juicy fruits, which engendered bad gastric juices and spoiled easily, as well as poultry and other delicate, easily digested meats like veal or kid, which nevertheless do not strike me as perishable. I doubt that these meats offered after beef, for instance, were in danger of rotting in the stomach. On the contrary, I believe that it was fine to eat them after the heavy meats because, being easier to digest, they would finish "cooking" at the same time.

Fowl and other delicate meats were the favorites for roasting, the point being that cooking method also influenced the sequence of dishes.

COOKING METHODS

Dietetic Principles

Cooking method constituted a third basis of classification. Both in France and in Italy, all dietitians repeatedly stated that boiled preparations were to be eaten before roasts.

WHAT IS NEEDED FOR A SUPPER (1555)

TABLE ENTRÉE
Green salads
Damascus plums
Venison loin
Parsnip salad
Sunburst of capon breasts
Parsnip jelly

SOUP
Frumenty
Boar navée
Larded boiled venison
Pigeons with cinnamon
Warm venison pâté
A hen pheasant

ANOTHER BANQUET OR WEDDING, FROM *LIVRE FORT EXCELLENT DE CUYSINE* (1555), FOL. LIX

FOR STARTERS
Good bread, good wine

TABLE ENTRÉE
Apricots
Damascus plums
Small hot venison pâtés
Shells of capon breasts

SOUPS
Larded boiled venison
Steamed poussins
Wild pigeons with cabbage

FIGURE B1. Two French menus from 1555.

According to Dr. Jacquelot, "Boiled meat comes next and precedes meats that are roasted, cooked on a spit, or grilled, it being digested more quickly and for fear it might cause roasts to descend prematurely, these being still raw and undigested."

Reiterating this centuries-old precept, the 1704 *Dictionnaire de Trévoux* points out, "Boiled meat is easier to digest. . . . Good tables always serve boiled meat before the roast." This is no longer evident to us, especially since, as Brillat-Savarin remarked in the early nineteenth century, boiled meat is meat that has lost its most digestive attributes, as these get transferred into the broth.

Could it be that roast is less digestible than boiled meat because not as well cooked, as Jacquelot claimed? I doubt it, especially because the Spaniards—just as mindful of dietetics as the French and Italians—served roasts before boiled meat.

Actual Practice

In France, theory and practice coincided perfectly on this point: the roasts course always followed the boiled meats and sauced meats (also moist) served during the soup and entrée courses. This was especially true in the seventeenth and eighteenth centuries, but perhaps less clear in the fourteenth, fifteenth, and sixteenth.

When there were spit-roasted entrées (seventeenth and eighteenth centuries),

· they followed the minor entrées;
· the roasted meat was less deeply browned and therefore less dry than for the roast course; and
· these spit-roasted entrées were always moistened with a sauce or a ragoût.

National Variations

The Italians and English agreed with the French about eating the roast after the boiled offering, in practice as well as in theory. Platina writes, "Roasts are more nourishing and more difficult to cook [= digest] than boiled meats; but meat cooked in its juices [is less filling and easier to digest] than fried meat." Further on he adds, "Roasted and fried flesh is much more filling and harder to digest for being too dry and without humors: but if boiled it is more moist and digestible, provided it is not too fat, in which case, as we said, better roasted than boiled."

Roasted meat, harder to digest than boiled meat, was logically to be eaten after it. Likewise for Castor Durante: "If there are roasted and boiled meats, start with the boiled ones, which are easier to digest." Thomas Cogan, in England: "Here in England, where we feed on divers sortes of meats at one meale, the order commonly is thus: that first we [?] eate Potage or Brothes, then boyled meats, after that rosted or baked, and in the end cheese and fruites."

But the Spanish boasted of a different practice. See *La Oposición y conjunción de los 2 grandes luminares de la tierra, o la antipatía de Franceses y Españoles,* by Carlos García (1617): "Frenchmen start with boiled meat, Spaniards with the roast." Did Spanish dietitians justify this practice the way their English counterparts justified equally aberrant dietetic practices (such as their predilection for beef)?

CONCLUSION

Although physicians did not all agree about the dietetic principles of meal sequencing, a certain number of ideas were rather generally accepted.

In France, principle and practice coincided on many points, including in the seventeenth and eighteenth centuries, when cooks distanced themselves from dietetics.

Contradictions nevertheless existed, or so research to date indicates. I remain hopeful that they will be resolved with further study.

Some differences did exist among the practices of various countries over the question of meal sequencing as well as cookery. But no physician admitted that his compatriots methodically violated basic principles. Instead, doctors generally rationalized the actual practice. This was certainly true of Thomas Cogan in England, and perhaps of Platina also. Further research must be conducted on how the Spanish explained their practices.

The Cuisine of the Renaissance

It is strange to see how much the sequencing of courses differed among countries in spite of being explicitly based on the same dietetic principles.

France

The prevailing order was very similar to that of the fourteenth and fifteenth centuries and not too different from that of the seventeenth and eighteenth.

- Entrées: raw fruits, hot or cold variety meats, hot pasties, large cuts of boiled meats, etc. (as in the Middle Ages)
- Soups (which will move to first position in the seventeenth century) and meats with sauces
- One or more roast courses (plus hot or cold pasties)
- Finish (= dessert)

Presented at the Symposium on the Renaissance and the Art of the Table, Brussels, 28 October 2000.

Judging by the banquet offered to Robert de Berges, count of Walhain, meal structure was very similar to that in France.

- First course: boiled meats, soups, and hot pasties
- Second course: hot roast meats
- Third course: cold roast meats and pasties, a few fish dishes
- Fourth course [dessert]: cakes, jams, fruits

England

Early in the century (9 March 1504, at the enthronement feast for Guillaume Warham, archbishop of Canterbury), some meals were still being served as in the fourteenth and fifteenth centuries, in two or three "courses" not distinctly different from one another in content. What characterizes these menus from the fourteenth to sixteenth centuries is the sequence of dishes within each course:

- "Soups" in the first two positions of each course
- "Sotelte" or "subtility" (in other words, entremets) in last position for each course, at least in the most elaborate feasts
- The other types of dishes distributed each in its position between the soups and entremets

On the basis of the 1591 *Book of Cookrye* and 1596 *The Good Huswifes Jewell*, it appears that English menus became more like French ones by the late sixteenth and early seventeenth centuries, even though they consisted of only two courses (figure C1). Instead of the repetitive courses of major medieval English feasts, we now see something closer to French meals, a sequence that progresses from the soups and boiled meats that introduce the first course to the pies that conclude the last. What is a bit strange in this progression is the way roasted meats straddle the first and second courses.

Italy

There would be much to say about Italy, since the sixteenth century is when the country saw its greatest proliferation of cookbooks, books for carving stewards, books for *maîtres d'hôtel*, etc. One of the traits of Italian meal organization throughout that whole period (even from the mid-fifteenth century to the mid-seventeenth) was candied specialties at the start of the meal—not only fruits as in French banquets, but assorted and sometimes very sweet confectioneries.

Still, menus do show some formal changes. Those of Messisbugo, from the

FIRST MENU FROM THE *BOOK OF COOKRYE*

FIRST COURSE
Potage or stewed broth
Boiled meat or stewed meat
Chickins and Bacon
Powdred Beefe
Pyes, Gooce, Pigge
Rosted Beefe
Rosted Veale
Custard

SECOND COURSE
Rosted Lamb
Rosted Capons
Chickins
Pehennes
Bakte Venison, Tart

And the same at supper:

FIRST COURSE
Potage or Sew *[sic]*
A Sallet
A Pigges petitoe
Powdred Beef sliced

And roasts:
A shoulder of Mutton or a brest
Vele, Lamb

And the inevitable:
Custard

SECOND COURSE

More roasts:
Capons rosted
Cunnies rosted
Chickins rosted

And then:
A Pye of Pigions or Chickins
Baked Venison, Tarte

FIGURE C1. A late sixteenth-century English menu, from *A Book of Cookrye* by A.W. (1591).

mid-sixteenth century, are often richer—like the 20 May 1529 menu featuring seventeen kitchen courses, not to mention the confectionery courses in between them. More striking yet are the menus in Vittorio Lancellotti's *Scalco prattico,* published in Rome in 1627 but containing some menus dating back to the early seventeenth century.

Here we see the culmination of Italian banquet structure:

- A credenza course consisting of cold dishes (meats, pasties, and confectionery selections) comparable to today's appetizer snacks
- Then two, three, four, five, or even more kitchen courses, consisting of all types of hot dishes whose principles of classification I have found difficult to identify
- And finally, a second credenza course, consisting mainly of cheeses, pastries, and entremets in the contemporary sense, such as blancmange and all sorts of fruits—including, to the surprise of the modern reader, chestnuts seasoned with salt and pepper, truffles, cardoons, chard pies, fresh fennel, and other selections

Additional Printed Sources

Books about How the Elements of Meals
Were Sequenced and Why

ARS = Bibliothèque de l'Arsenal; BN = Bibliothèque nationale; BHVP = Bibliothèque historique de la ville de Paris; BPI = Bibliothèque publique d'information

DICTIONARIES

Caraccioli, Louis Antoine de. *Dictionnaire critique, pittoresque & sentencieux, Propre à faire connaître les usages du Siècle, ainsi que ses bizarreries. Par l'Auteur de la conversation avec soi-même.* Lyon: Benoît Duplain, 1768. 3 vols. In-12°. BN [Z. 20458–20460] 20458 microfiche

Diderot, Denis. *Encyclopédie ou Dictionnaire raisonné des Sciences, des Arts, et des Métiers, par une société de gens de Lettres. Mis en ordre et publié par M. Diderot.* Orig. 1751–1780. New facsimile printing Stuttgart–Bad Cannstatt: Friedrich Frommann Verlag (Günther Holzboog), 1988. 26 vols. BPI [031 DID]

DIETETICS AND PHARMACOPOEIA

Buc'hoz, Pierre-Joseph. *L'Art de préparer les alimens, suivant les différens peuples de la Terre, Auquel on a joint une notion succinte sur leur salubrité ou insalubrité. Par M. Buc'Hoz, Auteur de différens ouvrages économiques.* 2nd ed. Paris: by the author, 1787. 2 vols. In-8°. BN [S. 14848]

Dufour de La Crespelière. *Commentaire en vers français sur l'École de Salerne. Contenant les moyens de se passer de Medecin, & de vivre longtemps en santé.* Paris: Gervais Clouzier, 1671. 714 pp., in-12°. BN [TC¹⁰. 57]

Lobera de Ávila, Luis. *Vanquete de Nobles Cavalleros e modo de bivir desde que se levantan hasta q se acuestan, y habla de cda* [sic] *manjar que complexion y propriedad tiene e que daños y provechos haze, e trata del regimiento curativo e prefarativo de las fibres Pestilanciales.* Augsburg: Heinricum Stainerum, 1530. In *El Vanquete de Nobles Cavalleros (1530), de Luis Lobera de Ávila y la Higiene individual del Siglo XVI.* Madrid: Ministerio de Sanidad y Consumo, 1991. 41 pp. & facsimile.

La Medecine domestique contenant le gouvernement de la Santé, l'Apothicaire, le Chirurgien, & le Medecin charitable. Avec une harangue sur la goutte à Messieurs ses Hostes. Geneva: Jean Herman Widerhold, 1673. 207 pp. In-8°. ARS (8° S. 9646)

La Chapelle, Vincent. *Le Cuisinier moderne qui apprend à donner toutes sortes de repas En Gras & en Maigre, d'une manière plus délicate que ce qui a été écrit jusqu'à présent. Divisé en quatre volumes, Orné de Figures en Taille douce, Dédié à Monseigneur le Prince d'Orange & de Nassau, & c., Par le Sieur Vincent La Chapelle, son Chef de cuisine & ci-devant de Mylord Chesterfield.* La Haye: A. van Dole, 1735. 4 vols. In-8°. ARS (8° S. 9808 [1–4])

La Chesnaye des Bois. *Dictionnaire portatif de cuisine, d'office & de distillation . . . On y a joint des observations médicinales qui font connaître la propriété de chaque aliment, relativement les plus convenables à chaque tempérament.* Paris: Latin le Jeune, 1770. 2 vols. In-8°. BHVP (717 444 [1–2–])

L'Escole parfaite des officiers de Bouche; contenant le Vray Maistre-d'Hostel, Le grand Escuyer-Tranchant, Le Sommelier Royal, Le Confiturier Royal, et le Patissier Royal. Paris: chez la Veuve Pierre David . . . et chez Jean Ribou, 1662. 494 pp. In-8°. BN [V. 37 608]

Gilliers. *Le Cannaméliste français, ou nouvelle instruction pour ceux qui désirent apprendre l'Office, rédigé en forme de dictionnaire, contenant les Noms, les descriptions, les usages, les chois, & les principes de tout ce qui se pratique dans l'Office— Par le sieur Gilliers, chef d'office & distillateur de sa Majesté le Roi de Pologne, Duc de Lorraine & de Bar.* Nancy: Jean Baptiste-Hiacynthe Leclerc, and Paris: Merlin, 1768. 238 pp. In-4°. BHVP (rés. 103 697)

Lamare, Nicolas de. *Traité de Police—avec un recueil de tous les status et réglemens des six corps des marchands et de toutes les communautés des Arts et métiers.* Paris: Jean et Pierre Cot, 1705–1738. 4 vols. In-folio. BN [2200–2203]

Liger, Louis. *Économie générale de la campagne, ou nouvelle Maison Rustique, Par le sieur Liger, d'Auxerre.* Paris: Charles de Sercy, 1700. 2 vols. In-4°. BN [S. 4459–4460]

———. *Le Ménage des champs et de la ville, ou nouveau Cuisinier françois accomodé au goût du temps. Contenant tout ce qu'un parfait chef de cuisine doit savoir pour servir toutes sortes de tables.* Paris: Micle David l'aîné, 1714. 584 pp. In-12°. BN [S. 1649]

———. *Le Voyageur fidele ou le Guide des étrangers dans la ville de Paris qui enseigne tout ce qu'il y a de curieux à voir. . . . les adresses pour aller de rües en quartiers, et y trouver tout ce que l'on souhaite, tant pour les besoins de la vie que pour autres choses. . . .* Paris: Pierre Ribou, 1715. 520 pp. In-12°. BN [Lk[7]. 6008]

Lune, Pierre de. *Le Nouveau et Parfait Maistre d'hostel.* Paris: Estienne Loyson, 1662. 357 pp. In-8°. ARS (8°S 9826)

Marin, François. *Les Dons de Comus ou les Délices de la table.* Paris: Prault fils, 1739. 275 pp. In-12°. ARS (8° 9809[1])

———. *Les Dons de Comus ou les Délices de la table—Suivi de la Lettre à un pâtissier anglais.* Paris, 1790. 2 vols. In-12°. ARS (8° 9811 [1–2])

———. *Suite des Dons de Comus, ou l'Art de la cuisine réduit en pratique. . . .* Paris: Vve. Pissot, 1742. 2 vols. In-12°. ARS (8° 9809 [2–3])

M. C. D. (pseud. Briand). *Dictionnaire des Alimens, vin et liqueurs, leurs qualités, leurs effets.* Paris: Gissey, 1750. 3 vols. In-8°. ARS (8°S. 9693 [1–3])

Menon. *Cuisine d'office et de santé propre à ceux qui vivent avec économie et régime.* Paris: Leclerc, 1757. 416 pp. In-12°. ARS (8°S 9822)

———. *Nouveau Traité de la cuisine, avec de nouveaux dessins de table et vingt-quatre menus.* Paris: Michel-Étienne David, 1739. 2 vols. In-12°. ARS (8°S 9817 [1–2])

———. *La Nouvelle Cuisine avec de nouveaux menus pour chaque saison—Pour servir de continuation au nouveau Traité de Cuisine.* Vol. 3. Paris: David père, 1742. 400 pp. In-12°. ARS (8°S 9817 [3])

———. *La Science du maître d'hôtel cuisinier avec des observations sur la connoissance et propriété des alimens.* Paris: Paulus du Mesnil, 1749. 552 pp. In-12°. ARS (8°S 9828)

———. *La Science du maître d'hôtel confiseur—Suite du Maître d'hôtel cuisinier.* Paris: Paulus du Mesnil, 1750. 525 pp. In-12°. BN [V.26999]

———. *Les Soupers de la Cour ou l'Art de travailler toutes sortes d'alimens.* Paris: Guillyn, 1755. 4 vols. In-12°. BN [V 26995]

———. *Traité historique et pratique ou le cuisinier instruit. De la connaissance des Animaux . . . de la façon de Préparer les divers Alimens, et de les Servir. Suivi d'un petit abrégé sur la manière de faire les confitures liquides et autres Desserts de toute espèces. . . .* Paris: O. J. B. Bauche, 1758. 2 vols. In-12°. BN [V. 26985–26986]

Le Petit Cuisinier économe ou l'art de faire la cuisine au meilleur marché mis à la porté de chacun et contenant l'indication des alimens les plus rapprochés des facultés de tous les citoyens. Paris: Janet, 1796. 105 pp. In-18°. BHVP (7 17 407)

Savary des Bruslons, Jacques. *Dictionnaire universel de commerce, d'histoire naturelle, et des arts & métiers. . . .* Paris: Nelle éd.; considerably expanded, Copenhagen: chez les frères CL and Ant. Philibert, 1759–1765. 5 vols. BHVP (F° B3)

Albert, B. *L'Art du cuisinier parisien ou manuel complet d'économie domestique contenant la cuisine, la charcuterie, la grosse pâtisserie finz, l'office dans toutes ses branches: la cuisine des malades—la conduite de la table.* Paris: Bab, uf, 1822. 578 pp. In-8°. BHVP (715 578)

Almanach bachique qui durera autant que le bon vin. Et le moyen tres-facile pour sçavoir en quel temps il faut planter & semer les choses nécessaires pour éguiser l'apetit et la soif. Ensemble les lois de Bacchus, prince de Nisse, Roy des Indes et des Buveurs. Rouen: Jean-B. Besongne, n.d. pet. 24 pp. In-12°.

Almanach de M. Ramponeaux, en vers et prose. Basse-Courtille, 1761. In-32°.

Almanach de santé. Paris: Rouault, 1774. 164 pp. In-16°. [Chapter VII is devoted to the selection of foods.]

Almanach des Marchés de Paris, étrennes curieuses et comiques, avec des chansons intéressantes, dédié à Marie Barbe, fruitière, orangère, dessiné et gravé par M. Quéverdo. Paris: Boulanger, 1782. In-24°.

Almanach des voluptueux ou les Vingt-Quatre Heures d'un sybarite, par un Épicurien. 12th year. Paris. In-18°.

Almanach de table. Paris: Duchesne, 1761. In-12°.

Almanach du comestible, nécessaire aux personnes de bon goût et de bon appétit; qui indique généralement toutes les bonnes choses que l'on pourra se procurer à la Halle et chez certains Débitans, dans le courant de chaque mois de l'année. En grosse viande, Volaille, Gibier, plume et poil, Oiseaux de rivière, Poisson de mer et d'eau douce, frais et salé. Légumes verds et secs; Vins de France et Etrangers; Liqueurs et ratafiats, Café, Chocolat, etc. Les Personnes qui aiment la Bonne Chère, y trouveront de quoi satisfaire leur goût; et celles qui aiment leur santé, y trouveront des préceptes pour la conserver. On a joint à cet ouvrage tout ce qui peut égayer le Lecteur et ceux qui aiment la joie dans les Repas. For the current year [1778]. Paris: Desnos, n.d. In-16°.

Almanach parisien en faveur des personnes curieuses contenant par ordre alphabétique, l'indication de tout ce qui est nécessaire & utile pour un Etranger. Ce qui comprend le Logement, la Nourriture, l'Habillement, les Voitures, les Emplettes qu'il a à faire, le Prix de toutes ces choses. L'Indication des Spectacles, des Promenades, & de tous les endroits dignes de sa curiosité. Les maîtres pour les Sciences. Les notions nécessaires à ceux qui ont des Affaires à Paris & ouvrage également utile aux François. . . . Paris: Duchesne, 1764. 183 pp. In-8°. BN [Lc³¹368]

Blegny. *Les Adresses de la Ville de Paris, avec le Tresor des Almanach. Livre commode en tous lieux, en tous temps & en toutes conditions, par Abraham du Pradel, astrologue Lionnois.* Paris: Veuve Denis Nion, 1691. 113 pp. In 8°. BN [8 Lc³¹. 365]

La Faye. *Catalogue et almanach du goût & de l'odorat. Donné par La Faye, Marchand.* Paris, 1773. 62 pp. In-16°. ARS (8°S 9835)

Lombard, L.-M. *Le Cuisinier et le médecin et le médecin et le cuisinier ou l'Art de conserver ou de rétablir la santé par une alimentation convenable à toutes les personnes qui veulent connaître leur tempérament, le gouverner en santé ou en maladie selon les règles de l'hygiène. Suivi d'un livre de cuisine d'économie domestique et d'hygiène alimentaire appliquée selon les divers tempéraments. Par une société de Médecins, de chimistes, de cuisiniers et d'Officiers de bouche. Sous la direction de MR. L-M. Lombard.* Paris: L. Curmer, 1855. Marseille: Jeanne Laffitte Reprints, 1980. 2 vols. BPI (641–1 CUI)

Viard, André. *Le Cuisinier impérial ou l'art de faire la cuisine pour toutes les fortunes; Avec différentes recettes d'office et de fruits confits, etc. etc.* Paris: Barba, 1806. Repr. Nîmes: Lacour, 1993. 459 pp.

OTHER BOOKS

Ancelin (L'abbé). *L'Eschole de Salerne ov Préceptes povr se conserver en bonne santé. le tout en quatrain François.* Paris, 1628. pet. 40 pp. In-4°.

Apologie des modernes ou réponse du Cuisinier françois auteur des Dons de Comus à un pâtissier anglois. No loc. [1740]. 44 pp. In-8°.

L'Art de conserver sa santé composé par l'école de Salerne, traduit en vers françois par B.L.M. [Bruzen de la Martinière]. La Haye: J. Van Duren, 1743. 104 pp. In-12°.

Athénée. *Les Quinze Livres des Déipnosophistes d'Athénée, traduits pour la première fois en françois par M. de Marolles, sur le grec original, après les versions latines de Natalis Comes, de Padoue et de Jacques d'Alechamp de Caen.* Paris: Jacq. Langlois, n.d. In-4°.

Aymes, J. *Bazar provençal rue du Bac, n° 104, tenu par J. Aymes. Succursale boulevart des Capucines, 23. Réunion des denrées du midi et recettes de tous les plats les plus renommés de la cuisine provençale.* Paris: Imprimerie de Poussielgue, 1835. 59 pp. in-16°. 1851 ed., 64 pp. In-16° [sold for the benefit of the poor who refrain from working on Sunday].

Balinghem, Antoine de. *Aprées dinées et propos de table contre l'excez au boire et au manger pour vivre longuement, sainement et sainctement dialogisez entre un prince et sept scavants personnages.* Lille: Pierre de Rache, 1615. In-12°. 2nd ed. S. Omer, 1624. pet. in-8°.

[Saint-Hilaire, Émile Marco de.] *L'Art de donner à dîner, de découper les viandes, de servir les mets, de déguster les vins, de choisir les liqueurs, etc., etc., enseigné en douze leçons, avec des planches explicatives du texte. Par un ancien maître d'hôtel du président de la diète de Hongrie, ex-chef d'office de la princesse Charlotte, etc., etc.* Paris: Urbain Canel, 1828. 141 pp. with engravings. In-18°. [See also Mangenville (le chevalier de). In his foreword, the author relates that he drew the idea of his work from an Italian manuscript in the State Council library titled *Catalogo dell'inventori delle cose qui si mangiano*, in-4°, including more than 50 color illustrations.]

NOTES

CHAPTER 1

1. Alexandre-Balthazar-Laurent Grimod de La Reynière, *Almanach des gourmands,* 3rd year (1805), p. 18.

2. These four culinary terms have been kept in the French and should be understood in their original, historical sense, not as used in modern French or in English. *Hors d'oeuvre:* Additional tidbits elaborating on the important offerings after the soup. Borrowed from the vocabulary of architecture, literally, "outside the main work." (In modern times, it has come to mean "appetizers.") *Relevé:* An intermediate course of dishes to replace (relieve) the soup or fish being removed. The most obsolete of these four terms and of the actual stages of a meal. Also called a remove, particularly in British usage. *Entrée:* The third course, after the hors d'oeuvre and relevé but before the roast. Literally, "entrance, beginning, introduction." (In English, the term has confusingly come to mean the main dish or *plat de résistance.*) *Entremets:* A spectacular offering of sweet and savory dishes after the roast course, accompanied by entertainment. Literally, "between dishes," like an intermezzo. (In modern times, it is part of dessert.)—*Trans.*

3. See the end of François Massialot's first menu (p. 3) in his 1691 *Le Cuisinier royal et bourgeois ou cuisinier moderne:* "THIRD COURSE. These are fruits and preserves, which go unmentioned because because they concern the Steward rather than the Cook." Most cookbook authors followed the same policy, though not in so many words. One notable exception: Menon, in *La Cuisinière bourgeoise suivie de l'Office* (1746), which, for once, also dealt with the pantry.

4. On pages 166 and 167 of *Le Nouveau et Parfait Maistre d'hostel royal. enseignant la maniere de couvrir les Tables dans les Ordinaires & Festins, tant en Viande qu'en Poisson, suivant les quatre Saisons de l'Année, Le tout représenté par un grand nombre de Figures. Ensemble un Nouveau Cuisinier à l'Espagnol, contenant une nouvelle façon d'apprester toutes sortes de Mets, tant en Chair qu'en Poisson, d'une méthode fort agréable* by Sieur Pierre de Lune, Kitchen Steward of the Duke of Rohan (Paris: at Charles de Sercy, Palais, Salle Dauphine, Bonne-Foy couronnée, 1662).

5. Menon, *La Cuisinière bourgeoise* (1746), pp. 14–15, 12–14.

6. Grimod de La Reynière, *Almanach des gourmands,* 2nd year (1804), pp. 45–46.

7. Philippe Mordacq, *Le Menu: Une histoire illustrée de 1751 à nos jours* (Paris: Robert Laffont, 1989), facing p. 1.

8. Grimod de La Reynière, *Almanach des gourmands,* 3rd year (1805), p. 20: "It is altogether wrong, in an important meal, to serve the entremets at the same time as the roast. The entremets, some of which should be eaten immediately, will languish as the roast is being carved and be cold by the time it is eaten. Thus it is better to present entremets as a separate course and accompany the roasts with salads only. . . . The entremets will be eaten as soon as served and as hot as they should be."

9. The practice occurs for example in the *Cuisinier économe* menu (Archambault, *Le Cuisinier économe, ou Élémens nouveaux de cuisine, de pâtiserie et d'office . . .* [Paris: Renard Baudouin, 1821]), where the second course successively mentions four major presentations—which are entremets because they consist of a brioche, a mound of crayfish, a "nougat or other pastry," and some "truffles in champagne"—the whole followed by two salads, four dishes of roast, and sixteen entremets.

10. Grimod de La Reynière, *Almanach des gourmands,* 3rd year (1805), p. 20: "Substantial pasties or other cold presentations like daubes, galantines etc., will serve as a centerpiece for the third course; and since the guests seldom touch these, the entremets will be eaten as soon as served and as hot as they should be."

11. Massialot, *Le Cuisinier royal et bourgeois,* p. 3: "For the entremets course: A cream pie for the center basin, garnished with flaky pastry strips and crescents, florets, and milk fritters. Two other secondary dishes: a ham loaf garnished with little toast points and a lemon loaf; the other, a ham and other salt-cured meat."

12. "This course being attractive to the eyes rather than the other senses, the faithful and true Gourmand simply admires it. A thirst-inducing or appetizing piece of cheese is worth more to him than all these showy, pretentious decorations" (Grimod de La Reynière, *Almanach des gourmands,* 2nd year [1804], p. 49).

13. Ibid., 3rd year (1805), p. 21.

CHAPTER 2

1. Boiled meats: The term *bouilli* does not appear in recipe titles either in François de La Varenne's *Cuisinier françois* (1651) or in Pierre de Lune's *Nouveau Cuisinier* (1660).

Meats in sauces: Considered entrées in *Le Nouveau Cuisinier* are "Lapereaux à la sauce blanche," "Lapereaux à la sauce brune," "Tétine de vache à la sauce douce," "Fricassée de poulet à la sauce blanche," "Fricassée de pigeonneaux à la sauce blanche," "Langues de veau à la sauce douce," "Langue de bœuf à la sauce brune," "Pieds de mouton à la sauce blanche," and "Canards farcis à la sauce douce"; while "Pieds de porc sur le grill à la sauce" is listed as an entremets. In *Le Cuisinier françois* (1651), pp. 36–37, no. 14, the "Pièce de bœuf à l'Angloise ou Chalonnoise" is boiled, then larded and spit-roasted, basted with marinade, and finally simmered in a terrine with the marinade, and served with capers, turnips, and such; it is clearly an entrée, as are the 5 braised meats in the same book: "Membre de mouton à la daube" (p. 39, no. 21), "Poulet d'Inde à la daube" (p. 39, no. 22), "Pièce de bœuf à la daube" (p. 41, no. 27), "Cochon à la daube" (p. 43, no. 32), and "Oye à la daube" (p. 43, no. 33).

Stewed meats: *Le Cuisinier françois* has "38 meats in ragoût," of which 29 are entrées and 9 are entremets. Out of 22 meats or fowls in ragoût in *Le Nouveau Cuisinier,* there are 9 entrées and 13 entremets.

The only example of steam-cooked meat, "Poulets à l'estuvée" (p. 53, no. 62), is also an entrée, as are the 3 dishes "à l'estoffade": breast of veal (p. 37, no. 15), beef (p. 50, no. 54), and partridge (p. 51, no. 57).

Likewise, the 4 meat or fowl fricassees are all entrées: "Foye de veau fricassé" (p. 45, no. 40), "Poulets fricassés" (p. 47, no. 43), "Pigeonneaux fricassés" (p. 47, no. 44), "Pieds de mouton fricassez" (p. 56, no. 70). The same goes for the 5 fowl fricassees in *Le Nouveau Cuisinier.*

Sautéed or fried meats: There are 2 entrées and 1 entremets among the 3 meats "à la poêsle" in Pierre de Lune's *Nouveau Cuisinier.* There are 4 entremets and 3 meat-day entrées among the 7 meats, fowls, or fried organ meats of *Le Nouveau Cuisinier.* In *Le Cuisinier françois,* there are 2 soups, 3 entrées, and 3 entremets.

Grilled meats: The 3 in *Le Cuisinier françois* are entremets. In *Le Nouveau Cuisinier* there are 2 entrées and 2 entremets.

Both *Le Cuisinier françois* and *Le Nouveau Cuisinier* have pastry chapters that do not indicate at what stage of the meal the pies and pasties were served. However, *Le Cuisinier françois* directly reveals the function of 4 meat pies, which are all entrées, and 9 pasties, of which 6 are entrées and 3 are entremets. *Le Nouveau Cuisinier* also gives the function of 3 meat pasties: 1 entrée and 2 entremets.

2. The 2 roasts are the "Pigeonneaux rostis" (p. 69, no. 9) and the "Espaule de veau rostie" (p. 83, no. 58). The roasted young pigeons, served on top of a pep-

per sauce, seem more like a spit-roasted entrée than a dish of roast. Two versions are offered for the veal shoulder: in one, it is also served on top of a pepper sauce; in the other, it is covered with bread and fine salt when nearly roasted, which was not incompatible with the roast function in the mid-seventeenth century. The stuffed meats are "Poictrine de veau farcie" (p. 78, no. 49) and "Membre de mouton farcy" (p. 81, no. 55), which cannot conceivably be roasts: they are meats in sauce, though they appear in the roast chapter. The "Cochon de lait au naturel" (p. 75, no. 40) is spit-roasted with a bouquet of herbs in its cavity. And the "Membre de mouton à la Royalle" (p. 81, no. 54) is also a meat with sauce— actually cooked in broth—and cannot therefore be a roast.

3. The "Espaule ou longe de sanglier" (no. 44), first recipe for "Poictrine de veau farcie" (no. 49), second recipe for "Haut costé de mouton" (no. 50), "Longe de mouton" (no. 51), "Alloyau" (no. 52), "Langue de bœuf fraîche, autre façon" (no. 53), "Membre de mouton à la Royalle" (no. 54), "Membre de mouton farcy" (no. 55), first through third versions of "Poularde grasse" (no. 56), "Batteurs de pavé" (no. 57), and first recipe for "Canard sauvage" (no. 61) are all meats simmered in sauce after roasting, or even cooked directly in the sauce.

4. Examples of entrées are the first through fourth versions of "Langues de mouton rosties" (pp. 57–58, no. 71), or "Queue de mouton rostie" (p. 42, no. 30), or "Achis de viande rostie" (p. 59, no. 72). Likewise, roasted entremets always came from cuts unsuitable for roast: "Jambon rosti" (pp. 96–97, no. 20), "Foye gras sur le gril" (pp. 107–108, no. 59), "Langue de mouton picquée" (p. 118, no. 89), and "Langue de mouton sur le gril" (p. 119, no. 90).

5. *La Cuisinière bourgeoise, suivie de l'Office* is attributed to Menon. The first edition is dated 1746. But the book was repeatedly reprinted until the end of the century and beyond, always with more recipes. My reference here is the very complete 1774 edition, reprinted in 1981 by Éditions Messidor–Temps Actuels.

6. "How can the roast . . . cook evenly, and how can it preserve the volatile qualities that account for its subtle flavor, when it turns constantly on a remote spit, wide open to a drafty, often cold kitchen? It is impossible. This is why roasts cooked in one of those tin receptacles known as 'Cuisinières' are far more succulent, far more evenly and swiftly cooked. Unfortunately, these Cuisinières (more accurately and justifiably called 'Rôtissoires' in other countries) are excluded from high-society households and relegated to modest ones, where the roast is not surprisingly far better than in upscale residences" (Grimod de la Reynière, *Almanach des gourmands,* 4th year [1806], pp. 17–18).

7. Ibid.

8. *La Cuisinière bourgeoise,* 1774 edition, pp. 56–57, 76, and the table on p. 463.

9. Menon uses this expression (ibid., pp. 217, 220, 225, 229) most often in connection with studded meats like pheasants, wood pigeons and their chicks, partridges, plovers, young rabbit, etc.; and in fact meat that has been studded

rather than barded is much easier to brown well without burning. Still, Menon sometimes mentions a "belle couleur" for birds wrapped in vine leaves and lard—like quail and their chicks, p. 222. The point is that a roast cannot be left pale.

10. So writes Menon about "Poulets au cerfeuil"—"bind this sauce over the fire and serve on spit-roasted chickens" (ibid., pp. 165–166)—or about "Poulets au réveil": "bind over the fire without boiling. Serve over the chickens" (ibid., pp. 166–167). But Massialot, in *Le Cuisinier royal et bourgeois* (1691), favors sauces poured underneath the roasted meat. Examples: the entrées of "Ris-de-Veau piquez, rôtis, une bonne sausse par dessous" and of "Deux Poulardes rôties, un ragoût dessous" in the "Soupé" on p. 11. This was not always so at the time of the *Cuisinier royal et bourgeois,* since the roasts for the "Dîné de Monsieur, le jour de Pâques 26 mars 1690" (p. 10) include a "dish of two roast ducks covered with a sauce." But this seems an isolated instance in the book.

11. *La Cuisinière bourgeoise,* p. 217.

12. Nicolas de Bonnefons recommends this for chickens, hens, and capons in *Les Délices de la campagne* (1654), p. 228: "They can also be roasted with butter instead of lard, an onion studded with two or three cloves inserted in the cavity, and some salt and pepper." La Varenne recommends the same in *Le Cuisinier françois* (1651), p. 69, no. 8: "Insert a studded onion, salt, and a little pepper"; so does Pierre de Lune in *Le Nouveau Cuisinier* (1660), p. 85, no. 23.

13. In the seventeenth century, *Le Cuisinier françois* almost never spit-roasted its stuffed meats and fowl. Nor did L. S. R.'s *L'Art de bien traiter* (1674), whose nine meat entrées are cooked in sauce or fried. But *Le Nouveau Cuisinier,* which likewise stuffs mostly soups and entrée meats cooked in sauce, nevertheless includes "Poulets farcis à l'Espagnolle" (p. 42), roasted and served "with lemon juice & lamb drippings," and some "Canards farcis à la sauce douce," also a spit-roasted entrée.

14. *La Cuisinière bourgeoise,* pp. 11, 220–225.

15. *Almanach des gourmands;* the 1704 *Dictionnaire de Trévoux* entry for "Pied" already defined the term "as applied to fowl or small game."

16. *Le Cuisinier françois* features 63 recipes for meat-day organ meats, including 3 under the roast chapter: 2 for "Langue de bœuf fraische" (p. 81, no. 53) and 1 for "Foye de veau" (p. 83, no. 59). In Pierre de Lune's *Nouveau Cuisinier,* none of the 60 organ-meat recipes constitutes a roast. There are none either among the 38 organ-meat recipes from *L'Art de bien traiter* (1674).

17. Massialot, *Le Cuisinier royal et bourgeois, ou cuisinier moderne qui apprend à ordonner toutes sortes de repas, en gras & en maigre & la meilleure manière des ragoûts les plus à la mode & les plus exquis & toutes sortes de pâtisseries, avec de nouveaux dessins de table. Ouvrage très utile dans les familles & singulièrement nécessaire à tous Maître d'Hôtel & Officiers de Cuisine. Augmentée de nouveaux ragoûts par le sieur Vincent La Chapelle, chef de cuisine de S.A.S. Monseigneur le Prince*

d'Orange & de Nassau (Paris: Claude Prudhomme, 1750–1751), 3 vols., Bibliothèque de l'Arsenal 8°S 9795.

18. *La Cuisinière bourgeoise*'s feathered game entrées: 5 of quail, 3 of thrushes, 3 of partridges or their chicks, 2 of woodcocks or their chicks, 2 of plovers, 1 of wild duck and 1 of wild duckling, 1 of pheasant, 1 of woodcocks or their chicks, 1 of robins, 1 of teal, and 1 of scoter. It also has 13 duck entrées; 20 entrées and 1 hors d'oeuvre of turkey; 6 goose entrées or hors d'oeuvres; 28 entrées and 1 hors d'oeuvre of pigeon; 1 entrée of guinea fowl; 19 entrées, 2 hors d'oeuvres, and 1 spit-roasted entrée of hen; and 18 entrées, 3 hors d'oeuvres, and 1 spit-roasted entrée of chicken.

19. Pierre de Lune, *Le Nouveau Cuisinier,* pp. 81–82, 89–90: roasts of "hares and their young," "rabbits and their young," "boars and their young," and "stags, does, and fawns."

20. La Varenne, *Le Cuisinier françois,* pp. 71–78: "18. Marcassin," "26. Longe de Cerf," "27. Filet de Cerf," "28. Longe de Chevreuil," "44. Espaule ou longe de sanglier," "46. Faon de biche," "47. Faon de chevreuil," and two versions of "Filet de chevreuil" (nos. 48 and 48 bis). Unlike today, shoulder was at the time routinely more prized than the hindquarter, except perhaps for pork (which usually referred to ham).

21. On this point, Menon's *Science du maître d'hôtel cuisinier* differs somewhat, since it suggests wild young hare, wild young rabbit, and "Lièvre mariné à la poivrade" as its three small furred game roasts.

CHAPTER 3

1. Sauces: For example, in *Le Cuisinier françois,* the "Membre de mouton à la Cardinale": "brown with lard & cook in broth well seasoned with bouquet of herbs, mushrooms, truffles, or mixed assorted well browned meat trimmings, & make sure the sauce is well thickened" (p. 31, no. 2). Or the "Jarrets de veau à l'épigramme": "reduce your sauce until tasty: add mushrooms if you have them, & serve" (p. 32, no. 3).

Ragoûts: For instance, "Langue de mouton en ragoust": "simmer in good broth, add together a little browned onion, mushrooms, truffles, and parsley, season well with a few drops of verjuice & vinegar" (pp. 38–39, no. 19). Or the "Queue de mouton en ragoust": "place in a heavy pot with a well-prepared broth, season well with mushrooms, capers, beef shoulder, & cover & let cook until well done" (p. 39, no. 20).

Garnishes: See the "Pièce de bœuf à l'Angloise ou Chalonnoise": "Garnish to taste, with capers or turnips or both, or parsley or even marinade" (pp. 36–37, no. 14).

Among the 86 *Cuisinier françois* meat-day entrées, there is only one instance of a vegetable ingredient mentioned in the name, in the "Poulet d'Inde à la framboise farcy" (p. 31, no. 1); out of the 102 comparable entrées from Pierre de Lune's *Nouveau Cuisinier,* there is just one, "Espaule de Veau aux champignons" (p. 192, no. 15); likewise, out of the 73 such dishes in *L'Art de bien traiter,* there is only one, "Eschignée aux pois" (p. 165). The vegetable ingredient seems to have been important only in this last, rather popular, recipe.

2. Recipe titles: "Langue de bœuf en persillade" (p. 38), "Culotte de bœuf à la braise aux oignons de Hollande" (p. 45), "Aloyau garni de légumes" (p. 50), "Gigot aux légumes glacés" (p. 54), "Gigot de Mouton à la persillade" (p. 55), "Gigot au Chou-fleurs" (p. 58), "Gigot aux Chou-fleurs glacés de Parmesan" (p. 58), "Gigot aux cornichons" (p. 59), "Carré de mouton en terrine à l'Angloise, aux lentilles" (p. 63), "Carré de mouton au persil" (p. 63), "Carré & Gigot de mouton aux concombres" (p. 64), "Cotelettes de mouton à la purée de navets" (p. 68), etc., as well as "Cailles au laurier" (p. 223), "Caille aux choux" (p. 223), "Lapereaux aux fines herbes" (p. 233), "Lapereaux roulés aux pistaches" (p. 235), "Lapin au coulis de lentilles" (p. 230), and "Lapins aux petits pois" (p. 232).

Quantity in the dish: The "Culotte à la braise aux oignons de Hollande" contains" about 30 Dutch onions or, if unavailable, . . . large red onions"; the "Gigot aux légumes glacés" calls for "half a cabbage, a dozen roots [carrots] that have been pared, six large onions, three bunches of celery, six turnips"; the "Carré de Mouton en terrine à l'Angloise," with lentils, takes "a liter's worth of lentils à la Reine"; the "Poulets aux petits pois" (p. 168) also require "a liter's worth of peas."

3. Pierre de Lune, *Le Nouveau Cuisinier,* pp. 47, 51, 56, 61–63, 65, 67, 71.

4. François Marin, *Les Dons de Comus* (Paris: Prault fils, 1739), pp. 118–120.

5. "Young green peas with lard": Pierre de Lune, *Le Nouveau Cuisinier* (1660), p. 67; "Pigeon with peas": Menon, *La Cuisinière bourgeoise* (1774), p. 209.

6. Herbs: "Salade de Chicorée" (p. 158), "Persil de Macédoine" (p. 158), "de Sellery" (p. 159), "Chicorée sauvage verte" (p. 159), "Chicorée sauvage blanche" (p. 160), "Salade de petites laictues, & autres" (p. 163), "Laictues pommées & autres" (p. 163), and "De Cresson" (p. 164). Root vegetables: "De Sellery cuit, & la racine" (p. 159), "De Racines de Macédoine" (p. 159), "Salade de betteraves" (p. 163), and "De Response" (p. 164). Fruits: "De Grenades," "Salade d'olives," "De pistaches" (p. 161), "Salade d'amandes," "Salade de citrons," "Salade d'écorce de citrons confits," "Salade de citrons doux, oranges & bigarades" (p. 162), and "Salade de concombres pour l'Hyver" (p. 163). Flowers: "Salade de capres" and "Capres au sucre" (p. 161), "De Brocolis" (p. 164), and "Salade de violettes" (p. 164). Anchovies: "Salade d'anchois" and "Autre salade d'anchois" (p. 160).

7. "De Chicorée cuite" (p. 58), "De Sellery cuit, & la racine" (p. 159), "De Macedoine cuit" (p. 159), and beet salad (p. 163).

8. *Le Cuisinier méthodique,* for example, suggests this. But we may legitimately question whether the French were widely accustomed to these sugared seasonings. In *Journal de voyage en Italie* (repr. Paris: Pierre Michel, 1974),

Michel de Montaigne does mention a sugared lettuce he ate in Italy around 1580; but Albert Jouvin de Rochefort in 1675 (*Le Voyageur d'Europe . . .*) found it incongruous and comical that the Irish sprinkled theirs with sugar.

9. Examples of each mode of preparation follow. Scrambled eggs: "œufs brouillés aux mousserons" (*Les Dons de Comus,* p. 198). Fried eggs: "Les œufs au plat, autrement dit, au miroir" (*La Cuisinière bourgeoise,* p. 315). With sauces: "Petits œufs et rognons à l'huile," "Petits œufs et rognons sauce verte," and "Petits œufs et rognons de coq en ragoût" (*Les Dons de Comus,* p. 117). With cooking juices: "œufs à la Huguenotte," cooked in mutton or beef juice (*Le Cuisinier françois,* p. 117, no. 83; and *L'Art de bien traiter,* p. 193). With meat: "Omelette de jambon de Mayence," "Omelette au foye de lapin, ou de levrault," and "Omelette de roignons cuits" (*Le Nouveau Cuisinier,* pp. 52, 66, 67). With fish: *Le Cuisinier royal et bourgeois* of 1691 mentions "œufs aux anchois" without a recipe and without saying whether it was suited for meat days as well as meatless ones; Pierre de Lune gives the recipe among fifty-six "meatless egg entrées or entremets" (pp. 290–308). *La Cuisinière bourgeoise* gives a herring omelet recipe, considered an entremets, "Omelette d'harengs sorés" (p. 317). With vegetables: "Omelette aux pointes d'asperges," "œufs aux champignons," and "œufs aux concombres" are listed as "hot entremets" in *Les Dons de Comus* (pp. 123, 197). With fruit: "œufs à l'orange" in Massialot's *Cuisinier royal et bourgeois* (p. 322) could be served for meat as well as meatless days and could thus be an entremets. Salt or sugar: "œufs à la Portugaise," "œufs mignons," "œufs filez," "œufs à la Varenne," "œufs à la neige" (*Le Cuisinier françois,* pp. 114–116, nos. 78–82); and "œufs ambrés" (*L'Art de bien traiter,* p. 194). For use as a main ingredient, see especially "Nulles," which were prepared with egg yolks, sugar, and macaroons and tinted either green with Swiss chard juice or red with gooseberry juice (*Le Nouveau Cuisinier,* p. 60).

10. *Le Cuisinier françois* has 11 egg recipes for meat days, compared to 29 for meatless ones; and *Le Nouveau Cuisinier* of Pierre de Lune lists only 6 egg recipes for meat days but 60 for meatless days.

11. "These egg dishes are served in many ways, with white or green sauce, coulis, caper and anchovy sauce, verjuice, sauce Robert, sauce ravigote; with ragoûts of mushrooms, veal sweetbreads, truffles, asparagus, cardoons, celery, lettuce, or chicory, for both meat and meatless days" (*La Cuisinière bourgeoise,* pp. 312–323).

12. These cuts were also used in hors d'oeuvres and relevés.—*Trans.*

13. From *Le Cuisinier françois:* "Pasté de jambon" (p. 91, no. 5); "Jambon en ragoust" (p. 96, no. 19); "Jambon en tranche" (p. 97, no. 21); "Omelette au jambon" (p. 113, no. 75); and "Méthode pour faire les jambons de Mayence" (p. 123). *Le Nouveau Cuisinier:* "Pan de porc" (p. 58); "Ragoust de tranches de jambon en pasté" (p. 74); "Ragoust de tranches de jambon à l'hypocras" (p. 75). From *L'Art de bien traiter:* three "Potage d'abattis d'agneau" (pp. 10, 93, and 95) and one

"Potage de menus d'agneaux" (p. 153). *La Cuisinière bourgeoise:* "Petits jambons nouveaux à la broche servis chauds ou froids" (p. 142), "Jambons cuits servis froids" (p. 143), "Jambon au cingarat" (p. 149), and "Roties au jambon" (p. 345).

14. The five suckling pig recipes are "Cochon de lait par quartiers au Père Douillet" (p. 150), "Cochon de lait en galentine" (p. 151), "Cochon de lait à la Lyonnoise" (p. 151), "Cochon de lait en pâté froid" (p. 152), and "Fromage de Cochon" (p. 152). As to the rest, there are "Rôties de toutes sortes de viandes," fried to "a nice color" (p. 348); and 14 recipes for cold meats, which will be discussed later.

15. For soups, *Le Cuisinier françois* offers "Potage d'abattis d'agneaux" (p. 15, no. 30), "Potage de teste de veau fritte" (p. 19, no. 43), "Potage de teste de veau desossée farcie" (p. 25, no. 8), and "Potage de teste d'agneaux désossées farcies" (p. 25, no. 9); Pierre de Lune's *Nouveau Cuisinier* has two versions of "Potage de ris de veau" (pp. 24 and 182), "Potage de teste de veau à deux fasses" (p. 146), "Potage de teste d'agneau" (p. 149), "Potage de pieds et fraise de veau" (p. 155), "Potage d'abatis d'oyson" (p. 184), "Potage de crestes ou bisque plate" (p. 205), and "Potage de testes d'agneau farcies" (p. 212).

16. "Ris de Veau à la Pluche verte" (p. 109), "Ris de Veau à la Lyonnoise" (p. 110), "Ris de Veau aux fines herbes" (p. 111), "Ris de Veau en Caisses" (p. 111), "Ris de Veau en Hatelet" (p. 112), and "Ris de Veau frits" (p. 113).

17. Feathered game: The 11 entrées of feathered game from *Le Cuisinier françois* include 5 hot pasties and 6 dishes described as entrées. The "Pasté de perdrix" (p. 135) is only to be eaten hot—while the other four can be hot or cold and are counted both among the entrées and among the entremets. They include "Pasté d'alouette" (p. 136, no. 16), "Pasté de cailles" (p. 137, no. 18), "Pasté de beccasses" (p. 137, no. 19), and "Pasté de merles" (p. 138, no. 20). The 6 entrée dishes are "Saucisses de blanc de perdrix" (p. 34), "Perdrix en ragoût" (p. 37), "Sarselles en ragoust" (p. 44), "Alouettes en ragoust" (p. 45), "Perdrix à l'estoffade" (p. 51), and "Allebrans en ragoust" (p. 52). The 10 entremets include the 4 cold pasties just mentioned plus the 6 following dishes, described as entremets: "Mauviettes" fricasseed and simmered (p. 97), "Alouettes en ragoust" (p. 98), "Achis de perdrix" (p. 101), "Ortolans en ragoust" (p. 105), "Grives," and "Perdreaux" fricasseed and simmered in a sauce (p. 122).

The 13 entrées of feathered game in *Le Nouveau Cuisinier* include 3 pasties to be eaten hot, 3 pies with pan juices added just before serving, and 7 dishes explicitly labeled as entrées. The 3 pasties are "Pasté de cailles" (p. 241), "Pasté d'alouettes" (p. 242), and "Pasté de bécasses" (p. 248). The 3 pies are "Tourte d'alouettes," served with a sauce of melted lard, fried flour, capers, and verjuice or lemon juice (p. 253); "Tourte de cailles" (p. 253); and "Tourte de ramiers" (p. 259). The 7 dishes identified as entrées are "Hachis de blanc de perdrix" (p. 35), "Perdrix en ragoust" (p. 39), "Ragoust d'alouettes à l'Angloise" (p. 42), "Grives en ragoust" (p. 192), "Perdrix à la daube" (p. 217), "Capilotade de perdrix" (p.

220), and "Marinade de perdrix" (p. 222). The entremets include 6 cold pasties and 3 dishes described as entremets. The pasties are "Pasté de perdrix" (p. 235), "Pasté de perdrix desossées" (p. 235), "Pasté d'ostarde" (p. 237), "Pasté de faisans" (p. 238), "Pasté de sarcelles" (p. 239), and "Pastez de sarcelles desossez" (p. 239). The entremets are "Ragoust de beccasines [sic]" (p. 72), "Ragoust de cailles" (p. 73), and "Roties de beccasses" (p. 73). Here again, ragoûts appear equally as entrées and entremets.

L'Art de bien traiter offers nearly any feathered game as roast. It does suggest 5 entrées of scoter (roasted, as ragoût, and as a daube), but they have not been tallied because they are meatless-day entrées. For entremets of feathered game, the book presents only a "Pasté de perdris froid" (p. 173, no. 2).

In La Cuisinière bourgeoise, the 2 entremets of feathered game are a pheasant pasty to eat cold (p. 217) and some game pasties (p. 358).

Domesticated animals: In addition to 4 dishes of foie gras (pp. 107–108, nos. 58–60), the 7 entremets from Le Cuisinier françois include a dish of "Poulets marinez," floured, fried, and simmered in their marinade (p. 97, no. 23) and 2 dishes of "Pigeonneaux" in ragoût, both versions floured, sautéed, and then simmered in broth with either capers, mushrooms, sweetbreads, etc. (p. 107), or mushrooms and truffles (p. 122). However, entrées in the same book include "Poulets marinez," which are also fried and simmered in their marinade (pp. 35–36, no. 12), and some "Pigeonneaux en ragoust" (p. 33, no. 6), again sautéed, then placed in a pot with broth and garnished with veal sweetbreads. Why serve these as entrées and those as entremets?

In Le Nouveau Cuisinier, domestic poultry accounts for 15 entremets, 8 of which consist of organ meats: "Foyes gras en ragoust" (p. 49), "Ragoust de béatilles" (p. 50), "Foyes gras à la broche" (p. 58), "Foye gras frits" (p. 66), "Rosties de foyes gras" (p. 74), "Ragoust de grosses crestes de cocq farcies" (p. 75), "Ragoust de roignons de cocq au jus de mouton" (p. 75), and "Boudins de foye gras et de chapon" (p. 76). There are 5 cold pasties: "Pasté de poullet d'Inde" (p. 235), "Pasté d'oye ou d'oyson" (p. 236), "Pasté de canards" (p. 236), "Pasté de poullet d'Inde desossez" (p. 236), and "Pasté de canards désossez" (p. 239). The last 2 entremets are "Saucisses de blanc de chapon" (p. 49) and "Ragoust de petits pigeonneaux" (p. 73). Note that the entrées include "Oysons en ragoust" (p. 163) and "Canards en ragoust" (p. 221).

Domestic poultry entremets in L'Art de bien traiter are also 4 organ-meat dishes: "Foyes gras frits," "en ragoust," or "picqués, rostis" (p. 18, no. 117), and "Foyes gras frits" (p. 193, no. 6); 2 "Gelées" made with capon (p. 17, no. 91 and p. 131, no. 4) of uncertain status; and some "Petits oisons à la daube" (p. 18, no. 110). Notice that a dish of "Petits oisons à la daube servis chauds" (p. 14, no. 19) and another of "Oison à la daube servis à chauds" (p. 168, no. 10) constitute entrées.

The poultry entremets in La Cuisinière bourgeoise include "Dindon en galentine" (p. 173) and a "Dindon en balon" (p. 174) that is served cold, although it would be an entrée when served hot; some "Vieux dindons" in cold daube (p. 175), "Pattes de dindons" (p. 181), "Canard en daube" (p. 196), "Oie à la daube" (p. 200), and "Pasté de poularde, chapon, etc, à manger froid" (p. 358); and lastly, "Foies gras des poulardes, chapon, dindons, et gros poulets cuits à la broche," "cuits en caisses" and "en papillote" (pp. 182–183), and a "Ragoût de foies gras" (p. 376).

Six furred game dishes are qualified as entrées in *Le Cuisinier françois:* "Civet de lièvre" (p. 40), "Longe de chevreuil en ragoust" (p. 49), 2 dishes of "Lapereaux en ragoust" (p. 50), "Espaule de sanglier en ragoust" (p. 54), and "Cuisseau de chevreuil" (p. 55) in ragoût or in sauce. Additionally, there is a hot version of "Pasté de lapereaux" to eat hot or cold (p. 136, no. 14). The 11 furred game entremets include 8 organ-meat preparations—"Menus droits de cerf" (p. 90, no. 2), 2 "Foye de chevreuil" (p. 94, nos. 13 and 14), "Tétine de chevreuil" (p. 94, no. 15), "Hure de sanglier" (p. 119, no. 92), "Tranche de hure," and 2 versions of "Tranche de hure en ragoust" (p. 120, no. 94)—as well as 3 pasties to be eaten cold: 2 versions of "Pasté de venaison" (p. 91 and p. 132) and the cold version of "Pasté de Lapereaux" already mentioned.

The 10 furred game entrées in *Le Nouveau Cuisinier* include a pie and 4 pasties to eat hot along with 5 dishes described as entrées. The latter are "Levraut à la Suisse" (p. 37), "Lapereaux à la sauce blanche" (p. 161), "Lapereaux à la sauce brune" (p. 163), "Lapereaux ou lapins en casserolle" (p. 189), and "Civé de lièvre" (p. 191). The former are "Tourte de Lapereaux" served with sauce and orange juice (p. 256), "Pasté de levreau à l'Angloise" (p. 243), "Pasté de lièvre" (p. 243), "Pasté de levreau en paste brisée" (p. 244), and "Pasté de lapins" (p. 248). The 11 entremets are 7 pasties to be eaten cold and 4 organ-meat dishes. They are "Pasté de cerf" (p. 232), "Pasté de chevreuil" (p. 233), "Pasté de sanglier" (p. 233), "Pasté de lièvre ou levrau" (p. 234), "Pasté de lièvre ou levrau desossé" (p. 234), "Pasté de lapins" (p. 235), "Pasté de hure de sanglier" (p. 238), "Omelette de foye de lapin ou de levraut" (p. 66), "Hure de sanglier par tranches" (p. 69), "Menus droits de cerf" (p. 70), and "Ragoust de tranches de hures de sanglier" (p. 70).

Furred game, in *L'Art de bien traiter,* produces no entrées, but 11 roasts and 2 entremets—2 versions of "Hure de sanglier" (pp. 18 and 189).

The entremets of furred game in *La Cuisinière bourgeoise* are "Pâté de lièvre à la bourgeoise" served cold (p. 226), "Filets de lapereaux aux concombres" (p. 231), "Lapereau en galentine" served cold (p. 234), "Hure de sanglier" served as a cold entremets (p. 238), boar's trotters à la Sainte-Menehould (p. 238), boar quarters as a cold pasty (p. 238), and cold pasties of fillets of hare (p. 358).

18. *Le Cuisinier françois,* respectively pp. 131–144 and 250–267.

19. *Le Nouveau Cuisinier,* respectively pp. 231–239, 240–251, 251–261, 261–269, 270–277.

20. This concept was to have been developed in part three.—*Trans.*

21. *Le Cuisinier royal et bourgeois*, p. 344.

22. *La Cuisinière bourgeoise*, pp. 226–227.

23. The entremets chapter lists "Pasté de jambon" (p. 91, no. 5), whose recipe concludes: "When cold, serve sliced." In the chapter on entrées, for example, "Pasté de chapon desossé," "Pasté de gaudiveau," "Pasté d'assiette," "Pasté à la marotte," and "Pasté à l'Angloise" (pp. 62–64) are all hot.

24. *Le Cuisinier françois*, p. 133.

25. Likewise for the "Pasté de poulet d'Inde, autre façon" (p. 134): "Serve hot with your choice of sauce"; and the "Pasté de gaudiveau": "When done, serve with sauce made of verjuice, egg yolks, & nutmeg"; or the "Pasté à la marote": "Next, prepare your pasty leaving a steam vent on top; take out of the oven after three hours, fill with strong broth, return to oven, & serve when quite done."

26. As an entrée, "Petits oisons à la daube servis chauds" (p. 14), or "Oisons à la daube servis chauds" (p. 168); as an entremets, a large platter of "Poictrine de veau avec quatre petits oisons à la daube servis à froid."

27. "Membre de mouton à la daube" (p. 39, no. 21), "Poulet d'Inde à la daube" (p. 39, no. 22), "Pièce de bœuf à la daube" (p. 41, no. 27), and "Oye à la daube" (p. 43, no. 33).

28. "Cochon à la daube" (p. 43, no. 32). The author does not say that this cold daube's function is different from that of a hot version. But we already know that, one idea leading to another, he slips entrées into the chapter on roasts. Here, he has probably slipped an entremets into the chapter on entrées.

29. Examples of those heated in a sauce are the "Gigot de veau piqué à la daube," which states, "When done, make a sauce with the pan juices, a little fried flour, capers, lemon slices, and mushroom juices, and simmer in the sauce; an anchovy is a good addition" (p. 160, no. 5); and the "Daube de veau hachée & piquée," whose recipe concludes, "When done, skim the fat from the sauce, and add Dijon mustard, orange juice & white pepper." For room temperature and plain: See the "Oysons à la daube" recipe, which states, "Cook in a pot with broth and white wine, let cool partly in the broth and serve on a napkin with lemon slices" (p. 166, no. 20). The same probably applies to "Perdrix à la daube" (pp. 217–218), since the instructions are to "Leave them in their broth until ready to serve on a napkin garnished with lemon and pomegranate slices."

30. Typical examples of this type of dish include "Casi de veau à la daube" (p. 116) and "Canard à la daube" (p. 196) under "Entremets froid"; and "Oie à la daube" along with probably older tom turkeys in cold daube and aspic served on a napkin under "Gros Entremets froids" (p. 175).

31. In *La Cuisinière bourgeoise* (p. 116), "Casi à l'étouffade" is described as "Entrée ou Entremets froids" and the recipe specifies, "To serve cold, do not add coulis, and reduce the sauce thoroughly until it gels." For the hares: "When your rabbits are done, if you want to serve them as an entrée, wipe off the fat while they are quite hot, and serve with a sauce à l'Espagnole; they are usually served

as cold entremets; in this case let them cool in their cooking juices as explained for the suckling pig," ibid., pp. 52, 96, and 234.

32. Dessert jellies: See *L'Art de bien traiter* under "Gelée de pomme" (p. 386), "Gelée de groseilles et de cerises" (p. 389), and "Gelée de verjus" (p. 391). To avoid ambiguities, *La Cuisinière bourgeoise* prefers names such as "Confiture de gelée de groseilles" (p. 417), "Confiture de gelée de pommes" (p. 418), "Confiture de gelée de groseilles à la Bourgeoise," and "Confiture de gelée de muscat & verjus" (p. 420). *Le Cuisinier françois:* all jellies for meat and meatless-day meals in this work are entremets—"Gellée" (p. 98, no. 26), "Gellée de corne de Cerf" (p. 99, no. 26 *[sic]*), "Gelée verte" (p. 100, no. 27), "Gelée rouge" (p. 100, no. 28), "Gelée jaune" (p. 100, no. 29), "Gelée violette" (p. 100, no. 30), "Gelée bleuë" (p. 100, no. 31), "Blanc manger" (p. 100, no. 32; p. 237, no. 17; and p. 300), which are also made from jellies; and "Gelée de poisson" (p. 237, no. 16).

33. In this chapter Pierre de Lune suggests (p. 344) "Gellée de citron," "Gellée de grenade," "Gellée verte," "Gellée jaune," all based on "rapelure de [corne de] cerf."

34. Refer to the end of the recipe for "Cochon à la daube" in *Le Cuisinier françois:* "The reduced sauce remains jellied for serving cold"; and a recipe in *La Cuisinière bourgeoise* for "Casi à l'étouffade" (p. 116): "If you want to serve it cold, do not add coulis, and reduce the sauce all the way to a gel." Also served in their jelly were "Cochon de lait par quartiers au Père Douillet" (p. 150), "Oie en daube" (p. 200), and "Canard en daube" (p. 196). We could no doubt also include other dishes without the term *jelly* used in their recipes, like the one for old tom turkeys on p. 175, which states, "Sieve the broth and reduce it to a glaze, let it cool, spread it over the turkey."

35. Examples: "Crême à l'Angloise," "Crême de Strasbourg," "Crême en rocher," "Crême noire," "Crême aux amandes," "Crême au cerfeuil," "Crême aux pistaches," "Crême au thé," "Crême à l'Allemande," "Crême à la Bourguignone," "Crême à la Polonoise," "Crême à la Sultane," "Crême ardoisée," "Crême au caffé," "Crême au lait de poule," "Crême brûlée," "Crême croquante," "Crême douce," "Crême fouettée," "Crême frite," "Crême jaspée," "Crême pâtisserie," "Crême souflée et sans sucre," "Crême vierge blanche," "Crême vierge jaune," "Crême de ris," "Crême au chocolat," "Crême d'épinars," "Crême au cellery," "Crême à l'estragon," "Crême au persil," "Crême au blanc de poulet," "Crême aux vermicelles," "Rissoles de crême," "Tourte de crême," "Tartelette de crême à la glace," etc.

36. *Le Cuisinier françois:* These include meatless-day "Baignets" (p. 235), "Baignets de moëlle," "Baignets de pommes," two "Baignets d'artichaux" (all three on p. 102), "Foye gras frit en baignets," "Baignets de pommes," and "Baignets de grenouilles." *La Cuisinière bourgeoise:* "Beignets de crême," "Beignets soufflés, ou pets, & petits choux," "Beignets de brioche," "Beignets de pommes et de pêches," "Beignets d'oranges," "Beignets de Blanc-manger,"

"Beignets de pain à chanter," "Beignets de feuilles de vigne," "Beignets mignons," "Beignets de pâte," and "Beignets à la crême."

37. *Le Cuisinier françois,* p. 104, no. 45.

38. Eight ramekins from *Le Cuisinier françois,* all as entremets, meatless and Lenten occasions included: "Ramequin de roignon," "Ramequin de chair," "Ramequin de fromage," "Ramequin de suye de cheminée," "Ramequin d'oygnon," "Ramequin d'aulx" (all on pp. 104 and 105), and twice, "Ramequins de toutes sortes" (pp. 231 and 301). For meat days, *Le Nouveau Cuisinier* offers "Roties de roignon de veau cuite," "Rosties de Becasse," and "Rosties de foyes gras" as entremets; for meatless days, "Rosties à l'hypocras," "Rosties au beurre," "Rosties aux pommes," and "Rosties au fromage de Milan" as entrées.

39. *Le Cuisinier royal et bourgeois:* "Rôties au jambon," two kinds of "Rôties au lard," "Rôties aux anchois," "Rôties de rognons de veau," "Rôties à la Minime," "Rôties de toutes sortes de viandes," and even "Rôties aux épinards," "Rôties aux haricots verts," and "Rôties aux concombres" (pp. 444–445, 448–449).

40. Quoting from *La Cuisinière bourgeoise* (p. 300 of the 1774 edition): "Tender purple artichokes as well as small green ones are eaten with pepper sauce: place them on a plate with some ice; they accompany the soup as a little hors d'oeuvre." But it is in the entremets chapter (p. III, no. 69) that La Varenne's 1651 *Le Cuisinier françois* places the following instruction: "Artichokes with pepper sauce. Cut your artichokes in quarters, remove the chokes, blanch in fresh water and when ready to serve, place on a plate with pepper and salt."

CHAPTER 4

1. The *Cuisinier françois* chapter titled "Table de ce qui se peut trouver dans les jardins, dont on se peut ayder au besoin: & servir aux Entrées & Entre-mets des jours maigres, & autres de charnage, ou de Caresme" presents meatless-day recipes exclusively, with a *charnage* version allowing eggs and cheese. See for example the recipe for fried skirret (p. 241, no. 1). After blanching and peeling, the recipe goes on: "For *charnage,* make a fairly runny batter with eggs, a little salt, and a little flour; mix in some crumbled cheese to make it fancier, dip your skirret in it, fry and serve. For Lent, dilute your flour with a little milk or verjuice and more salt: moisten your skirret in this preparation and fry it in clarified butter to make it tastier." Another example is "Bouillie de fleur de bled" (p. 242, no. 2): "Mix it with a little milk and some salt, or add egg yolks, a little butter and some sugar if not for Lent; let it cook." None of these recipes contains meat, lard, or any other animal fat except butter, which had become permissible during Lent.

2. The cooking water for split peas was called *purée* and has served as broth for meatless dishes since the Middle Ages. In the seventeenth century it was ob-

tained by cooking the peas until they became a purée, which was then sieved to keep the liquid and solid particles while removing the skins (*Le Cuisinier françois,* p. 279).

3. The vegetables included dishes of peas, purée, beets, turnips, carrots, parsnip, Jerusalem artichokes, salsify, skirret, Swiss chard, lentils, spinach, and fricasseed potatoes.

4. Spinach: In *Le Cuisinier françois,* the spinach pie "Tourte d'espinars" is served on meatless days and during Lent (pp. 263 and 300), and the spinach "Espinars" only during Lent (p. 296, no. 2) and especially on Good Friday (p. 307). *Le Nouveau Cuisinier* gives a recipe for a spinach pie that can be served both as a meat-day and as a meatless entremets, but there are also 4 other recipes reserved for Good Friday. *L'Art de bien traiter* has 4 spinach recipes, all for meatless meals.

Brassicas: "Potage de choux au lait" (p. 155, no. 16), "Potage de choux au pain frit" (p. 155, no. 17 and p. 283, no. 13), "Potage de choux à la purée" (p. 155, no. 18 and p. 284, no. 15) are all cabbage soups for meatless and Lenten meals; "Potage de Brocolis" (p. 304) and "Potage de brocolis au lait" (p. 305) are broccoli soups for Good Friday; the "Potage de choux fleurs," a cauliflower soup, appears as a meatless, Lent, and Good Friday recipe (pp. 167, 289, and 305). *Le Nouveau Cuisinier* gives 2 broccoli recipes, both for Good Friday.

Pumpkin: Seven out of 11 pumpkin recipes in *Le Cuisinier françois* are for meatless days, 2 for Lent and 2 for Good Friday. *Le Nouveau Cuisinier* does have one for meat days—a "Potage de petites citrouilles farcies à l'Espagnole," which contains more than just pumpkins—but it also gives 1 for meatless meals and 4 for Good Friday.

Celery: Celery appears only twice in *Le Cuisinier françois:* as a meatless entremets (p. 239, no. 22) and as a Lenten entremets (p. 300).

Leeks: *Le Cuisinier françois* gives a meatless recipe for leek soup, "Potage de poireaux" (p. 165, no. 38), and 2 for "Potage de poireaux à la purée" (pp. 170 and 171); it gives another for Lent (p. 290, no. 40), along with 1 for "Potage de poireaux au laict" (p. 288, no. 32); it contains no meat-day leek dishes.

Greens: *Le Cuisinier françois* has a recipe for a "Tourte d'herbes" for Good Friday, and 7 assorted recipes for soups with greens for meatless, Lenten, and Good Friday meals.

Lentils: There are 2 lentil recipes in *Le Cuisinier françois,* both for Lent: one is a soup (p. 289, no. 43) and the other an entrée (p. 295, no. 1). *Le Nouveau Cuisinier* also has 2 (pp. 315 and 360), both for Good Friday.

Carrots: While *Le Cuisinier françois* mentions carrots twice in a chapter that applies to meat as well as meatless days, it gives 1 carrot recipe for Lent and 7 for Good Friday. *Le Nouveau Cuisinier* has only 2 carrot recipes, both for Good Friday.

Turnips: The 7 *Cuisinier françois* turnip recipes are all for meatless, Lenten, or Good Friday meals.

Salsify: *Le Cuisinier françois* has 5 salsify recipes: 1 meatless (p. 244), 2 for Lent (pp. 294 and 300), and 2 for Good Friday (p. 307). *Le Nouveau Cuisinier* has 3 salsify and 3 black salsify recipes, all 6 for Good Friday.

5. *Le Cuisinier françois* gives no morel recipe for meat days, just 1 for a Lenten entremets (p. 300), and 3 for Good Friday (p. 309): "Morilles à la cresme," "Morilles en ragoust," and "Morilles farcies." It does give recipes for St. George's wild mushrooms (p. 232, no. 1): 2 for meatless days and 1 for Good Friday (p. 308); and 5 skirret recipes designed for meatless days or Lent (pp. 241, 294, and 300). In *Le Nouveau Cuisinier,* the 3 recipes are for Good Friday.

6. Pierre de Lune's 3 fava bean recipes appear in the chapter on "Entremets tant gras que maigres" (p. 68): "Febves à l'italienne," "Febves au lard," and "Febves tendres à la cresme."

7. For examples of humble vegetable dishes well suited to serving with salted meat, see *Le Cuisinier françois* for "Potage de salé au pois" (p. 15); and *Le Nouveau Cuisinier* for "Febves au lard" as well as "Faufrache à l'Espagnolle" and "Febves tendres à la cresme," which are also sautéed in a skillet with lard.

8. The 7 cabbage recipes in *Le Cuisinier françois* include 6 soups, 1 preserve, no entrée, and no entremets. Similarly, broccoli is used only for 2 Good Friday soups. *Le Cuisinier françois* mentions lettuce in the names of 2 soups, 1 soup garnish, and 1 preserve; its 4 meatless onion and 5 leek recipes are for soups.

9. For cauliflower, *Le Cuisinier françois* has 2 entremets—1 for meat days, the other meatless—and 3 soups; *Le Nouveau Cuisinier* 2 entremets and nothing else; *L'Art de bien traiter* just 1 recipe, also an entremets. *Le Cuisinier royal et bourgeois* has 2 entremets (pp. 192–193) and 1 salad; *La Cuisinière bourgeoise* considers them useful for "making entremets [meat or meatless] and garnishing meat entrées" (p. 287).

Spinach is, unusually, used for a soup in *Le Cuisinier royal et bourgeois.* But generally it is used for entremets and entrées: 3 entrées and 1 entremets in *Le Cuisinier françois;* 4 Good Friday entrées and 1 meat or meatless entremets in *Le Nouveau Cuisinier;* 2 entremets and 2 meatless entrée pies in *L'Art de bien traiter.*

Artichokes likewise produce 8 entremets, 1 preserve, and 2 entrées for Good Friday in *Le Cuisinier françois;* an isolated Good Friday soup in *Le Nouveau Cuisinier,* compared to 3 entremets (meat or meatless) and 4 entrées; and entremets only (4) in *L'Art de bien traiter.*

The 2 *Cuisinier françois* celery recipes are entremets, but celery is not mentioned in *Le Nouveau Cuisinier, L'Art de bien traiter,* or *Le Cuisinier royal; La Cuisinière bourgeoise* uses it for salad and occasionally as a meat garnish (p. 293).

The 4 chard and cardoon recipes in *Le Cuisinier françois* include 3 entremets (1 for meat days, 2 for Lent) and 1 Good Friday entrée; there are 3 soups and 2 entremets in *Le Nouveau Cuisinier,* 3 entremets and 1 soup in *L'Art de bien traiter.*

Mushrooms, often used from the seventeenth century onward, provided Good Friday soups, entremets, and entrées: 3 meatless or Lenten soups in *Le*

Cuisinier françois as well as 4 meat-day and 3 Lenten entremets, and 3 Good Friday entrées. In *Le Nouveau Cuisinier,* we find 4 soups including 1 for meat days, 6 entremets potentially for meat days, and 9 Good Friday entrées; and only 4 recipes, all entremets, in *L'Art de bien traiter.*

10. Four skirret recipes out of 5 in *Le Cuisinier françois* are entrées, all 3 in *Le Nouveau Cuisinier.*

11. The other books do not lend themselves to such statistics: *Le Nouveau Cuisinier* because most of its meatless egg recipes (numbering 56) are found in an ambiguous "Traité particulier d'œufs pour les entrées et les entremets des jours maigres" (pp. 290–308) and because the 9 entrée egg recipes for Good Friday are far fewer; *Le Cuisinier royal* and *La Cuisinière bourgeoise* because they do not specify whether their dishes are for meatless or nonfasting meals nearly as systematically.

12. *La Cuisinière bourgeoise* (1774); *L'Art de bien traiter* (1674), p. 276.

13. Crayfish were used a great deal in elegant cuisine and were often served as entremets from that time on. See *Le Cuisinier françois* with recipes for "Escrevisses en ragoust" and "Escrevisses fricassées" as Lent entremets (p. 300). See the same work for frog and turtle entremets as well: "Grenouilles en ragoust" (p. 300) and "Baignets de grenouilles" (p. 302), turtles as entremets for meat days (p. 113) and for Lent (p. 300); as well as "Tortuës en ragoust" as a meatless entremets (p. 239). Also see *L'Art de bien traiter,* with its "Escrevisses au naturel" (p. 283); *La Cuisinière bourgeoise,* which shows crayfish in court bouillon served on a napkin (p. 274), and "Des écrevisses de mer, des homars & des crabes," all boiled in salt water and served cold on a napkin (p. 263); and *Le Nouveau Cuisinier*'s "Gellée de Garnulles pour les malades."

14. Anchovies were used mostly for sauces and salads. But they were also served as entremets, like the anchovies soaked in water and fried in dough in *La Cuisinière bourgeoise* (p. 260).

15. Monkfish: *Le Cuisinier françois* has a dish of "Lottes frittes" (p. 300) and four of monkfish liver: "Foye de lotte" (p. 236 and p. 301), "Foye de lotte autre façon" (p. 237), and "Foye de lotte fritte *[sic]*" (p. 301). Carp: In the same work, see also "Laittances de carpes frittes" (p. 236), "Laittances en ragoust" (p. 236, no. 14 and p. 300) and probably "Laittances frittes" and "Nulle de laittances" (p. 300), while *L'Art de bien traiter* has "Laictances de carpes en ragoust" (p. 279) and probably "Laictances frites" (p. 280). Examples of delicacies include the oven-baked rissoles (p. 301) and the fried "Petites rissoles" (p. 302) in *Le Cuisinier françois.* Eel: The same work also suggests a "Servelast d'anguille" as an entremets for meatless days (p. 235) as well as for Lent (p. 300). Anchovies: See "Rôties d'anchois" (p. 261) and the "Rôties aux anchois" variation in *La Cuisinière bourgeoise* (p. 346). Salmon: See the meatless entremets chapter "Pasté de saulmon frais" (article VII) and article VIII, in *L'Art de bien traiter,* p. 283.

16. *Le Cuisinier françois* gives recipes for "Gelée de poisson" (p. 237) and

"Gelée de toutes sortes de poissons" (p. 300); "Jambon de poisson" (p. 239, no. 24); and a "Servelast" recipe with eels (pp. 192, 235, 293, and 300). *L'Art de bien traiter* also has a recipe for "Gelée de poisson" at the beginning of its chapter on meatless entremets (pp. 278–279), its own very detailed recipe for "Jambon de poisson" (pp. 281–282), and one for "Servelats" on p. 282. *Le Nouveau Cuisinier* has a recipe for "Jambon de poisson" on p. 130 and one for "Servelats de poisson" with fish (p. 131).

17. "Sturgeon" (p. 244): "Marinate it two or three hours . . . until ready, then cook it on the spit & and serve with any good meatless sauce." "Eel" (p. 268): "large ones can be cooked on the spit, wrapped in well-buttered paper, and served with the same seasonings as when they are grilled," that is, "with a white sauce, capers and anchovies, or other sauces."

18. *La Cuisinière bourgeoise* lists twenty-one recipes for grilled fish, all served as entrées, with a sauce or a ragoût.

19. For example: "Morue fraîche en Dauphin au ragoût de laitances de carpes & pointes d'asperges" (p. 247); or "This [tuna] is a large ocean fish shipped already marinated from Provence that can also be served as an entrée: arrange it on the serving dish with good butter, parsley, and chopped chives; cover it with bread crumbs, and toast it until golden in the oven or under a pie pan lid" (ibid.).

20. Ibid., p. 269.

21. Poached: "Turbot ou Barbue court-bouillonés" (p. 241), "Saumon frais au court-bouillon" (p. 243), "Alose court-bouillonée" (p. 246), "Bar dans un court-bouillon au vin blanc et au beurre" (p. 261), "Brochet au court-bouillon" (p. 267), and "Carpe au bleu" (p. 269). Fried: "Limande, sole, carlet et plie frits" (p. 246), "Éperlans frits" (p. 257), "Merlans frits" (p. 261), "Lote ou barbote frite" (p. 272), "Brème frite" (p. 275), and probably "Goujons frits" (p. 275).

22. Ibid., pp. 249, 255, 256, 261 and 386, 260, 277.

23. Considered as entrées are dabs, sole, plaice, and flounder in white court bouillon served in sauce, shad cooked and served the same way (p. 246), red gurnard (or sea robin, p. 259) and freshwater cod or catfish (p. 272).

24. *La Cuisinière bourgeoise*, p. 243.

25. Ibid., p. 170.

26. Ibid., p. 169.

27. Ibid., p. 255–256.

28. Ibid., p. 272.

29. Ibid., p. 252.

30. Very few fish cooked *au bleu* are found in the books consulted, but they yield the highest proportion of meatless roasts, with no variation from the mid-seventeenth century to the mid-eighteenth. *Le Cuisinier françois* has recipes for "Brochet au bleu" (p. 225, no. 20), and for "Carpe au bleu" (p. 227, no. 27); *Le Nouveau Cuisinier* for "Brochet au court bouillon ou au bleu" (p. 136); *L'Art de bien traiter* for "Brochet au bleu, ou au court boüillon" (p. 202) and "Carpe au

bleau ou au sel" (p. 248); *Le Cuisinier royal et bourgeois,* for "Brochet au Court-boüillon, ou au Bleu"—freely borrowed from Pierre de Lune (p. 164)—and for "Carpe au Court-boüillon" (p. 178). This is the only instance where the pike and the carp in court bouillon are served "à sec, pour entremets." Note that *La Cuisinière bourgeoise* (1777 edition) has a recipe for carp *au bleu,* with its scales, served as roast (p. 269); and that the recipe ends with these words: "All manner of fish fried and cooked in court bouillon are served as meatless roasts."

Fish in court bouillon dishes were more numerous and also frequently served during the second course: nearly half the time in *Le Cuisinier françois* and every time in the listings of Massialot's *Cuisinier royal et bourgeois.* When served as entrées they came with a sauce, as in *Le Cuisinier françois,* "Vilain au court bouillon" (p. 186, no. 23), "Barbeaux au court bouillon" (p. 187, no. 31), and "L'Aloze au court bouillon" (p. 191, no. 44). But for the second course, they were generally served plain, for example in the same work's "Saumon au court bouillon" and "Bescard au court bouillon" (pp. 221–222, nos. 5, 6, 8, and 9) and more explicitly the "Esturgeon au court bouillon" (p. 221, no. 6), whose recipe states, "once cooked, place them on top of two or three folded napkins, sprinkle with parsley, and serve."

The figure given for fried meatless roasts in *L'Art de bien traiter* cannot be compared with other figures because the author did not include these dishes in his chapter on second-course fish dishes, but in a chapter on fried recipes that were not necessarily served for the second course.

Among second-course fishes, the *rostis* and *à la broche* appear most often in *Le Cuisinier françois:* "Alloze rostie" three different ways (p. 218, no. 48 and p. 223, no. 17), "Huistres rosties" (p. 219, no. 55), "Plies rosties en ragoust" (p. 219, no. 58), "Vives rosties sur le gril" (p. 220, no. 3), "Bresme rostie" (p. 224, nos. 19 and 19 bis and p. 299, no. 30), and "Dorade rostie" (p. 299, no. 38). The book gives recipes for only six of these dishes, and in each, the fish is covered with sauce after roasting. *Le Nouveau Cuisinier* gives a recipe for "Brochet lardé d'anguille, cuit à la broche" (p. 140) served in the second course with a sauce of anchovies, capers, and oysters; there is also an entrée of "Macreuse à la broche" with a sauce made from its liver and bitter orange juice (p. 127). Other second-course recipes from that book are "Alose rostie" (p. 137)—actually grilled and served with sauce or ragoût—and an entrée of "Bremmes rosties" (p. 125), both also served with sauce. Furthermore, a reading of the recipes themselves, rather than merely the titles, reveals that both the "Brochet picqué de menu lard" (p. 140, no. 21) and "Saumon au lard" (p. 141, no. 23) were also spit-roasted and served with sauce. In *Le Cuisinier royal et bourgeois,* the roasted shad and pike, whose recipes are incidentally freely borrowed from *Le Nouveau Cuisinier,* are also served with sauce or ragoût.

Le Cuisinier françois has two second-course grilled fish: "Vives rosties sur le gril" simmered in a red sauce (p. 220, no. 3) and "Louxtre de mer sur le gril," also simmered in a highly seasoned sauce (p. 222, no. 13). There are three in *Le Nou-*

veau Cuisinier: "Carpes sur le gril" in caper and anchovy sauce (p. 137); "Vives sur le gril," in thickened sauce (p. 139); and "Maquereaux sur le gril" in brown butter (p. 142). We find two in *L'Art de bien traiter,* "Vives grillées" (p. 202, no. 51) and "Vives rosties sur le gril," served in a "sauce blanche" (p. 271, no. 48); and six in *Le Cuisinier royal et bourgeois:* "Carpes sur le gril" (served in brown or clarified butter, p. 178); "Esturgeon de même"; "Maquereaux sur le gril," served with brown butter and gooseberries (p. 298); "Soles grillées"; "Tanches de même"; and "Vives sur le gril sausse aux Anchois" (p. 69). It is clear that even though grilled fish were accompanied by a (usually spicy) butter sauce from 1651 to 1691, they were nevertheless served in the second course.

For the second course, *Le Cuisinier françois* serves 14 of its 57 fish dishes in ragoût; nine of them are suitable for meatless meals of which five are also suitable for Lent: "Macreuse en ragoust" (p. 218, no. 32), "Lotte en ragoust" (p. 218, no. 36 and p. 299, no. 25), "Tanches frittes en ragoust" (p. 218, no. 38 and p. 299, no. 34), "Barbeaux en ragoust" (p. 218, no. 39 and p. 299, no. 34), "Solles en ragoust" (p. 218, no. 41 and p. 298, no. 6), "Vilain en ragoust" (p. 218, no. 42 and p. 299, no. 36), "Plies rosties en ragoust" (p. 219, no. 58), "Marsouin en ragoust" (p. 222, no. 10), "Limandes frittes en ragoust" (p. 222, no. 11).

It is no exception but almost a rule in *Le Cuisinier françois* to serve fish in casserole for the second course, as it does seven out of ten times: "Barbuë en castrolle" (p. 218, no. 33 and 298, no. 3) whose recipe appears only under entrées (p. 188, no. 33); "Barbeau en castrolle"; "Turbot en castrolle"; "Plies en castrolle"; "Grenost en castrolle"; and "Lotte en castrolle." But fish prepared in this manner is not served as a second course in any of the other books we have examined.

"Demy court bouillon" is not only a cooking liquid but also a sauce served with the fish cooked in it. See for instance the "Carpe au demy court bouillon" (*Le Cuisinier françois,* pp. 180–181): "Gut the carp fresh out of the water; section it according to its size; add vinegar, very little salt, pepper and chopped onion, capers, and fresh butter; cook with the mixture in a heavy pot until the sauce has thickened; transfer to a serving platter . . . and serve." This is the usual procedure for entrées, in *Le Cuisinier françois* (seven times out of nine) as well as in *Le Nouveau Cuisinier* (p. 108), *L'Art de bien traiter* (p. 200, nos. 19 and 20; p. 244, no. 9; and p. 245, no. 10), and *Le Cuisinier royal et bourgeois* (p. 178). But it is no longer found in *La Cuisinière bourgeoise. Le Cuisinier françois* is the only one to serve a fish in demi–court bouillon as a meatless roast: only for carp, once for meatless days (p. 218, no. 37) and once for Lent (p. 299, no. 33).

The "Perches au beurre blanc" in *Le Nouveau Cuisinier* (p. 137) were first scaled and cooked in a court bouillon of "vin, verjus, eau, sel, cloux [de girofle], laurier," then served "with a thickened sauce made of butter, vinegar, nutmeg, and lemon slices."

The second course in *Le Nouveau Cuisinier* features "Brochet à la sauce d'Alemagne" (p. 136) with this recipe: "Poach the pike au bleu as above; place it in a fish pot with white wine, nutmeg, a little pepper, a piece of lime, and a little salt, and cook over high flame, covered; when the broth is reduced to a cup, take out the pike, add a pound of good fresh butter well creamed with nutmeg, capers, and lemon slices, mix well and you will see that the sauce will thicken; serve with fried bread and slices of lemon." Second-course fish dishes in *L'Art de bien traiter* were "Rougets à la saulce" (p. 202, no. 53), "Maquereau frais à la saulse" (p. 202, no. 54), and "Raye à la saulse rousse, & blanche" (p. 202, nos. 53, 54, and 55); among second-course fish dishes, *Le Cuisinier royal et bourgeois* lists "Vives sur le gril, sausse aux Anchois" (p. 69). *La Cuisinière bourgeoise* is alone in serving no fish *à la sauce* for a meatless roast.

31. *Le Cuisinier royal et bourgeois,* p. 73:

Le Rôt
Deux moiens plats, composez de deux Brochets, & de huit Soles chacun.
Le grand, d'une Carpe, & six Brochetons autour.
Et le reste de ce service, de pièces d'Entremets, & filets en Salade,

and on p. 74:

Pour le Rôt
Deux moiens plats; d'Esturgeon, & des Rougets autour.
Deux petits; de cinq Soles à chacun.
Le reste de ce Service, de pièces d'Entremets.

32. Menon, *Les Soupers de la Cour* (1755), vol. 1, pp. 17–20.

33. Cf. Philippe Mordacq, *Le Menu: Une histoire illustrée de 1751 à nos jours* (Paris: Robert Laffont, 1989), facing p. 1.

CHAPTER 5

1. Alfred Franklin, *La Vie privée d'autrefois,* vol. 3, *La Cuisine* (Paris: Plon, 1888), pp. 47–48: "While our ancestors were hearty eaters . . . they knew nothing about the culinary arts. They liked to be served huge platters loaded with meats, fish and vegetables, and to combine these disparate elements. Dishes were not presented separately as they are today; instead, several were combined on a single platter that was called a dish *(mets).* For instance, all of the roasts piled together constituted a single dish, their greatly varied sauces being offered on the side. In fact, it was not unusual for a single platter to hold the entire meal, a horrible hodgepodge also called a dish."

2. See for instance Fernand Braudel, *Civilisation matérielle et capitalisme* (Paris: Armand Colin, 1967), p. 139: "No refined cuisine in Europe before the end of the fifteenth century. . . . Let not the reader be dazzled in retrospect by feasts such as those at the sumptuous court of Valois de Bourgogne: the fountains of wine, the set pieces, the children in angel costumes lowered from heaven on cables. . . . The ostentatious quantity belied its quality."

3. Franklin, *La Vie privée d'autrefois,* vol. 6: *Les Repas* (1889): "For a long time, the courses and dishes followed each other in no established order." But he immediately adds, "However, Olivier de la Marche tells us that in general, the soup was served first, followed in turn by eggs, fish and meats" (p. 60).

4. Bridget Ann Henisch, *Fast and Feast: Food in Medieval Society* (University Park: Pennsylvania State University Press, 1978), p. 146.

5. *Le Viandier de Taillevent* (ca. 1486), ed. Jérôme Pichon and Georges Vicaire (Paris, 1892); new ed. rev. Sylvie Martinet (Geneva: Slatkine Reprints, 1967). I am not considering the menus of Maître Chiquart, which cover only a small number of feasts. Similarly, the six *Taillevent* menus printed one century after *Le Ménagier de Paris* do not contain enough dishes (115, of which 84 are dissimilar) to yield solid conclusions.

6. Menus 3–4, 6–13, 15, and 18–24.

7. I am inclined to count 4 dishes in the first "platter" of menu 1, "Grenache wine and toast," "veal pasties," "pompano pasties," and "black puddings and sausages"; 4 in the second, "Hare stew and ribs," "strained peas," "salted and coarse meat," and "smoked eels and other fish"; 3 in the third platter, "Roast: coneys, partridge, capons, etc.," "burbot, sea bass, carp," and "shredded meat soup"; 4 in the fourth platter, "Water fowl in a white sauce," "smothered rice," "bourrée in hot sauce," and "jellied eels"; 4 in the fifth platter, "shad pasties," "rissoles," "sugared milk," and "sugared flans"; and 3 in the sixth platter, "Pears and sugared almonds," "loquats and shelled nuts," and "*hypocras* and wafers." This adds up to only 22, not 30 dishes; the correct figure would be obtained by counting 7 dishes on the third platter—hares, partridge, capon, burbot, sea bass, and carp representing 1 dish each—and 6 on the sixth platter. But then what does "etc." represent at the end of the list of meat roasts? And why are the dishes of fruits in the sixth platter paired by the word *and,* which in the first two platters appears to link foods comprising a single dish? In menu 2, I count between 4 and 6 dishes in the first platter, 4 in the second, 3 in the third, 4 in the fourth, 6 in the fifth, and 7 in the sixth, which would add up to 28 or 30 dishes instead of the 24 indicated in the title.

8. Menu 2 calls for "sixth and last platter for the finish"; and in 5, the "Fourth platter" consists of "*Hypocras* and sweet wafers for the finish."

9. Menus 9 and 19 have only two courses; menus 4, 6, 8, 10, 12, 15, 17, 18, 21, and 23 have three. But I find four sequences in menus 3, 5, 11, 20, 22, and 27; five in menus 13, 14, and 16; six in menus 1, 2, and 7; seven in menus 24 and 26; and nine in menu 25.

10. Menu 20 actually refers extensively to menu 19 for its first and last courses: e.g., "First course. Cooked apples, etc. as above." The first course of menu 19 indeed begins with cooked apples and includes six other dishes. The four-course menu 20 again refers to 19 for the fourth: "Finish: figs and raisins, *hypocras* and sweet wafers, as above." But neither of these dishes appears in menu

19. Thus it is likely that menu 19 also consisted of four courses, the last two omitted by the copy clerk.

11. Menu 24: "Third dish. Frumenty with porpoise, breaded meat balls and fritters and young lamprey, roast fish, jelly, lamprey, conger and turbot in green sauce, bream in verjuice, fried bread slices, meat tarts and entremets." Menu 10: "Third dish. Frumenty, venison . . . fried bread slices, meat tart, and large entremets." Menu 13: "Fourth dish. Frumenty, venison, breadings, jellied eels, bream roast. Boar's head entremets."

12. "Second dish: Capons . . . jellied meat and fish" (7 platters). "Entremets: Burbot and carp" (2 platters?). "Special entremets: Swan, peacocks, bitterns, herons, and other things" (more than 4 platters?). "Finish."

13. I have counted 5–5–7–4–4–3 in menu 1; 6–5–5–4–6–5 in menu 2; 8–9–9–7 in menu 3; 7–7–7 in menu 4; 9–11–10 in menu 6; 5–4–6–6 in menu 7; 7–8–8 in menu 8; 10–12–11 in menu 10; 7–8–8–8 in menu 11; etc. But, still using the numbered courses, 8–6–10–1 in menu 5; 6–13 in menu 9; 8–5–12 in menu 15; 5–11–11 in menu 18; etc.

14. Their absence in menu 10 does not challenge this rule because, contrary to the menu's title, it describes a meatless meal. But the meat-day dinners in which the courses are named but not numbered (menus 26 and 28) also do not show boiled coarse meats, as if these could be included neither in the "Platter" nor among the "Soups."

15. Sendoff: Explicitly in menus 7, 24, 25, and 26; and implicitly in 27 and 28. Finish: Menus 2, 5, 7, 14, 16, 20, and 24–28.

16. See menus 2, 5, 7, 25, and 26.

17. "Finish: apples and cheese without *hypocras,* which is out of season" clearly does not literally refer to a season, as *Le Ménagier*'s coeditor, Jerôme Pichon, believed, since *hypocras* was served at a dinner on the same day in May.

18. Cf. Jean-Louis Flandrin, "Le Sucré dans les livres de cuisine français, du XIVe au XVIIIe siècle," in "Le Sucre et le sel," special issue, *JATBA: Travaux d'Ethnobiologie* 35 (1988): 215–232.

19. The six menus are 1, 2, 14, 18, 26, and 28. The specified types are capons [roasted] (4/4), a pheasant (1/2), *hétoudeaux* (i.e., pullets ready to be caponized; 1/1), small birds (2/2), nestlings (1/1), chicks (1/1), young partridges (1/1), partridges (4/4), and plovers (2/2), for a total of 17 presumably roasted birds out of 18 mentioned in all of the courses combined; as well as coneys [roasted] (4/4), a deer (1/1), a quarter of roe deer (1/1), a suckling pig [roasted] (2/2), and veal [roasted] (1/1), for a total of 8 presumably roasted quadrupeds out of 8 mentioned in all of the courses.

20. The two dishes of organ meats are a platter of "Organs with parsley and vinegar" and a platter of "Meat tripe." But note that while *Le Ménagier de Paris* indicates no recipe for the latter dish, the chapter on meat roasts in all versions of *Viandier de Taillevent* starts with a recipe for "veal tripe," even though this is not a roast.

21. This separation is normal because the dietitians of the time prescribed that certain fruits should be eaten at the start of a meal and others at its end. Cf. Jean-Louis Flandrin, "Médecine et habitudes alimentaires anciennes," in J.-C. Margolin and R. Sauzet, eds., *Pratiques et discours alimentaires à la Renaissance*, Actes du Colloque de Tours 1979 (Paris: Maison-neuve & Larose, 1982), pp. 85–95.

22. The dietetic principles of the time were not without influence on these distributions: the comments about fruits apply equally to boiled meats and particularly to "coarse meats" deemed less indigestible if eaten before the roast. This point will be discussed further in the last part of this volume.

CHAPTER 6

1. *Livre fort excellent de cuysine tres-utile & profitable contenant en soy la maniere dabiller toutes viandes. Avec la maniere deservir es banquets & festins. Le tout veu & corrige oultre la premiere impression par le grant Escuyer de Cuysine du Roy* (Lyon: Olivier Arnoullet, [1555]). The first edition of this work, titled *Le Livre de cuysine très utile et profitable,* was published about 1540. These twelve menus—or rather, eleven, since the last one is not a true menu—are composed as follows:

"*1. Cest que fault pour faire ung banquet ou nopces après pasques.* Et premièrement. Bon pain. Bon vin. Entrée de table. Potages. Rost. Second rost. Tiers service de rost. Issue de table. *2. Ung aultre bancquet ou nopces.* Bon pain. Bon vin. Entrée de table. Potaiges. Rost. Second rost. Tiers service. Quart service. Cinquiesme service. Sixiesme service. Issue de table. *3. Autre bancquet.* Bon pain. Bon vin. [Entrée de table]. Potages. [Rost]. Second service. Issue de table. *4. Aultre service.* Bon pain. Bon vin. Entrée de table. Potaiges Rost. Second service. Entremetz troussez. Tiers service de rost. Quart service de rost. Issue de table. *5. Un aultre bancquet ou nopce.* Bon pain. Bon vin. [Entrée de table]. Potaiges. Rost. Second Rost. Issue de table. Boucherie pour faire boullon. Pour lespicerie. *6. Aultre feste ou bancquet desté.* Bon pain. Bon vin. Entrée de table. Aultre entrée de table pour yver. Potaiges. Rost. Issue de table. *7. Ledit jour à soupper.* Bon pain. Bon vin. Entrée de table. Potaiges. Rost. Aultre service. Issue de table. *8. Pour une aultre feste ou bancquet.* Bon pain. Bon vin. Assiette de table. Potaiges. Rost. Issue de table. *9. [Souper].* Entrée de table pour le souper. Rost. Issue de table. *10. [Banquet d'hiver].* Entrée de table dyver. Entrée de cuisine. Potaiges. Issue de table. Dixième mets. *11. Cest qui fault pour ung souper.* Entrée de table. Potaiges. Premier rost. Second rost. Issue de table. Espices de chambre. *12. Memoire quant du vouldras faire un bancquet regarde en ce chapitre tu trouveras des memoires pour faire ton escripteau.* Et premièrement . . . Autrement trouveras . . . Patisserie. Aultrement. Plus rissollées."

2. *Le Viandier de Taillevent* (Geneva: Slatkine Reprints, 1967), p. 197: "FRUICTERIE. Cresme blanches, et fraises, jonchée, et amandes."

3. As note 1 above demonstrates. The "Sixth course" in menu 10—which is actually the fifth course—is too atypical to contradict this conclusion.

4. Grimod de La Reynière, *Almanach des gourmands,* 2nd year (1804), pp. 45–46. Recall, for instance, the menu for a royal supper at Choisy on Monday 21 June 1751, which began with "2 Grandes Entrées," namely, "Un Quartier de Veau du Roy, une Blanquette" and "Une Culotte de Bœuf au Bain marie" followed by 2 geese and 2 soups, 16 entrées, and 4 relevés. (This menu is published by Philippe Mordacq in *Le Menu,* facing p. 1.)

5. There the "Première table à cinq bassins, & quatre assiette" successively presents a course of nine soups, a course of nine entrées, a third course of nine roasts, followed by one of countless entremets, and very likely a dessert.

6. Menu 1: "Rost" (third course), "Second Rost" (fourth), "Tiers service de rost" (fifth). Menu 2: "Rost" (third course), "Second rost" (fourth), "Tiers service" (fifth), "Quart service" (sixth), "Cinquiesme service" (seventh), "Sixieme service" (eighth). Menu 3: [Roast: six platters at the end of the soup course], "Second service" (third or fourth). Menu 4: "Rost" (third course), "Second service" (fourth), "Entremets troussez" (fifth), "Tiers service de rost" (sixth), "Quart service de rost" (seventh). Menu 5: "Rost" (third course), "Second rost" (fourth). Menu 6: "Rost" (fourth course). Menu 7: "Rost" (third course), "Aultre service" (fourth). Menu 8: "Rost" (third course). Menu 9: "Rost" (second course). Menu 11: "Premier rost" (third course), "second rost" (fourth). Menu 10 starts with two entrée courses—one a table entrée and the other a kitchen entrée—Italian style, as we will see in the third part of this book. I have already pointed out the very strange tenth dish, "Dixième mets," which doubles as the finish and which, if I am counting properly, is nothing more than a fifth course. But most important here, and exceptionally, this menu has no roast course. Could this be a printer's error?

7. See for example *Le Viandier de Taillevent,* "Chapitres d'entremès" (pp. 14–20), "Entremetz" (p. 75), "Ensuivent les entremez" (pp. 91–100); or *Le Ménagier de Paris,* ed. Jérôme Pichon and Georges Vicaire (Paris: Crapelet, 1846), "Entremès, fritures et dorures" (pp. 210–224), "Autres entremès" (pp. 224–229).

8. *Le Ménagier de Paris,* "L'entremets. Lus et carpes. L'entremets eslevé. Cine, paons, butor, hérons et autres choses" (p. 99); "Faisans et cines pour entremets" (p. 101); "Entremès: plays, lemproie à la bœ" (p. 107); "Entremès: gelée d'escrevices, de loches, lapereaulx et cochon" (p. 108).

9. There are indeed 3 dishes of "Bécasses à lesquesal," which are roasted woodcocks covered with a sauce; 1 "Canard à la dodine"; 1 "Chevreaulx au verjus d'ozeille"; 1 "Héronneaulx saulce réalle"; 3 "Hétoudeaux au moût" and 1 "Hétoudeaux au saulge"; 1 "Lapereault de garenne aulx oranges"; 1 "Levreaulx sauce royale"; 3 "Oisons à la malvoisie" and 2 "Oisons farcis"; 2 "Perdrix aux oranges"; 1 "Pigeons au sucre"; 1 "Poulet au vinaigre rosat"; 4 "Poussins au vinaigre rosat"; and 1 "Venaison de rost saulce realle."

10. See, for example, the "third platter" in the first menu of *Le Ménagier de Paris* ("Rost: connins, perdris, chappons, etc., lux, bars, carpes, et un potage escartelé"); the "third dish" in the second menu ("Rost: chappons, connin, veel et perdris, poisson d'eau doulce et de mer, aucun taillis avec doreure"); the "second dish" in the third menu ("Rost de char, poisson d'eau doulce, poissons de mer, une cretonnée de char, raniolles, un rosé de lapereaulx et de bourrées à la sausse chaulde, d'oiselets tourtes Pisaine"); and the "second dish" in the fourth menu ("Rost le meilleur que on peut et poisson doulx, un bouli lardé, un tieule de char, pasté de chappons et crespes, pasté de bresmes, d'anguilles et blanc mangier"). Another example is the second dish in the fourth menu of the printed *Viandier de Taillevent* ("Rost le meilleur, paons au scelereau, pasté de chapons, levreaulx au vin aigre rosac, chapon au most iehan").

11. The 41 organ-meat dishes are cow's udder; beef palate; 2 beef marrow presentations; 6 beef and 4 sheep tongues; 1 shank of beef, 5 of sheep and 2 probably of pig; 8 calf livers, 1 of sheep, 1 of deer or kid or beef, and 1 of capon or chicken; and 4 heads of boar and 4 of kid. The only lamb mentioned is a roast; likewise for 8 suckling pigs out of 13; but there is only 1 roast out of 2 beef dishes (organ meats excluded); 1 out of 14 veal dishes; 2 out of 13 sheep dishes; and 3 out of 14 kid dishes.

12. There is no roast listed for doe, nor for any of the 3 "deer" dishes, and only 2 out of 7 boar dishes and 8 out 41 "venison" dishes.

13. At least 2 larks out of 4; at least 4 woodcocks or woodcock chicks out of 5; the 1 pheasant; the 3 herons or heron chicks; at least 6 partridges or partridge chicks out of 12; 2 dishes of sparrows out of 5; 1 dish of teal out of 2; 1 of doves out of 2, etc.; in other words, at least 20 roasts out of 34 wild bird preparations. Of the ducks, 3 or 4 were roasts; 7 of 27 capons; all 5 pullets; 5 of 10 chickens; all 6 gamy chickens; 4 of 11 pullets; 4 of 9 nestlings; 9 of 19 pigeons; and 2 of 4 peacocks. A minimum of 4 coneys out of 6; all 6 young rabbits; and 4 young hares out of 5.

14. The *Ménagier de Paris* menus mention lettuce three times toward the middle of the meal: twice in the roast course (menus 10 and 24, second course) and once in the next course (menu 16, third course). In addition, for the "Bancquet de Monseigneur de Foyes," the published edition of *Le Viandier de Taillevent* mentions watercress in the meal's penultimate "fourth course," together with "poires à l'ypocras, lesches dorées, gelée" and other sugared selections. However, in *Le Ménagier de Paris,* watercress is mentioned five times, always with the first course. But was it a salad? It is served once as a purée, once in connection with chicken, and three times with salt herring. Still, two out of three times this watercress early in the meal was explicitly dressed with vinegar.

15. "The fifth" in the first menu; the "Fourth dish" and "Fifth dish" in the third menu; the "Fourth dish" in the fourth; "Third dish" and "Fourth dish" in the fifth; and the second part of the "Third course" in the sixth of the menus.

CHAPTER 7

1. *L'Escole parfaite des officiers de Bouche; contenant le Vray Maistre-d'Hostel, Le grand Escuyer-Tranchant, Le Sommelier Royal, Le Confiturier Royal, Le Cuisinier Royal, et le Patissier Royal* (Paris: chez la Veuve Pierre David . . . et chez Jean Ribou, 1662).

2. See the first course of the 21 June menu (published by Philippe Mordacq, *Le Menu,* facing page 1, with successive listings for the standing centerpiece ("le Dormant"), two main entrées (a veal blanquette and "Une Culotte de Bœuf au bain marie"), followed by two stews ("Une Oille au Riz" and "Une Brunoise"), two soups ("Une Julienne au Pois" and "Un Potage au Navets"), then sixteen entrées and four relevés.

3. Grimod de La Reynière, *Almanach des gourmands,* 2nd year (1804), p. 43.

4. Massialot, *Le Cuisinier royal et bourgeois* (1st ed., 1691), p. 29.

5. Ibid., pp. 17–18.

6. Menon, *Les Soupers de la Cour ou l'Art de travailler toutes sortes d'alimens,* 4 vols. (Paris: Guillyn, 1755).

7. See for example the "Spring dinner for seven" (pp. 545–546), the "Summer dinner for seven" (pp. 548–549), and the "Fall & Winter meatless dinner for eleven" (pp. 551–553).

8. Examples: the "Spring supper for nine" (pp. 547–548); "Summer supper for nine" (pp. 549–551); "Fall & Winter meatless supper for nine" (pp. 553–554).

9. In this "Fall & Winter meat-day dinner for seven" (p. 555), the four hors d'oeuvres follow "A stew à la Fonbonne, for the centerpiece [pièce de milieu]," and precede "Two entrées," one being "de beccasses à la sauce à la beccasse," and the other "d'ailerons de dindons à l'étuvée," both as part of the first course.

10. Archambault, *Le Cuisinier économe, ou Élémens nouveaux de cuisine, de pâtisserie et d'office* (Paris: Renard Baudouin, 1821). "Pickles. Olives. Marinated tuna fish. Young rapes. Butter loaves. Pepper dressing. Anchovy fillets. Radishes."

11. Meals: January (pp. 2–4), February and March (pp. 5–8), March (pp. 9–11), April (pp. 16–17), May (pp. 21–25, 26–28), June (pp. 28–30, 31–32, 33–35), July and August (pp. 38–41, 42–45), October and November (pp. 49–50), and December (pp. 51–54). See also "Repas en Maigre" (pp. 72–73). Ordinaries: pp. 75–76 and 78–79. Dinners: April (pp. 17–18 and 19–20). Suppers: March (pp. 11–12) and a meatless supper (pp. 73–75 and 76–77).

12. The "Spring supper for nine" (pp. 547–548), "Summer supper" (pp. 549–551), "Fall & Winter meatless supper" (pp. 553–554), and "Fall & Winter meat-day supper" have no soup for the first course, only a centerpiece *[pièce de milieu],* four entrées, and four hors d'oeuvres.

13. Chapter 2, "Eighteenth-Century Roasts and Spit-Roasted Entrées."

14. Menon, *Les Soupers de la Cour,* pp. 14, 28, 30, and 21.

15. After 1850, for instance, Vuillemot had a dinner for forty at La Tête noire

restaurant in Saint-Cloud, with just a "Bisque d'écrevisses tapioca" by way of soups, but four relevés: first, "Truite saumonnée sauce génoise"; second, "Turbot à la hollandaise"; third, "Filet de bœuf à la régence"; and last, "Quartier de chevreuil sauce poivrade" (Alexandre Dumas, *Grand Dictionnaire de cuisine* [repr. Paris: Phébus, 2000], p. 601). Similarly, in a menu for the Austrian imperial family recorded by Urbain Dubois and Émile Bernard, there is only one soup—"Consommé printanier aux quenelles de volaille"—but two relevés, one being "Saumon sauce [sic] génevoise et hollandaise," and the other, "Filet de bœuf à la financière" (Urbain Dubois and Émile Bernard, *La Cuisine classique,* 3rd ed. [Paris: by the authors, 1868], p. 53). It does appear that the initial meaning of the term *relevé* fell into oblivion during the years 1867–1868. In the Philippe Mordacq book (*Le Menu,* p. 17), I even found notes for a "Lunch for 16 October 1867" whose menu includes no soup at all but starts directly with two relevés, followed by four entrées, two roasts, and so on.

16. Pierre de Lune, *Le Nouveau et Parfait Maistre d'hostel royal* (1662), pp. 19–20.

17. Choisy supper: Mordacq, *Le Menu,* facing p. 1.

18. Fish has not completely disappeared: there is still some sturgeon in the "third roast course" of menu 1 and in the "Sixth Course" roast of menu 2, but these are the exceptions.

19. *Le Cuisinier gascon* (1740), p. 102.

20. J. Lebas, *Festin joyeux, ou La cuisine en musique: en vers libres* (Paris: Lesclapart, 1738), pp. 137, 139, and 155.

21. Menon, *La Cuisinière bourgeoise,* pp. 242, 245, 268, 270, 271, and 272.

22. Pierre de Lune, *Le Nouveau et Parfait Maistre d'hostel royal,* pp. 17–18.

23. Menon, *La Science du maître d'hôtel cuisinier,* new revised and corrected edition (Paris, 1789), pp. 549–551.

24. This diversity is amply illustrated in chapter 3 of the present work.

25. Quoted in A. B. de Périgord, *Nouvel Almanach des gourmands, servant de guide dans les moyens de faire excellente chère. Dédié au Ventre,* 1st year (1825), p. 106.

26. *Le Cuisinier méthodique* (1685 ed.).

27. As early as 1672, in *Le Voyageur d'Europe,* Jouvin de Rochefort was already ridiculing the sugared salads he had been served in Flanders (vol. 1, p. 612) and in Ireland (vol. 3, p. 486): "I recall eating there a salad prepared in the local style . . . without oil or salt but only with a little beer vinegar, the salad topped with a quantity of sugar worthy of Mount Etna covered with snow, such that it is impossible to eat if you have never experienced anything like it. I gave my host much merriment . . . when I asked for oil to dress the salad in the French way."

28. *L'École des ragoûts ou le Chef-d'œuvre du cuisinier, du pâtissier & du confiturier . . . . ,* 11th ed. (Lyon: Jacques Canier, 1685), pp. 156–165. The first edition of this work apparently dates from 1668.

29. The menus I used for this study are those in *Le Ménagier de Paris* (ca. 1393) that indicate desserts or *issues de table;* those from the published version of *Le Viandier de Taillevent* (1486); those from *Le Livre fort excellent de cuysine* (1555); three menus from *La Cuisinière bourgeoise* (1746); and five menus from *Les Soupers de la Cour* (1755). In addition to these period publications, I also used a few manuscript menus published in the twentieth century: one for a dinner offered in 1656 to Louis XIV at Pontchartrain Castle (*Larousse gastronomique* [1967 ed.], "Menus" article, p. 662); one for a dinner for sixteen guests and seven servants at a residence in Laval on 18 November 1686; and another for a wedding feast for twenty-three guests, given in the same region on 1 September 1785. These last two menus were published by Jules-Marie Richard in *La Vie privée dans une province de l'Ouest: Laval aux XVIIe et XVIIIe siècles* (Paris: Champion, 1922), pp. 130 and 131.

CHAPTER 8

1. Archambault, *Le Cuisinier économe, ou Élémens nouveaux de cuisine, de pâtiserie et d'office . . .* (Paris, 1821), in-8°; Alexandre Dumas, *Grand Dictionnaire de cuisine* (repr. Paris: Phébus, 2000), p. 597.

2. Dumas, *Grand Dictionnaire de cuisine,* p. 599.

3. Urbain Dubois and Émile Bernard, *La Cuisine classique: Études pratiques raisonnées et démonstratives de l'École française appliquée au service à la russe,* 3rd ed. (Paris: by the authors, 1868 [orig. 1856]), p. LXIII.

4. Archambault, *Le Cuisinier économe,* p. 405.

5. Dumas, *Grand Dictionnaire de cuisine,* p. 600.

6. Dubois and Bernard, *La Cuisine classique* (1856), p. 6. On the same page, in a menu for twenty whose courses are not named, he offers "Turbot sauce aux crevettes" and "Dorade garnie de filets de rougets en caisse" between "Petites bouchées à la Montglas et cromesquis," which is certainly an hors d'oeuvre, and "Longe de veau à la Toulouse"—the first of two relevés that, in the first course, precede two entrées and a vegetable.

7. Ibid., pp. 8 and 10.

8. The 4 May 1894 banquet of the gastronomic association La Poule au pot lists "Poularde à la Belgrand," "Selle de Chezelle purée Marie-Jeanne," and roast ducks "Rouennais farcis à la bonne femme"; the menu of 22 June of the same year shows a "Selle de pré-salé avec flageolets nouveaux," some "Poulardes truffées," a "Canetons nouveaux sauce au sang" duckling roast, and a cold roast of "Ortolans en chaudfroid"; lastly, the menu of 28 April 1899 includes an entrée of "Selle de pré-salé avec morilles à la crème," a roast of "Canetons nouveaux sauce Rouennaise," and a cold roast of "Poulardes Rossini en gelée."

9. Dubois and Bernard, *La Cuisine classique,* pp. 3 and 6.

10. Ibid. (1856), p. VII.

11. We should point out that during the seventeenth and eighteenth centuries, aristocratic meals were eaten much more rapidly in France than in most other European countries. In *Le Nouveau Cuisinier royal et bourgeois,* Massialot wrote, "Do not keep the masters of the house too long at each course, lest they become bored: allow only a quarter hour or quarter hour and a half." This certainly did not leave much time to taste the variety of dishes placed on the table for each course. The same conditions do not appear to have prevailed during the nineteenth century, at least in the social circles that the *Almanach des gourmands* used as a model.

12. Dubois and Bernard, *La Cuisine classique* (1856), p. IX.

13. Grimod de La Reynière, *Almanach des gourmands,* 2nd year (1804), pp. 43f.

14. This is a kind of soup of Spanish origin (the *olla*), frequently served in France from the late seventeenth to early nineteenth centuries.

15. *Le Conservateur,* containing as part three a "Wine Monograph" by Messrs. Joubert, Bouchard, and Louis Leclerc (Paris: Dentu, 1842), pp. 375–376.

16. In the menus of *L'Art culinaire* of 1893 to 1899, we find "Punch à la Romaine" (15 February 1897, p. 29; 15 June 1897, p. 111; 31 October 1897, p. 214; etc.), "Punch à la Reine" (30 June 1897, p. 124), "Punch à la Russe" and "Punch au Champagne" (31 January 1897, p. 16), "Sorbets au Clicquot rosé" (30 June 1897, p. XXII), "Sorbets à la fine Champagne" (15 November 1897, p. 52), "Granité à l'Armagnac" (15 June 1897, p. 114), "Sorbets au Champagne" (30 June 1897, p. 125), "Sorbets à l'Orientale" (31 June 1897, p. 140), "Sorbets au Lunel" and "Spooms au Roederer" (15 September 1897, p. 174), "Spooms au vin de Samos" (October 1897, p. 190), "Punch suédois" (15 October 1897, p. 203), "Granités au Clicquot," etc. Similarly, in the 1897 menus of *La Cuisine française et étrangère,* where this midway pause is a little less frequent, we also find "Punch à la romaine" (no. 65, p. 187), "Punch au Champagne" (no. 68, p. 59), "Sorbets au kirsch" (no. 34, p. 66), "Granité à la fine champagne" (no. 35, p. 90), "Sorbets Marquise" (no. 55, p. 27), "Grande fine" (no. 66, p. 2), "Punch à la Russe" (no. 68, p. 39), "Rhum de Mana en Sorbets" (no. 86, p. 141), etc.

17. Philippe Mordacq, *Le Menu,* p. 22.

18. Grimod de la Reynière, *Almanach des gourmands,* 3rd year (1805), pp. 18–23.

19. Grimod de La Reynière, *Manuel des amphitryons* (repr. Paris: A. M. Métailié, 1983 [orig. 1808]), pp. 108–109 and 178–180.

20. Archambault, *Le Cuisinier économe,* pp. 403–405. The menu presented already contained eight cold hors d'oeuvres between the two relevés and the twelve entrées.

21. Dubois and Bernard, *La Cuisine classique* (1856), p. 7.

22. Dumas, *Grand Dictionnaire de cuisine,* pp. 597–598. For instance, in Dugléré's "Menu for 15" (p. 597), the "Two soups" are preceded by hors d'oeu-

vres consisting of "Small canapés, marinated oysters, anchovies, stuffed olives"; in the "Menu for 15–20" (p. 598), the hors d'oeuvres of "Melon, smoked salmon, canapé, butter" precede "Two soups," one *à la Demidoff* and the other *à la princesse;* in the "Menu for six," hors d'oeuvres of "Spanish melon, Ostend oysters, smoked salmon and caviar" precede the "Two soups"; etc. All these hors d'oeuvres served before the soups appear to be cold.

23. Verdier's "Two soups" in the "Dinner menu for 15" at La Maison dorée (ibid., p. 599), a "Poultry consommé" and a "Turtle consommé," are followed by an "Hors-d'œuvre," probably hot, and by "Noodle timbales chasseur"; and those in the "Dinner menu for 24" are followed by "Four hors-d'œuvres" consisting only of "Bouchées à la Monglas." Note that in Dugléré's "Menu for 15 to 20" (p. 598), soups preceded by cold "Hors-d'œuvres" are followed by "Two hot hors-d'œuvres,"—"Soufflés à la Reine" and "Bâton de Charles VII."

24. The Dumas menu (ibid.) begins with "Ostend and Marenne oysters," followed by "Two soups." The banquet for the Saxe royal family (Dubois and Bernard, *La Cuisine classique* [1868], vol. 1, p. 49) began with "Oysters, butter, lemon," then "Consommé with lettuce," and a hot hors d'oeuvre of "Small timbales à la Reine." The banquet for the Hesse-Darmstadt family (ibid., p. 61) also began with "Oysters and lemons," followed by two soups—"Game consommé primavera" and "Cream of poultry à l'Allemande"—and by an hors d'oeuvre of "Caviar and blini" that could qualify as cold for the caviar or as hot for the blini. As for the dinner served to the court of Carlsruhe (ibid., p. 55), it began with "Oysters," followed by "Crécy rice soup" and two hot hors d'oeuvres: "Small pasties of young partridge purée" and "Sole à la Vénitienne."

25. Dumas, *Grand Dictionnaire de cuisine,* p. 600: "Marenne oysters, lemon. HORS-D'ŒUVRE: Butter, tuna, shrimp."

26. Dubois and Bernard, *La Cuisine classique* (1868), vol. 1, pp. LI and LVIII.

27. Dubois and Bernard, *La Cuisine classique* (1856), p. 1.

28. Dumas, *Grand Dictionnaire de cuisine,* p. 601.

29. Dubois and Bernard, *La Cuisine classique* (1868), vol. 1, p. LIII.

30. Mordacq, *Le Menu,* p. 17.

31. Ibid. [*sic;* Dumas, *Grand Dictionnaire de cuisine,* may have been intended—*Trans.*], p. 599.

32. In fourth position for instance, after the soups, hors d'oeuvres, and relevés, in the dinner for the Belgian royal family whose menu is published by Dubois and Bernard in *La Cuisine classique,* p. LXIII; in Dugléré's "Menu for 15" at Café anglais, after the "Hors-d'œuvre," "Two soups," and "Two large joints" (Dumas, *Grand Dictionnaire de cuisine,* p. 597); and in the "Dinner menu for 15" by Verdier at La Maison dorée (ibid., p. 599), where the entrées are preceded by "Two soups," "Hors d'oeuvres," and "Two relevés"; etc. They are even found in fifth position, after "Hors-d'œuvres," "Two soups," "Two hot hors d'oeuvres," and "Two large joints" in Dugléré's "Summer menu for 15 to 20" (ibid., p. 598),

in his "Winter menu for six" (ibid.), and in Verdier's "Dinner menu for 24" (ibid., p. 599), where "Four entrées" are mentioned after "Two soups," "Four hors-d'œuvres," "Two relevés," and "Two flans," etc.

33. Dumas, *Grand Dictionnaire de cuisine*, p. 599.

34. Mordacq, *Le Menu*, p. 25. "GD. DÎNER PARISIEN. Les Clients devront apporter leur Pain. POTAGES. Purée Crouton—Impérial. Bisque-Bismarck. Consommé de Tire-Fiacre. HORS-D'ŒUVRES. Sardines antédiluviennes. Beurre de Coco. ENTRÉES. Galantines de Mufles. Andouillette et Boudins de Dada. Rats à la Crapaudine. Haricot de Chien. Cheval à la Mode. Civet de Lapin de goutière. RÔTS. Gigot d'Antilope. Mulet. Ane. Cheval. Filet d'Éléphant. POISSONS. Morue au beurre de cacao. Harengs & Maquereaux. Merluche au Cérat. Phoque savant. LÉGUMES. Cardons à la mouëlle de Mulet. Pois, conserve de 1814. SALADES. Céleris, Mâches, Barbe de capucin, à l'huile Carcel, 1re qualité. ENTREMETS. Bombes glacées à la Krupp. Crêpes au suif. Plum-pudding à la graisse de bosse de Chameau. DESSERTS. Mendiants assortis. Confiture de Gélatine. Gâteaux Bretons-Trochu, avec fèves pour tirer les Rois. Prunes à la Dreyse. Café & Liqueurs. Certifié conforme. LE MAÎTRE-D'HÔTEL, Ch. Blocqend."

35. Ibid., facing p. 1.

36. Mordacq shows them in 1889, 1892, 1895, 1896, 1898, 1902, etc., as well as in 1923.

37. Ibid., p. 31. Other examples: a "Lunch in honor of the Italian National Holiday on 3 June 1888, in Nice," whose menu ends with "Dolce alla Romana.— Frutta e Formaggio" (p. 28); a menu for King Humbert II on 29 May 1898 in Naples (p. 52) that ends with "Salade Palestine. Glace Orientale. Gâteau romain"; the lunch at Windsor Castle (p. 53) on 20 November 1899 ending with "Gâteau créole à l'Ananas. Pommes à la D'Aremberg"; the menu of a dinner given by King Peter I of Serbia (p. 56) on 3 October 1904, ending with "Croûtes à la Parisienne. Bombe de pistache. Fromages. Fruits," etc. For the twentieth century, there is also a communion meal in 1948 (p. 61) that, after a "Salade de saison," ends with "Fromages variés. Bombe Jacqueline. Le Mont 'Martre.' Corbeille de fruits"; a 1929 Christmas lunch at Gometz-le-Châtel (p. 78) that ends with "Fromages. BÛCHE DE NOËL. Fruits. Friandises"; a 1938 Christmas Eve dinner at the Brasserie royale in Paris (p. 79): "Salade Egyptienne. Pouding Anglais Flambé. Glace Lorraine. Gaufrette. Café"; a 1939 Christmas menu for the armed forces (p. 45) that concludes with "Plateau de fromages. Buches de Noël. Ananas au Kirsch. Petits fours abondants et variés. Fruits. Café"; the Masonic menu for a family lunch on 22 April 1982 (p. 93): "Salade. Plateau de fromages. Sorbet au cassis. Petits fours secs. Café," etc.

38. According to today's [French] dictionaries, the term *hors-d'œuvre* is invariable. The rule now applies without exception, as it did in all of the menus from the 1860s published in *Le Grand Dictionnaire de cuisine* by Dumas, all of the editions of *La Cuisine classique* by Dubois and Bernard, the menus published

between 1893 and 1898 in *La Cuisine française et étrangère,* and in *L'Art culinaire* of 15 October 1897. However, the word has sometimes been written [in French as it is in English] with a terminal *s.* Examples include certain menus published by Philippe Mordacq: the great Parisian dinner of 1870–1871 (p. 25); the dinner of 30 May 1892 given in London by Lord Goldschmidt (p. 50); and the menu of a first communion meal in 1948 (p. 61). Now considered erroneous [in French], this spelling appears to have been correct in the eighteenth century: it appears in all of the 1789 menus published in *La Science du maître d'hôtel cuisinier* (pp. 545, 547, 548, 550, 551, 554, 555, 556, and 558), the 1755 menus published in *Les Soupers de la Cour* (pp. 14, 17, 32, 35, 54, etc.), and the three menus of *La Cuisinière bourgeoise* (pp. 13, 14, and 16 of the 1774 edition). It even appears in the menus of Massialot's *Cuisinier royal et bourgeois* (pp. 2, 3, 18, 22, 23, etc.), the earliest occurrence I have found. It thus seems that *hors-d'œuvre* evolved in a direction opposite that of other words designating courses: although it no longer carries the *s* typical of plurals, it has certainly remained a plural noun, as evidenced by the plural form of adjectives sometimes associated with it.

CHAPTER 10

1. Michel de Montaigne, *Journal de voyage en Italie,* Le Livre de poche no. 3957 (Paris: Pierre Michel, 1974), p. 92: "They mix cooked plums, pear tarts, and apples in with the meat course, and sometimes place the roast first and the soup last, sometimes backwards."

2. The distribution of the 38 dishes explicitly called roasts merits closer examination. In the three-course meals, we find 6 in the first, 8 in the second, and 6 in the third. For the meals with only two courses, 6 roasts are mentioned in the first and 12 in the second. Thus, while the roasts are distributed among all of the courses, they are nevertheless most often presented in the second, whether the latter constitutes an intermediate or a last course. On the other hand, the menus published by Richard Warner (n. 7 below) show 14 roasts in the first course, 15 in the second, and 16 in the third. The increasing number of dishes from first course to second and from second to third indicates no preference for any course and supports the notion of English menus being circular.

3. Thomas Austin, ed., *Two Fifteenth-Century Cookery-Books* (London, 1888; facsimile ed. London, Early English Text Society, 1964), pp. 57–64.

4. Venison: The four mentions of "Fromentée et venaison" always occur in the first course, but the two mentions of "Venaison et fromentée" appear in the second. How should this difference be interpreted? The "Venaison en brothe" is found once in the first and once in the second position. The baked venison appears in the first (a single occurrence), the roasted venison in the second (9 times) or the third (twice).

Fowl: Of 16 kinds mentioned 2 or more times, just 2 are presented in only the first course, 7 in only the last, and none in only the intermediate course. If we add to these 16 kinds of fowl those mentioned only once, we find that 29 dishes of fowl were presented in the first course, 30 in the second, and 32 in the third—which can also be read as 29 in the first, 20 in the intermediate, and 42 in the last [depending on the total number of courses in the meal].

Fish: Among the freshwater fishes, pike was presented at the beginning of the meal 5 times out of 5, while tench, trout, perch, and shad were presented at the end. What these 4 fish had in common that pike did not is a mystery. Among the unsalted ocean fish, fried or poached whiting was served in the first course, as were ling or "Milwell" tails and a large flounder; fried or not, common flounders, hake, halibut, poached sole, and conger eel were served in the second course; sea bream, cod, porpoise, and plaice, in the last. And among the fish caught either in salt or fresh water, eels and lampreys were served 3 times in the first course, 4 times in the second, and 3 times in the last; salmon 3 times in the first, 1 time in the second, and 1 time in the last; sturgeon 1 time in the first and 4 times in the last. Of the 77 fish dishes overall, 25 were presented in the first course (including the 8 cured), 23 in the second, and 29 in the third. Alternatively: 25 in the first, 16 in the intermediate, and 36 in the last.

5. Boiled: Of the 7 dishes described as boiled ("y-boylid") or in broth ("y-sothe"), 5 were presented in the first course and 2 in the second.

Sauced: The sauced dishes in the Austin menus are too rare (4, including 3 in the first course) for their distribution to be of any significance; but they occur 16 times in the Warner sample, including 11 in the first course, 5 in the second, and none in the third.

Dishes in crust: Of the 5 dishes that appear to be pasties, 2 were in the first course, 2 in the second, and 1 in the third. If we add the "Crustades" (5 in the first, 2 in the second, and 1 in the third) and the tarts (2 in the first, 1 in the second), these dishes in crust were unevenly distributed among the three courses: 9 in the first, 5 in the second, and just 1 in the third.

6. Oven-baked: The Austin menus include 8 other oven-baked dishes, 3 in the first course and 5 in the second. In the published Warner menus, the 17 occurrences are fairly evenly spread among all the courses: 7 in the first, 6 in the second, and 4 in the third.

Fried: Of the 19 explicitly fried dishes, 3 were presented in the first course, 6 in the middle course, and 10 in the final course, which was the second course 3 times and 7 times the third. But they appear more frequently in Warner's second courses.

7. Richard Warner, ed., *Antiquitates Culinariae, or, Curious Tracts Relating to the Culinary Affairs of the Old English* (London, 1791; facsimile ed. London: Prospect Books, 1981), pp. 97–99 and 113–21.

8. I use the term *function* because a soup is not defined only as a kind of culinary preparation but also as a dish with a specific place in the structure of a meal.

This is suggested by the fact that all of the soups in the 13 Austin menus occupy the first position, or the second position after another soup. Also, the expressions "to potage" or "for potage" are used 7 times in the Warner menus following the name of a first- or second-position dish.

9. As we have seen, this entremets holds the nineteenth position in a 22-dish course. It is reasonable to suppose that the three dishes that follow—fruits, sweet wine, and waffles—were not part of this last course but served after the conclusion of the meal proper, as was common practice in England.

CHAPTER II

1. Jędrzej Kitowicz, *Opis obyczajów za panowania Augusta III* (A Description of Customs during the Reign of Augustus III, 1733–1763), first published in 1840.

2. Le sieur de Hauteville [pseud. of Gaspard de Tende], *Relation historique de la Pologne* (Paris, 1686), chap. 27.

3. Ulrich von Werdum, *Das Reisejournal des Ulrich von Werdum, 1670–1677* (Frankfurt: P. Lang, 1990), p. 298.

4. Charles Ogier, *Le Journal du voyage en Pologne, 1635–1636.* According to *Cudzoziemcy o Polsce: Relacje i opinie,* ed. Jan Gintel, vol. 1 (Kraków: Wydaw, 1971), p. 230.

5. Hauteville, *Relation historique,* chap. 27.

6. S. Czarniecki, *Stół obojetny to jest pański oraz y pacholski abo sposób gotowania rozmaitych potraw* (Sandomierz, 1784).

7. Hauteville, *Relation historique,* chap. 27.

8. Guillaume Le Vasseur, Sieur de Beauplan, *Description de l'Ukraine, depuis les confins de la Moscovie jusqu'aux limites de la Transylvanie,* new ed. (Paris: J. Techener, 1861), p. 194.

9. Ibid., p. 195.

10. Ibid., p. 109.

11. Ibid., pp. 195–196.

12. Ibid., p. 196.

13. Werdum, *Das Reisejournal,* p. 298.

14. Hauteville, *Relation historique,* chap. 27.

15. Ibid.

16. Beauplan, *Description de l'Ukraine,* pp. 196–197.

17. Hauteville, *Relation historique,* chap. 27.

18. Beauplan, *Description de l'Ukraine,* p. 109.

19. Grimod de La Reynière, *Almanach des gourmands,* 3rd year (1805), p. 19.

20. L. Sébastien Mercier, *Tableau de Paris,* vol. 2 (1781), p. 258.

21. C. Calviac, *La Civile Honesteté* (Paris, 1560), fols. XIX et XVIII, v°.

22. Denis Fonvizin, *Lettres de France de D. I. Von Vizine à sa sœur à Moscou, traduites par une Russe* (Paris: H. Champion, 1888), pp. 36, 38.

23. Michel de Montaigne, *Journal de voyage en Italie,* p. 65.

24. Marx Rumpolt, *Ein new Kochbuch* (1581; facsimile ed., Hildesheim: Olms Presse, 1980), prologue.

25. Werdum, *Das Reisejournal,* p. 298.

26. Johann-Joseph Kausch, *Nachrichten über Polen* (Salzburg, 1794); according to *Cudzoziemcy o Polsce: Relacje i opinie,* ed. Jan Gintel, vol. 2 (Kraków: Wydaw, 1971), p. 133.

27. Beauplan, *Description de l'Ukraine,* pp. 193, 195, 197.

28. Ibid., pp. 193–194.

29. Hubert Vautrin, *La Pologne du XVIIIᵉ siècle* (Paris: Calmann-Lévy, 1966), pp. 142–144.

WORKS CITED

This bibliography has been newly compiled for the English-language edition. It includes works cited in the notes but not those named in the appendixes. For Flandrin's own partial list of sources, see Appendix D.

Archambault. *Le Cuisinier économe, ou Élémens nouveaux de cuisine, de pâtiserie et d'office* . . . . Paris: Renard Baudouin, 1821.

Austin, Thomas, ed. *Two Fifteenth-Century Cookery-Books*. London, 1888. Facsimile ed. London, Early English Text Society, 1964.

Beauplan, Sieur de (Guillaume Le Vasseur). *Description de l'Ukraine, depuis les confins de la Moscovie jusqu'aux limites de la Transylvanie.* New ed. Paris: J. Techener, 1861.

Bonnefons, Nicolas de. *Les Délices de la campagne.* Paris: Pierre Des-Hayes, 1654.

Braudel, Fernand. *Civilisation matérielle et capitalisme.* Paris: Armand Colin, 1967.

Brisse, Léon, baron. *La Cuisine en carême avec obédience aux Commandements de l'Église . . . Menus et recettes pour le déjeuner et le dîner de chaque jour du carême.* Paris, 1873.

———. *Les 366 Menus du baron Brisse.* Paris, 1867.

Calviac, C. *La Civile Honesteté.* Paris, 1560.

Le Cuisinier gascon. Amsterdam: n.p., 1740.

Le Cuisinier méthodique. . . . Paris, 1660. Also cited: 1685 ed.

Czamiecki, S. *Stół obojetny to jest pański oraz y pacholski abo sposób gotowania rozmaitych potraw.* Sandomierz, 1784.

Dictionnaire de Trévoux (=Dictionnaire universel françois et latin). 1st ed. Trévoux: Estienne Ganeau, 1704.

Dubois, Urbain, and Émile Bernard. *La Cuisine classique: Études pratiques raison-nées et démonstratives de l'École française appliquée au service à la russe*. Orig. 1856. Also cited: 3rd ed. Paris: by the authors, 1868.

Dumas, Alexandre. *Le Grand Dictionnaire de cuisine*. Paris: Lemerre, 1873. Repr. Paris: Phébus, 2000.

L'École des ragoûts ou le Chef-d'œuvre de cuisinier, du pâtissier & du confiturier . . . . 1668. Also cited: 11th ed., Lyon: Jacques Canier, 1685.

L'Escole parfaite des officiers de Bouche; contenant le Vray Maistre-d'Hostel, Le grand Escuyer-Tranchant, Le Sommelier Royal, Le Confiturier Royal, Le Cuisinier Royal, et le Patissier Royal. Paris: chez la Veuve Pierre David . . . et chez Jean Ribou, 1662.

Flandrin, Jean-Louis. "Médecine et habitudes alimentaires anciennes." In J.-C. Margolin and R. Sauzet, eds., *Pratiques et discours alimentaires à la Renaissance*, pp. 85–95. Actes du colloque de Tours 1979. Paris: Maison-neuve & Larose, 1982.

―――. "Le Sucré dans les livres de cuisine français, du XIVe au XVIIIe siècle." In "Le Sucre et le sel," special issue, *JATBA: Travaux d'Ethnobiologie* 35 (1988): 215–232.

Fonvizin, Denis. *Lettres de France de D. I. Von Vizine à sa sœur à Moscou, traduites par une Russe*. Paris: H. Champion, 1888.

Franklin, Alfred. *La Vie privée d'autrefois*. Vol. 3, *La Cuisine;* vol. 6, *Les Repas*. Paris: Plon, 1888, 1889.

Grimod de La Reynière, Alexandre-Balthazar-Laurent. *Almanach des gourmands*. Annual: 2nd, 3rd, 4th years. 1804, 1805, 1806.

―――. *Manuel des amphitryons*. 1808. Repr. Paris: A. M. Métailié, 1983.

Hauteville, Sieur de (Gaspard de Tende). *Relation historique de la Pologne*. Paris, 1686.

Henisch, Bridget Ann. *Fast and Feast: Food in Medieval Society*. University Park: Pennsylvania State University Press, 1978.

Joubert, Bouchard, and Louis Leclerc. "Wine Monograph." In *Le Conservateur*, pt. 3. Paris: Dentu, 1842.

Jouvin de Rochefort, Albert. *Le Voyageur d'Europe*. 3 vols. Paris, 1672.

Kausch, Johann-Joseph. *Nachrichten über Polen*. Salzburg, 1794. In *Cudzoziemcy o Polsce: Relacje i opinie*, ed. Jan Gintel, vol. 2 (Kraków, 1971).

Kitowicz, Jędrzej. *Opis obyczajów za panowania Augusta III* (A Description of Customs during the Reign of Augustus III, 1733–1763). Orig. ed. 1840. Warszaw: Państwowy Instytut Wydawniczy, 1985.

La Varenne, François Pierre de. *Le Cuisinier françois*. 1st ed. Paris: P. David, 1651.

Lebas, J. *Festin joyeux, ou La cuisine en musique: en vers libres*. Paris: Lesclapart, 1738.

Livre fort excellent de cuysine tres-utile & profitable contenant en soy la maniere dabiller toutes viandes. Avec la maniere deservir es banquets & festins. Rev. ed. Lyon: Olivier Arnoullet, 1555 (orig. ca. 1541).

L. S. R. *L'Art de bien traiter, divisé en trois parties: ouvrage nouveau, curieux, et fort galant, utile a toutes personnes, et conditions.* Paris: Frédéric Léonard, 1674.

Lune, Pierre de. *Le Nouveau Cuisinier ou il est traitté de la veritable methode pour apprester toutes sortes de viandes.* . . . Paris: Pierre David, 1660. Orig. ed. 1656.

———. *Le Nouveau et Parfait Maistre d'hostel royal enseignant la maniere de couvrir les Tables dans les Ordinaires & Festins.* . . . Paris: Charles de Sercy, 1662.

Marin, François. *Les Dons de Comus ou les Délices de la table.* Paris: Prault fils, 1739.

Massialot, François. *Le cuisinier royal et bourgeois.* . . . Orig. ed. Paris, 1691. Also cited: rev. ed., 3 vols., Paris: Claude Prudhomme, 1750–1751.

Le Ménagier de Paris, Traité de morale et d'économie domestique composé vers 1393, par un bourgeois parisien, ed. Jérôme Pichon and Georges Vicaire. Paris: Crapelet, 1846.

Menon. *La Cuisinière bourgeoise, suivie de l'Office, À l'usage de tous ceux qui se mêlent de dépenses de Maisons, Contenant la manière de disséquer, connoître & servir toutes sortes de Viandes.* 1746. Also cited: 1774 ed., repr. Éditions Messidor–Temps Actuels, 1981.

———. *La Science du maître d'hôtel cuisinier avec des observations sur la connoissance et propriété des alimens.* Paris: Paulus du Mesnil, 1749. Also cited: a revised and corrected 1789 ed.

———. *Les Soupers de la Cour, ou l'Art de travailler toutes sortes d'alimens.* 4 vols. Paris: Guillyn, 1755.

Mercier, Louis-Sébastien. *Tableau de Paris.* Hamburg, 1781.

Montaigne, Michel de. *Journal de voyage en Italie.* Le Livre de poche 3957. Paris: Pierre Michel, 1974.

Mordacq, Philippe. *Le Menu: Une histoire illustrée de 1751 à nos jours.* Paris: Robert Laffont, 1989.

Ogier, Charles. *Le Journal du voyage en Pologne, 1635–1636,* in *Cudzoziemcy o Polsce: Relacje i opinie,* ed. Jan Gintel, vol. 1 (Kraków: Wydaw, 1971).

Périgord, A. B. de. *Nouvel Almanach des gourmands, servant de guide dans les moyens de faire excellente chère. Dédié au Ventre.* 1st year (1825).

Richard, J. M. *La Vie privée dans une province de l'Ouest: Laval aux XVIIe et XVIIIe siècles.* Paris: Champion, 1922.

Rumpolt, Marx. *Ein new Kochbuch.* 1581. Facsimile ed. Hildesheim: Olms Presse, 1980.

Vautrin, Hubert. *La Pologne du XVIIIe siècle.* Paris: Calmann-Lévy, 1966.

Le Viandier de Taillevent (= *Le viandier de Guillaume Tirel dit Taillevent,* ca. 1486). Ed. Jérôme Pichon and Georges Vicaire. Paris: Techener, 1892. New ed. rev. Sylvie Martinet. Geneva: Slatkine Reprints, 1967.

Viard, André. *Le Cuisinier impérial ou l'art de faire la cuisine pour toutes les fortunes; Avec différentes recettes d'office et de fruits confits, etc. etc.* Paris: Barba, 1806. Repr. Nîmes: Lacour, 1993.

Warner, Richard, ed. *Antiquitates Culinariæ, or, Curious Tracts Relating to the Culinary Affairs of the Old English.* London, 1791. Facsimile ed. London: Prospect Books, 1981.

Werdum, Ulrich von. *Das Reisejournal des Ulrich von Werdum, 1670–1677.* Repr. Frankfurt: P. Lang, 1990.

INDEX

Page references in *italics* indicate figures and tables.

baked dishes: medieval English menus, 112–14, 116. *See also* pasties; pastries; pies

barding, 14, 77, 162n9

Beauplan, Sieur de, on Polish food and eating, 119–20, 121, 122, 124

Benzo, Ugo: *Regole della sanità et natura dei cibi*, 138

Bernard, Émile. See *La Cuisine classique*

beverages, 122–23, 142, 143; *coup du milieu*, 96–98; wine in medieval meals, 50, 51, 53, 55

birds. *See* fowl

bitter foods, 137–38, 139. *See also* astringent foods

blancmange, blancmanger, 54, 56, 114, 131, 140, 141

boar, 16, 18

boiled dishes, 13, 68, 71, 112, 161n1; dietetic principles, 145–48; Spanish menus, 131

Bonnefons, Nicolas de. See *Les Délices de la campagne*

A Book of Cookrye, 150, 151

Bouchard. See *Le Conservateur* wine monograph

boute-hors. See sendoff

braised meats, 28, 29

Braudel, Fernand, 179n2

Brillat-Savarin, 147

Brisse, Léon, baron, 93

broths, 119, 142. *See also* soup(s); stock

butcher's meats, 15, 17–18, 23–24, 65, 66

butter, 33, 34, 121

cakes, 66, 69, 122

Calviac, C., 123

Charles IX, 59, 78, 91

charnage, 33

cheeses, 3, 10, 122, 140; dietetic considerations, 138, 140, 152; dissociated from dessert, 88–89, 105, 108; Italian meals, 138, 152; medieval meals, 70, 87; Spanish meals, 135

cherries, 137, 139

Chinese menus, 137

Church food prohibitions, 32–33, 60, 90, 92–93. *See also* meatless meals

citrus fruit, 138, 139

Civilisation matérielle et capitalisme (Braudel), 179n2

classical period, defined, 42

classical-period meals: meal sequence overviews, 3–5, 33–34, 42–43, 95–96; menu examples, *6, 7, 8, 74*; seventeenth-century developments toward, 72–89. *See also specific ingredients and functions*

Cogan, Thomas: *The Haven of Health*, 145, 147, 148

cold dishes, 10, 107; meats, 24, 25–26, 67; pasties, 9, 27–28, 64. *See also* salads; serving temperature

confections, in Italian meals, 140–41, 150

Le Conservateur wine monograph (Joubert, Bouchard, and Leclerc), 97, 98

cookbooks: cooking techniques in recipe titles, 19–20, 34; dessert in, 5, 159n3; meatless menus in, 41–42; meats in, 13, 17–18, *18, 19*; recipe functions in, 11. *See also* recipe titles; *specific authors and titles*

cooking methods. See preparation methods; *specific preparations*

coup du milieu, 96–98. *See also* midway pause

course *(service)*, as term, 57, 61

course composition and sequence: author's notes about, 128; classical period overviews, 3–5, 33–34, 42–43, 95–96; English menus, 111–17, 150; flavor distinctions and, 136–41; gastronomic concerns, 91–92, 98, 122, 127–28; medieval French menus, 47–56, 58–59, 116–17; nineteenth-century developments, 9, 59, 92, 94–99, 105; number of dishes per course, 50, 58, 72, 78, 98–99; order of dishes within courses, 5, 7, 9–10, 112–17; presentation order vs. consumption order, 7, 9–10; seventeenth-century developments, 72, 73–77; in sixteenth century, 57–71, 149–52; Spain, 131–35; twentieth-century developments, 106–8. *See also specific courses, types of dishes, and periods*

dietetic principles, 136–48; cooking methods, 145–48; Flandrin's notes about, 127, 128; flavor distinctions, 136–41; lighter/heavier foods, 140, 141–45
digestion, meal sequence and, 137–38, 141–42, 145, 146–47
dishes *(mets),* 47, 48, 61
diversity of dishes, 91–92, 128
Les Dons de Comus (Marin), 11, 22, 29, 166n9
dried fruits, 139–40
drinks. *See* beverages
Dubois, Urbain. *See La Cuisine classique*
duck, 16
Dumas, Alexandre. *See Le Grand Dictionnaire de cuisine*
Durante, Castor: *Il Thesoro della sanità,* 137–38, 142, 143, 147

Eastern menus, flavor distinctions in, 136–37
L'École des ragoûts . . . , 86
eel, 37
eggs, egg dishes, 23, 34, 35, 82, *83. See also* custards
eighteenth-century meals: menu examples, *7, 8, 74. See also* classical-period meals
England, English meals: dietetic principles, 145, 147, 148; English table service, 92, 116–17; medieval meals, 111–17; in sixteenth century, 150, *151;* sweetened dishes, *81*
entrées, 3–4, 5, 9, 21–31, 59; aspics, 29; definition, 159n2; egg dishes, 23, 34, 35; fish and seafood, 37, 178n30; fritters, 29–30; fruits, 66, 71, 139, 140, 143; meatless meals, 34, 37; medieval French menus, 59, 86; nineteenth-century developments, 102; pasties and pies, 27–28, 66–67; preparation methods, 21, 27–31, 38; vs. roasts, 13–15; serving temperature, 27–29; seventeenth-century developments, 72, 73, 75; sixteenth-century meals, 57, 58, 59, 60, 66–68, 71, 86, 100–101, 149; sweet dishes, 86, 140–41, 150; types, 21; vegetables, 22, 34–35. *See also* meat entrées

entremets, 3, 4, 5, 9–10, 21–31; aspics, custards, and fritters, 29, 71; definition, 159n2; egg dishes, 23, 35; fish and seafood, 37–38, 41; Italian versions, 152; meatless meals, 34, 37–38; medieval English menus, 111, 115–16, 117; medieval French menus, 49–50, 52, 54–55, 55–56, 60; pastics and pies, 27–28; preparation methods, 12–13, 26–31, 37–38; roasts and, 9, 79–80, 96, 97–98; salads as, 4, 22–23, 31, 107; serving temperature, 27–29; seventeenth-century developments, 72, 79–80; sixteenth-century precursors, 58, 60, 64, 66, 68, 69, 70, 150; sugared entremets, 10, 29, 72–73, 79, 85, *86,* 87, 88; toasts and ramekins, 30; types, 21; vegetables, 22–23, 29, 34. *See also* meat entremets; salads
Escoffier, Auguste, 93
L'Escole parfaite des officiers de bouche, 59
étouffades, 28–29

Fast and Feast: Food in Medieval Society (Henisch), 47
fasting, 32–33
fats, 33, 34, 121
fava beans, 35, 144
Felipe II, banquet menu for, 131, *132–33*
Festin joyeux (Lebas), 79
fifteenth-century meals. *See* medieval meals
final course: dietetic considerations, 137, 138, 140, 142. *See also* dessert(s); finish
finish: medieval meals, 49, 50, 53, 58; sixteenth-century meals, 58, 60, 61, 69–70, 149
first course: classical period, 3, 72, 73–77; flavor considerations, 137, 138, 139–41; light foods for, 141–43, 145; medieval menus, 48–49, 51–52, 59, 112; nineteenth-century developments, 92; Polish menus, 118–20; seventeenth-century developments, 72, 73–77; sixteenth-century meals, 57, 58–59; sweets in, 140–41, 150. *See also* entrées; hors d'oeuvres; relevés; soup(s)

fish: aspics, 29, 37; eggs with, 166n9; fritters, 29, 30; during Lent, 33; in meat-
day meals, 59, 78–79, 91–92; in meatless meals, 34, 35–38, 39, 40–42;
medieval English menus, 111, 112, 113,
192n4; medieval French menus, 52,
54, 55, 59, 78; pasties and pies, 11, 27,
34, 37, 77; post-Revolutionary developments, 91–92, 105; preparation
methods, 37–39, 40, 54, 176–79n30; as
relevé, 77, 91; as roast, 34, 36–37,
38–39, 40, 43, 54, 59, 78, 91; sixteenth-
century meals, 59, 78; soups, 34, 37,
52, 79; sugared fish dishes, 80, 81, 82;
twentieth-century meals, 107
flavor distinctions, 136–41. See also
sweet/salty opposition
Fonvizin, Denis, 123, 124
fourteenth-century meals. See medieval
meals
fourth course, 3. See also dessert(s); final
course; finish
fowl: as entrées/entremets, 16, 26–27, 27,
39, 167–68n17; as light meat, 143, 145;
medieval English menus, 112, 113,
191–92n4; medieval French menus,
52, 54, 55; Polish menus, 120; preparation methods, 14–15, 161n1; scoter, 16,
37, 168n17; sixteenth-century meals,
65, 66, 67; sugared fowl dishes, 82;
suitability for roasts, 15–16, 17, 19, 19,
65, 163n10. See also meat entries;
roast(s)
Franklin, Alfred, 47
French service, 3, 48, 92; drawbacks, 94,
122–23; replaced by Russian service, 5,
7, 94–95, 105
fricassees, 161n1
fried dishes, 30, 107; medieval English
menus, 112, 113, 116. See also fritters
fritters, 29–30, 131
frogs, 37
fruicterie, fruiterie, 58, 61, 69
fruit(s), 3, 10, 82, 83, 86, 159n3; as dessert, 31,
71, 82, 96, 103, 122; dietetic principles,
137, 138–40, 142; dried fruits, 139–40;
eaten as savories, 70, 108; eggs with,
166n9; as entrées, 66, 71, 139, 140, 143;

flavor distinctions, 137, 138–40; Italian
meals, 137, 138, 152; jellies, 29, 171n32;
meat with, 66, 71; medieval English
menus, 112, 115; medieval French
menus, 53, 55, 61; pies, 69; Polish fruit
sauces, 119; salads, 82, 84; sixteenth-
century meals, 58, 66, 68, 69; Spanish
menus, 131, 135
frumenty, 55, 114, 116, 121, 144
functions: defined, 4; indications in
cookbooks, 11; medieval English
menus, 111–12; order of presentation/
consumption, 3, 5, 7, 9–10. See also
course composition and sequence;
specific functions

galantines, 28
game: as entrées/entremets, 16–17, 19, 21,
26–27, 27; game organ meats, 25;
medieval French menus, 54, 55;
Polish menus, 120; as roasts, 15–17,
18–19, 65, 78; sixteenth-century meals,
66, 67
García, Carlos, 141, 147
garnishes: for roast course, 54, 62, 108; vegetables as, 22
gastronomic considerations, meal organization, 91–92, 98, 122; Flandrin's notes,
127–28
Germany: table service in, 123–25
Good Friday meals, 29–30, 33, 35
The Good Huswifes Jewell, 150
goose, 16
grain-based dishes, 84, 84, 120, 121, 144
Grand Dictionnaire de cuisine (Dumas), 91,
92, 93, 99–100, 103
Grimod de La Reynière, A.-B.-L. See
Almanach des gourmands; Manuel des
amphitryons

ham, 24, 131
hare, 16, 17, 19
Hauteville, Sieur de, on Polish food and
eating, 118, 119, 120–21
The Haven of Health (Cogan), 145, 147,
148
heavy/light opposition, 140, 141–45
Henisch, Bridget Ann, 47

hors d'oeuvres, 3, 5, 72, 75–76, 159n2;
meats as, 17, 19, 25–26; medieval
precursors, 52; nineteenth-century
developments, 99–101; raw, 30, 31;
serving temperature, 75, 100,
101; singular vs. plural forms,
190–91n38; twentieth-century
meals, 107
hot/cold conventions. *See* serving
temperature
hypocras, 50, 53, 55, 58, 66, 71

ice creams, 10
Indian meals, 137
innards. *See* organ meats
issue de table, 61. *See also* finish
Italy, Italian meals: dietetic considerations,
137–38, 141, 142, 143, 145; influence in
France, 66, 68, 71, 141; in sixteenth
century, 137–38, 150, 152; sweetened
dishes, *81,* 150

Jacquelot, Dr., 146, 147
jellies, jellied dishes, 28, 29, 70; medieval
English menus, 113, 114, 115. *See also*
aspics
Joubert. *See Le Conservateur* wine
monograph
Journal de voyage en Italie (Montaigne), 111,
165n8
Jouvin de Rochefort, Albert: *Le Voyageur
d'Europe,* 84, 166n8

Kausch, Johann-Joseph, 124
kidneys, 25, 26
Kitowicz, Jędrzej, 118

La Framboisière, Sire de, 141
La Varenne, François de. *See Le Cuisinier
françois*
Lancellotti, Vittorio: *Lo Scalco prattico,*
140–41, 152
lard, 33, 34
larding. *See* barding
Leclerc, Louis. *See Le Conservateur* wine
monograph
legumes, 143, 144. *See also* fava beans;
peas

Lenten meals, 32, 33, 34, 93. *See also* meat-
less meals
Libro de cozina (Nola), 131
Libro intitolato il perche (Manfredi), 138
light/heavy opposition, 140, 141–45
liquids: as light foods, 142, 143. *See also*
beverages; moist foods
Le Livre fort excellent de cuysine, 57, 59, 73,
78, 138; menu analysis, 57–70; menu
example, *146*
Louis XV, menus for, 9, 43, 73, *74,* 103
Louis XVI, menu for, 4
Lune, Pierre de. *See Le Nouveau Cuisinier;
Le Nouveau et Parfait Maistre d'hostel
royal*
Luther, Martin, 33

Manfredi, Gieronimo De': *Libro intitolato
il perche,* 138
Manuel des amphitryons (Grimod de La
Reynière), 93, 98
Marin, François. *See Les Dons de Comus*
marinated dishes, 26, 38, 39
marine mammals, 36. *See also* porpoise
Martínez Montiño, Francisco, *134,* 135
Massialot, François. *See Le Cuisinier royal
et bourgeois; Le Nouveau Cuisinier
royal et bourgeois*
Mazars, Guy, 137
meal sequence. *See* course composition and
sequence
meat aspics, 29
meat entrées, 12–13, 21, 23; braises, 28, 29;
game and fowl, 16–17, 19, 26–27, *27;*
organ meats, 13, 17, 24–26, *25,* 67, 71;
preparation methods, 12–15, 25–27; vs.
roasts, 13–15; sixteenth-century meals,
67–68; spit-roasted, 13–15, 19–20, 39,
65, 77, 147
meat entremets, 17, 24, 28–29, 30, 162n4;
game and fowl, 19, 26–27, *27;* meal
position, 9–10; organ meats, 13, 17,
24–26, *25;* preparation methods,
12–13, 25–27
meat hors d'oeuvres, 75
meat pasties and pies, 9, 13, 24, 27–28; medieval and sixteenth-century meals,
13, 51, 54, *63,* 64, 65, 69

meatless meals, 32–43, 59–60; course sequence, 33–34, 42–43; dessert, 34; eggs in, 23, 34, 35; entrées and entremets, 29, 30, 34, 37–38; fish and seafood in, 34, 35–38, 39, 40–42; medieval and sixteenth-century meals, 59–60, 113; menus, 41–42; Poland, 121; after the Revolution, 90, 92–93, 105; roasts in, 34, 35, 37, 38–42, 43, 78; scoter allowed for, 16, 168n17; soups in, 33, 34; vegetables in, 34–35

meats, 12–15; affordability, 90; braises, 28; dietetic principles, 143, 144–48; digestion of, 142, 146–47; eggs with, 166n9; English menus, 112, 113, 150; with fruit, 66, 71; Italian meals, 137, 152; light/heavy distinction, 143, 145; medieval menus, 51–52, 53, 54, 64, 68, 144–45; Polish menus, 119, 120; as relevés, 77; sauced, position of, 54, 64, 68, 71, 85–86, 149; sugared meat dishes, 80, *81,* 82, 88; suitability for roasts, 15–20, 53–54, 65–66; toasts/ramekins, 30; vegetables served with, 35, 68; young vs. adult animals, 18, 19. *See also* roast(s); *other* meat *entries and specific types*

medical principles. *See* dietetic principles

medieval meals, 47–56; before- and after-meal food and drink, 50, 51; course distribution of meats, 144–45; dessert precursors, 49, 53, 55, 60–61; "dishes" vs. "platters," 47, 48–50; English menus, 111–17; entrées, 59, 86; entremets, 49–50, 52, 54–55, 55–56, 60, 111, 115–16; finish and sendoff, 49, 50, 53, 58; flavor distinctions in, 137–40; identification and number of courses, 48, 49–50, 56, 57, 58–59; inaccurate notions of, 47, 56; Italian meals, 137; legumes, 144; number of dishes per course, 50; opening course, 48–49, 51–52, 59; overview, 47–50, 56; roasts, 51, 53–55, 59, 64, 65, 78, 111, 112, 113, 116; salads, 138; savory desserts in, 87, *88;* significance of position in, 116–17; soups, 52, 54, 59, 64, 85–86, 111, 114–15

medlars, 139, 140

Le Ménagier de Paris, 57, 59, 60–61, 65, 78; menu analysis, 48–56

Menon. See *La Cuisinière bourgeoise, suivie de l'Office; La Science du maître d'hôtel cuisinier; Les Soupers de la cour*

menu examples: of nineteenth century, *99, 100;* of seventeenth and eighteenth century, *6, 7, 8, 74, 134;* of sixteenth century, *132–33, 146, 151;* Spanish banquets, *132–33, 134;* of twentieth century, *107*

Mercier, L. Sébastien, 122–23

Messisbugo, 150, 152

mets. See dishes

midway pause, 96–98, 102

moist foods, for start of meal, 142, 143, 147. *See also* boiled dishes; broths; sauced dishes; soup(s)

monkfish, 37

Montaigne, Michel de, 111, 124, 127–28, 165n8

mushrooms, 35, 120–21

Netherlands: sixteenth-century meals, 150

nineteenth-century developments, 90–105; *coup du milieu,* 96–98; diversification of dishes, 91–92; entrées, 102; fish dishes, proliferation of, 90, 91–93, 105; reduction trends, 95–96, 98–99, 105; relevés, 101–2, 185–86n15; singular-to-plural shift, 102–5; Russian service, adoption of, 5, 7, 94–95, 105; soups, 59, 99–101, 102. *See also* Russian service

nineteenth-century menu example, *99, 100*

Nola, Roberto de, 131

Le Nouveau Cuisinier (Lune), 11; aspics and custards, 29; braised meats, 28; butcher's meat, *18,* 24, *24;* eggs, 166n9, 166n10; fish, 41, 177–79n30; fritters, 29–30; game and fowl, 18, 19, *19,* 163n13, 167n17, 169n17; hors d'oeuvres, 75; legumes, 144; meat entrées, 161n1, 163n13; meat entremets, 24, 26, 161n1; number/position of entremets, 79; organ meats, 17, 25, *25,* 26, 163n16, 167n15; pasties and pies,

Le Nouveau Cuisinier (continued)
27; roasts, 17, 18, *18,* 19, 20; serving
temperature of entrées/entremets,
28–29; soup/entrée order, 73; soups,
167n15; toasts/ramekins, 30; vegetables, 22, 165n1, 173n4
Le Nouveau Cuisinier royal et bourgeois
(Massialot), 40, 41, 78, 95
Le Nouveau et Parfait Maistre d'hostel royal
(Lune): course composition/sequence,
5, *6,* 73, 95; meatless menus, 41–42;
roasts, 78, 102–3; soups, 59
number of courses. *See* courses, number of
number of dishes: per course, 50, 58, 72,
78, 98–99, number of guests and,
98–99
nuts, 55, 139

Ogier, Charles, 119
oil, 33, 34, 121
oilles (ollas), 96, 188n14
olive oil, 33
La Oposición y conjunción de los 2 grandes
luminares de la tierra . . . (García), 141,
147
order of consumption, vs. order of presentation, 7, 9–10
organ meats, 24–26, 67; fish organs, 37;
medieval meals, 54; sixteenth-century
meals, 61–62, 66, 71; toasts and
ramekins, 30; unsuitability for roasts,
13, 15, 17, 24, 65
oven-baked dishes: medieval English
menus, 112–14, 116. *See also* pasties;
pies
oysters, 30–31, 101

pantry staff responsibilities, 5, 21, 82, 86
pasties, 3, 21, 24, 26, 27–28; fish, 11, 27, 34,
37; game/fowl, 167n17; medieval
meals, 13, 51, 54, 112; sixteenth-century
meals, 13, 149, 150; unsuitability for
roasts, 13
pastries, 71; Italian meals, 140–41, 152;
medieval English menus, 113, 116;
sixteenth-century meals, 66–67, 69;
sweet, 66, 69. *See also* dessert(s);
pasties; pies

Patin, Guy: *Traité de la conservation de la*
santé, 140, 141–42
pears, 137, 138, 139, 140
peas, 35, 120, 144, 172n2. *See also* purée
pies, 21, 27–28, 37; medieval meals, 51, 52,
53, 56, 112; as relevés, 77; sixteenth-
century meals, *63, 64,* 65, 69, 70. *See*
also pasties
Platina: *De honesta voluptate et valetudine,*
1, 137, 140, 141, 147, 148
platters *(assiettes),* 48–49, 57, 61, 116
Polish banquets, 118–25; dishes and presentation order, 118–22; table service, 123,
124–25
poppy seeds, 120, 121
pork, 24, 164n20; organ meats, 25; suckling
pig, 24, 28, 65, 66. *See also* ham
porpoise, 36, 70, 114
potage, 4. *See also* soup(s)
poultry. *See* fowl
preparation methods: cooking techniques
in recipe titles, 13, 19–20, 34; dietetic
principles, 145–48; entrées and entremets, 12–15, 26–31, 37–38; fish,
37–39, 40, 54, 176–79n30; hot vs. cold
foods, 28; medieval English menus,
112; roasts, 12–15, 19–20, 38–40,
61–62, 64–65; sugar use, 80–84, *81, 83.*
See also specific preparations
preserves, 29, 31, 115, 159n3; Italian meals,
137, 138. *See also* dessert(s)
purée, 33, 34, 172n2

quinces, 137, 138, 139, 140

rabbit, 16–17, 19
ragoûts, 14, 15, 27, 39; fish in, 37, 38,
178n30; vegetables in, 22. *See also*
stews
raw foods, 30–31; fresh fruit, 31, 82, 86;
salads, 22–23, 31
recipe titles: cooking techniques in, 13,
19–20, 34; vegetables in, 22
Reformation, 33, 60
Régime du corps. See Aldebrandin of
Siena
Regole della sanità et natura dei cibi
(Benzo), 138

relevés, 72, 76–77, 159n2; meal position, 3, 5, 9, 10, 77; post-Revolutionary developments, 91, 96, 101–2

religious food prohibitions, 32–33, 60, 90, 92–93. *See also* meatless meals

removes, 159n2. *See also* relevés

Renaissance meals. *See* sixteenth-century meals

Revolution, fish and meatless meals after, 90, 91–93

roast(s), 3, 4, 5, 9, 12–20; after boiled dishes, 145–48; changing definitions of, 13–14, 40, 43, 70–71; changing number of, 72, 78; characteristics of, defining, 14, 39–40; classical period overview, 4, 12–20, 78; dishes served with, 3, 5, 54, 62, *63,* 64, 108; entremets and, 9, 79–80, 96, 97–98; fish or seafood, 34, 36–37, 38–39, 40, 43, 54, 59, 78, 91; meatless meals, 34, 35, 37, 38–42, 43, 78; meats suitable for, 15–20, 53–54, 65–66; medieval English menus, 111, 112, 113; medieval French menus, 51, 53–55, 59, 64, 65, 70, 78, 116; nineteenth-century meals, 91; Polish menus, 120; preparation methods, 12–15, 19–20, 38–40, 61–65; salads and, 5, 22, 31, 62, 78, 141; singular-to-plural shift, 102–3; sixteenth-century meals, 57–58, 59–60, 61–66, *62, 63,* 70–71, 78, 149, 150; Spanish menus, 131; sugared roasts and roast sauces, 85, *86;* twentieth-century meals, 108

Rousseau, Jean-Jacques, 123

Rumpolt, Marx, 124

Russian service, 94–95, 116; adoption of, 5, 7, 94–95, 105; characteristics, 90–91, 94, 122; in Germany and Poland, 123–25; number of dishes and, 98–99

Sabban, Françoise, 137

salads, 4, 5, 22–23, 31, 41, 107; dietetic considerations, 138, 141; medieval meals, 51–52, 54; national variations, 120, 141; as pantry responsibility, 21, 86; roasts and, 5, 22, 31, 62, 78, 141; sixteenth-century meals, 62, 68, 71, 138; sugared salads, 4, 23, 82, 84

salted foods, 25, 26, 35; in medieval meals, 51–52, 112; Polish menus, 120

salty/sweet opposition. *See* sweet/salty opposition

sauced dishes: as entrées/entremets, 13, 14, 17, 37–38, 39, 67–68; fish, 177–79n30; medieval menus, 54, 55, 64, 68, 112, 113; as roasts, 13, 37, 62, 64–65; sauce placement, 14; sixteenth-century menus, 62, 64–65, 67–68; as soups, 54, 64, 68, 71, 85–86, 147; spit-roasted meat entrées, 14, 15, 77; vegetables, 22. *See also* sauces

sauces: for pasties, 28; Polish fruit sauces, 119; sugared roast sauces, *86. See also* sauced dishes

savory dishes: consumption order of sweets/savories, 10, 53, 70, 72–73, 85–87, 88–89, 105, 108, 140–41; separation of sweets from, 71, 72–73, 80–84, 88, 105, 108, 141

Lo Scalco prattico (Lancellotti), 140–41, 152

La Science du maître d'hôtel cuisinier (Menon): course composition/number, 95–96; entremets, 79; meatless menus, 60; relevés, 77; roasts, 18, 164n21; soups, 76

scoter, 16, 37, 168n17

sea otters, 36

seafood, 92; marine mammals, 36, 70, 114. *See also* crustaceans; fish; shellfish

second course: classical period, 3, 40–42; hors d'oeuvres in, 75, 76; Polish menus, 120–21; relevés in, 77. *See also* roast(s); salads

sendoff, 50, 53, 58

servants, table service style and, 122–23, 124, 125

service. *See* French service; Russian service; table service

service à la française. *See* French service

service à la russe. *See* Russian service

services, 57, 61

serving sequence. *See* course composition and sequence

serving temperature: consumption order and, 10, 64, 65, 70, 101, 160n8; entrées and entremets, 21, 25–26, 27–29; hors

banquets, 122–25. *See also* French service; Russian service

"Tables d'hier, tables d'ailleurs" (Sabban), 137

tarts, 21, 56, 69. *See also* pastries; pies

temperature of foods. *See* serving temperature

Il Thesoro della sanità (Durante), 137–38, 142, 143, 147

third course, classical period, 3. *See also* entremets

Traité de la conservation de la santé (Patin), 140, 141–42

Les 366 Menus du baron Brisse, 93

Troy, Jean-François de: *Déjeuner d'huîtres,* 31

turtles, 37

twentieth-century developments, 89, 106–8

Two Fifteenth-Century Cookery-Books (Austin): menu analysis, 113–16

variety of dishes, 91–92, 128

Vautrin, Hubert, 124–25

Vedic Indian meals, 137

vegetables, 22–23, 29, 34–35; fritters, 30; greens as light foods, 142–43; in meatless meals, 34–35, 69; medieval French menus, 52; Polish menus, 120–21; raw, 30, 31; in recipe titles, 22; served with meats, 35, 68; sixteenth-century meals, 68–69; sugared vegetables, 84, 88; twentieth-century meals, 107–8; vegetable soups, 22, 34, 35, 68–69. *See also* salads

venison, 55, 61, 111, 114, 116, 191n4

Le Viandier de Taillevent, 48, 58, 61, 69

Viard, André: *Le Cuisinier impérial,* 97

La Vie privée d'autrefois (Franklin), 47

Le Voyageur d'Europe (Jouvin de Rochefort), 84, 166n8

"vyands," 114

Warner, Richard. See *Antiquitates Culinariæ*

Werdum, Ulrich von, on Polish food and eating, 118, 120, 124

"Western Views of Poland's Banquets in the Sixteenth, Seventeenth, and Eighteenth Centuries" (Flandrin and Flandrin), 109–10. *See also* Polish banquets

wild boar, 16, 18

wild mushrooms, 35, 120–21

William I, coronation menu for, 97

wine: medieval meals, 50, 51, 53, 55. *See also* *hypocras*

Text:	11.25/13.5 Adobe Garamond
Display:	Perpetua, Adobe Garamond
Compositor:	Binghamton Valley Composition
Indexer:	Thérèse Shere
Printer/Binder:	Maple-Vail Manufacturing Group